Improving Literacy Achievement

Urban Schools
IN

Critical Elements in Teacher Preparation

Louise C. Wilkinson

Lesley Mandel Morrow

Victoria Chou

EDITORS

INTERNATIONAL
Reading Association
800 BARKSDALE ROAD, PO BOX 8139
NEWARK, DE 19714-8139, USA
www.reading.org

The International Reading Association attempts, through its publications, to provide a forum for a wide spectrum of opinions on reading. This policy permits divergent viewpoints without implying the endorsement of the Association.

Executive Editor, Books Corinne M. Mooney
Developmental Editor Charlene M. Nichols
Developmental Editor Tori Mello Bachman
Developmental Editor Stacey Lynn Sharp
Editorial Production Manager Shannon T. Fortner
Design and Composition Manager Anette Schuetz

Project Editors Stacey Lynn Sharp and Rebecca A. Fetterolf

Cover Design, Linda Steere; Photograph, JupiterImages

The publisher would appreciate notification where errors occur so that they may be corrected in subsequent printings and/or editions.

Library of Congress Cataloging-in-Publication Data

Improving literacy achievement in urban schools : critical elements in teacher preparation / Louise C. Wilkinson, Lesley Mandel Morrow, Victoria Chou, editors.
    p. cm.
  Includes bibliographical references and index.
  ISBN 978-0-87207-459-0
  1. City children—Education—United States. 2. Reading—United States.
3. Literacy—United States. 4. Urban schools—United States. 5. Teachers—Training of—United States. I. Wilkinson, Louise Cherry. II. Morrow, Lesley Mandel. III. Chou, Victoria.
  LC5128.5.I47 2008
  372.6'044—dc22

                                                                    2008013278

This volume is dedicated to Jim Flood, our dear colleague, friend, and mentor, whose work has resulted in increasing the chances for struggling readers to succeed in our schools.

CONTENTS

SECTION 1

How Context Influences the Preparation of Teachers of Reading for Urban Settings

SECTION 2

Effective Preparation of Teachers of Reading for Urban Settings

SECTION 3

Key Resources for the Preparation of Teachers of Reading for Urban Settings

ABOUT THE EDITORS

 ouise C. Wilkinson is a distinguished professor of education, psychology, and communication sciences at the School of Education at Syracuse University in Syracuse, New York, USA. Wilkinson has focused her scholarship on language and literacy learning among school-age children. An internationally recognized leader in education, Wilkinson is best known for her extensive research on children's language and literacy learning and has been published in 145 articles, chapters, and volumes. She coauthored *Communicating for Learning* (1991); edited *Communicating in the Classroom* (1982); and coedited *The Social Context of Instruction* (1984), *Gender Influences in Classroom Interaction* (1985), *The Integrated Language Arts* (1994), and *Language and Literacy Learning in Schools* (2004). She currently teaches courses on literacy learning for English-language learners and on literacy studies.

She has served on the editorial boards of major research journals and on the advisory or governing boards of the National Reading Research Center, National Association of Universities and Land-Grant Colleges' Commission for Human Resources and Social Change, and the U.S. Department of Education's Laboratory for Student Success. She is a fellow of the American Psychological Association, the American Psychological Society, and the American Association of Applied and Preventative Psychology, and she has chaired panels for the U.S. Department of Education and the National Science Foundation. She has served as dean of the schools of education at both Syracuse University and Rutgers University, vice president and national program chair of the American Educational Research Association, honorary professor at Beijing Normal University, and education advisor for the New Jersey Legislature. She cochairs Literacy Leadership for Urban Teacher Education (International Reading Association commission) and is a member of the Alumni Executive Board of Oberlin College in Oberlin, Ohio, USA.

She has taught at Harvard University, Massachusetts Institute of Technology, Boston University, University of Wisconsin–Madison, City University of New York–Graduate Center, Rutgers University, and Syracuse University. She holds a bachelor's degree in psychology from Oberlin College and both the Master of Education and Doctor of Education in human development from Harvard University.

Lesley Mandel Morrow is a distinguished professor of literacy at the Graduate School of Education at Rutgers, The State University of New Jersey in New Brunswick, New Jersey, USA, where she is chair of the Department of Learning and Teaching. She began her career as a classroom teacher, then became a reading specialist, and later received her PhD from Fordham University in New York City, New York, USA. Her area of research deals with early literacy development and the organization and management of language arts programs. Her research is carried out with children and families from diverse backgrounds.

Morrow has more than 300 publications that appear as journal articles, book chapters, monographs, and books. She received Excellence in Research, Teaching and Service Awards from Rutgers University, and she was the recipient of the International Reading Association's Outstanding Teacher Educator of Reading Award and Fordham University's Alumni Award for Outstanding Achievement. In addition, Morrow has received numerous grants for research from the federal government and has served as a principal research investigator for the Center of English Language; the Center for the Study of Reading; the National Reading Research Center; and the Center for Instruction for Early Reading Research, Achievement, and Assessment. Presently she is a researcher with the BELLE project for the Bellevue Hospital Project for Early Literacy, Language and Education, working with pediatricians to provide language and literacy information for at-risk mothers during primary pediatric care. She served on the Board of Directors of the International Reading Association and served as president of the organization in 2003–2004. She was elected into the Reading Hall of Fame in 2006.

Victoria Chou has served as dean of education at the University of Illinois at Chicago in Chicago, Illinois, USA, since 1996. She has led a sustained faculty effort to demonstrate how an urban land grant research college of education can be responsive to Chicago's neighborhood schools. The college has been recognized among *U.S. News and World Report's* Best 50 Graduate Schools of Education and has been honored with three American Association of Colleges of Education Best Practice Awards.

Chou served for three years as cochair of the steering committee of the Consortium on Chicago School Research and for three years as chair of the governing board of the National Teachers Academy-Professional Development School in Chicago. She coedited a section of the recent *Handbook of Research on Teaching Literacy Through the Communicative and Visual Arts: Volume II* (2008). She has contributed recent publications to the *Handbook of Research on Teacher Education: Enduring Issues in Changing Contexts* (2008, 3rd ed.), *Partnering to Prepare Urban Teachers: A Call to Activism* (2008), and *Teacher Education Quarterly* (2008).

A former classroom teacher and reading specialist, Chou received her PhD in curriculum and instruction, with a specialization in developmental and remedial reading, from the University of Wisconsin–Madison, USA. She began her university teaching at American University in Washington, DC, before relocating to the University of Illinois at Chicago Circle (UICC), now the University of Illinois at Chicago (UIC), in 1978. At UIC she conducted research on and published in the area of reading comprehension, twice receiving the campus award for teaching before turning to administration.

CONTRIBUTORS

Richard L. Allington
Professor of Education
University of Tennessee,
    Knoxville, Tennessee, USA

Patricia L. Anders
Professor and Head of the
    Department of Language,
    Reading, and Culture
University of Arizona, Tucson,
    Arizona, USA

Kathryn H. Au
Chief Executive Officer
SchoolRise, LLC, Honolulu,
    Hawaii, USA

Diane Barone
Professor of Literacy Studies
University of Nevada, Reno,
    Reno, Nevada, USA

Jeanine Beatty
Doctoral Student
Rutgers, The State University of
    New Jersey, New Brunswick,
    New Jersey, USA

Erica C. Boling
Assistant Professor of Literacy
    Education
Rutgers, The State University of
    New Jersey, New Brunswick,
    New Jersey, USA

Amy D. Broemmel
Assistant Professor of Theory and
    Practice in Teacher Education
University of Tennessee,
    Knoxville, Tennessee, USA

Julie Esparza Brown
Director, Bilingual Teacher
    Pathway Program
Portland State University,
    Portland, Oregon, USA

Heather Casey
Assistant Professor of Literacy
    Education
Rider University, Lawrenceville,
    New Jersey, USA

Victoria Chou
Dean and Professor, College of
    Education
University of Illinois at Chicago,
    Chicago, Illinois, USA

James Flood
Distinguished Professor of
    Education
San Diego State University,
    San Diego, California, USA
(Deceased)

Linda B. Gambrell
Distinguished Professor of
    Education
Clemson University, Clemson,
    South Carolina, USA

Kathleen A. Hinchman
Professor and Chair, Reading and
    Language Arts Center
Syracuse University, Syracuse,
    New York, USA

Diane Lapp
Distinguished Professor of
    Education
San Diego State University,
    San Diego, California, USA

Susan Lenski
Professor
Portland State University,
    Portland, Oregon, USA

Jill Lewis
Professor of Literacy Education
New Jersey City University,
    Jersey City, New Jersey, USA

Richard Long
Director of Government Relations
International Reading Association,
    Newark, Delaware, USA

Carol L. Mack
Vice Provost of Academic
    Administration and Planning
Portland State University,
    Portland, Oregon, USA

Wendy B. Meller
Doctoral Candidate
University of Tennessee,
    Knoxville, Tennessee, USA

M. Kristiina Montero
Assistant Professor, Reading and
    Language Arts Center
Syracuse University, Syracuse,
    New York, USA

Kathleen C. Mooney
Doctoral Student
University of Illinois at Chicago,
    Chicago, Illinois, USA

Lesley Mandel Morrow
Professor of Literacy
Rutgers, The State University of
    New Jersey, New Brunswick,
    New Jersey, USA

Taffy E. Raphael
Professor of Literacy Education
University of Illinois at Chicago,
    Chicago, Illinois, USA

Cynthia Hynd Shanahan
Professor of Literacy, Language,
    and Culture; Executive
    Director of Council on Teacher
    Education
University of Illinois at Chicago,
    Chicago, Illinois, USA

Elaine R. Silliman
Professor of Communications
    Sciences and Disorders
University of South Florida,
    Tampa, Florida, USA

Louise C. Wilkinson
Distinguished Professor of
    Education, Psychology, and
    Communication Sciences
Syracuse University, Syracuse,
    New York, USA

FOREWORD

Some books are ahead of the times. Some books are forward thinking and address issues that will become more significant with the passage of time. Some books help to move us forward with respect to our thinking about critical issues in reading. This is such a volume, and as such it should be required reading for literacy leaders who are committed to best practices in preparing pre-K–12 teachers of reading to students in U.S. urban communities.

This book shouts hope, promise, and potential for literacy leaders who strive to make a difference in the preparation of teachers of reading. The acknowledged goal of reading instruction is that all students reach their full literacy potential. The position taken by the chapter authors in this book is that enhancing the quality of teaching is the most important way of reaching this goal.

There are a number of reasons why this volume makes a substantial contribution to the field. First, context matters, and different contexts dictate different instructional approaches. Today, we must prepare teachers who can effectively teach reading to diverse populations, in particular those in urban settings, and they must do so in ways that students find engaging, relevant, and understandable.

Second, accountability has hit higher education. Teacher educators are being held accountable for their own performance, the performance of their teacher education graduates, and ultimately the performance of students in classrooms. This accountability comes at a time when the challenges that face teachers of reading are greater than at any time in the history of the teaching profession.

Third, this text provides models of transformative professional development—new repertoires of instructional practices and opportunities for the intellectual growth of teachers as they take on the challenges of teaching reading in urban settings.

The authors of the chapters use a research-informed lens for looking at the comprehensive design of effective reading instruction. They challenge literacy leaders to engage in more deliberate planning in the preparation of teachers in urban settings. And now I invite you to join the chapter authors on a journey toward a deeper understanding of and appreciation for what is needed if we are to have teachers who provide engaging and effective reading instruction for all students.

Linda B. Gambrell, Distinguished Professor of Education
Clemson University, Clemson, South Carolina, USA

PREFACE

Louise C. Wilkinson
Syracuse University

Lesley Mandel Morrow
Rutgers, The State University of New Jersey

Victoria Chou
University of Illinois at Chicago

We are pleased to offer you this volume representing the work of the International Reading Association's Commission on Literacy Leaders for Urban Teacher Education. The commission was initiated in 2005 as a task force, and it was formally established in May 2007 to develop ways to improve the preparation of classroom teachers who develop children's literacy in urban settings and to disseminate key information on the issue. The commission's work focuses on students and youth whose progress in learning to read is not adequately supported by current teaching practice, and it focuses on both the initial and continuing preparation of teachers and those in allied professions.

The theoretical framework of this volume is that the preparation of urban teachers of language and literacy must take into account the urban contexts in which they work, including what we know about students who attend urban schools. Still, few state policies for initial teacher certification make a distinction between those preparing to teach in urban schools and those who plan to work in other communities. We believe that context matters and that different contexts dictate different instructional approaches. Moreover, we recognize that the very term *urban* refers to a multiplicity of contexts, each of which must be well understood when making recommendations for practice. Furthermore, we count ourselves among a wide and dedicated group of educators who believe that preparing urban teachers to teach reading well must be a top priority if national and state goals for "leaving no child behind" are to be realized.

Although some research on urban reading instruction exists, the corpus is limited, and the best way to prepare teacher candidates for positions in urban settings has not yet been completely or clearly defined.

Indeed, many teachers graduate from our programs without ample knowledge of how such issues as social class, dialect and first language, and power and privilege affect literacy teaching and learning.

The focus of this volume is on ways to tie ideas about the specifics of teaching and learning in urban contexts to the preparation of teachers of reading in urban settings. The first two parts of the book describe the pedagogical, curricular, and policy challenges we face; the third provides practical information—model syllabi—to guide those involved in this important work.

Following the Foreword by Linda B. Gambrell, president of the International Reading Association (2007–2008), the overview and context for this volume is provided in the Introduction, authored by the three coeditors.

Chapters in Sections 1 and 2 follow a similar outline that, for the most part, includes a statement of purpose; review of research and theory on the topic; a discussion of best practices on the topic; a summary of main ideas; implications for research, practice, and policy; and a list of references. The chapters in Section 1 address how context influences the preparation of teachers of reading in urban settings and consider such issues as policy, research, and culture.

Chapter 1, "Legislative Context and Policy Issues Concerning the Preparation of Teachers for Urban Settings" by Jill Lewis and Richard Long, considers the effects of legislation and current education policy on the preparation of teachers who will teach in urban settings where students are disproportionately poor and disproportionately members of ethnic minority groups. Major challenges facing such schools include recruiting and retaining highly qualified teachers, providing effective leadership, providing adequate working conditions, and establishing and sustaining a professional learning community. This chapter contains specific recommendations for revised state-level, urban-focused, pre- and post-certification requirements.

In Chapter 2, "The Promise of Multiliteracies for the Preparation of Urban Classroom Teachers of Reading," Diane Lapp, James Flood, and Victoria Chou emphasize the importance of the urban instructional context when it comes to the preparation of literacy teachers. They also acknowledge the need for teaching and learning in urban classrooms to incorporate aspects of youth culture and the widespread influence of multiliteracies. They conclude the chapter with suggestions to support necessary further research in this area.

In Chapter 3, "Critical Elements for Literacy Instruction of Teacher Candidates for Urban Settings," Susan Lenski, Carol L. Mack, and Julie Esparza Brown review the pertinent research on urban literacy practices and present a set of much-needed recommendations for practice, policy, and further research on teacher preparation programs that target successful practices in urban settings. The primary purpose of their chapter is to describe the elements in literacy teacher preparation that are essential for the literacy learning of students in urban settings. The authors point out that while there is a considerable research base on the teaching of reading and a growing research corpus on teacher preparation, we know little about how best to prepare literacy teachers for urban settings.

The second section of the volume addresses effective preparation of teachers of reading in urban settings, and it includes consideration of the social, cultural, and classroom context in which urban teachers work. Also discussed are the multiple pathways available to urban literacy teacher candidates, issues related to their fieldwork, and the role of professional development in enhancing the effectiveness of urban teachers.

In Chapter 4, "Preparing Expert Teachers of Reading for Urban Schools: Models and Variations in the Literature," Amy D. Broemmel, Wendy B. Meller, and Richard L. Allington begin with an overview of teacher preparation in the context of current policy and law. They identify what we know about preparing expert teachers of reading and the current status of reading achievement in urban settings. The chapter examines specific models of urban teacher preparation, identifies the common strengths in the literacy components of the programs, and then offers advice on where we need to go from here in order to meet the literacy needs of urban students effectively.

In Chapter 5, "Essential Fieldwork for the Preparation of Teachers of Reading for Urban Settings," Cynthia Hynd Shanahan focuses on preparing teachers of reading to teach in complex urban environments where a substantial number of low-income and minority families are served by large, unwieldy, bureaucratic, and highly politicized school districts. Her chapter discusses research on fieldwork models for preservice reading teachers working in such settings, the tensions and opportunities related to urban fieldwork, and the characteristics of quality urban fieldwork sites.

In Chapter 6, "Academic Language Proficiency and Literacy Instruction in Urban Settings," Louise C. Wilkinson and Elaine R. Silliman identify a major goal of education: academic language proficiency that is sufficient to meet the increasingly complex academic discourse requirements of schooling. The chapter defines academic language proficiency and academic discourse requirements and their importance to students' achievement in school. It also reviews both the theory behind and relevant research on each concept, with an emphasis on English-language learners. The authors go on to clarify the distinction between the everyday oral language register and the academic language register and discuss best practices in the development of academic language proficiency. Gaps in the research literature are identified, and implications for both policy and teacher practice in urban areas are raised.

In Chapter 7, "The Importance of Professional Development for Teachers of Reading in Urban Settings," Lesley Mandel Morrow, Heather Casey, and Linda B. Gambrell begin with the observation that after initial teacher preparation, professional development becomes crucial for creating exemplary teachers of reading in urban settings. They then discuss the theory behind and research on exemplary professional development programs. The chapter, guided by sociocultural theory that defines the link between teaching and learning, includes a discussion of successful professional development models as well as evidence from a survey conducted by the authors on the needs and concerns of urban reading teachers.

In Chapter 8, "What We Have Learned About Teacher Education to Improve Literacy Achievement in Urban Schools," Kathryn H. Au, Taffy E. Raphael, and Kathleen C. Mooney assert that teachers of literacy working in such settings should be prepared to deal effectively with what will be their biggest challenge—improving student achievement. The authors share what they have learned about teacher education from working with urban schools to improve students' literacy achievement through the Standards Based Change Process. Their view builds on and extends concepts central to the professional development school model that seeks to improve achievement through partnerships between teacher education programs and P–12 schools.

Section 3 provides practical information in the form of syllabi representing "best practices" for teaching particular courses. The first three syllabi focus specifically on urban teaching, while the final two focus on urban schooling through the wide-angle lenses of culture and context. Each syllabus includes a succinct description of the course, its main themes, and objectives; lists of required and supplemental texts and other resources; an outline of the main topics covered and related readings; and a description of major assignments.

In Chapter 9, "Literacy Development in the Urban Elementary and Middle School: A Syllabus," Erica C. Boling and Jeanine Beatty present their course, which serves as an introduction to the teaching of literacy in urban schools, with a focus on grades 4 through 8. The course is designed to assist future teachers in developing the fundamental knowledge, skills, strategies, and dispositions needed to carry out a literacy program where students' expertise in reading, writing, and oral language is nurtured.

In Chapter 10, "Content Area Literacy in the Multicultural Secondary School: A Syllabus," Patricia L. Anders and Kathleen A. Hinchman outline their course for middle and high school teachers. Their specific goal is to familiarize teachers with the nature of diverse school populations and to explore principles of literacy that support the teaching of reading comprehension, composition, and study skills within the various subject areas.

In Chapter 11, "Children's Literature for Urban Classrooms: A Syllabus," Diane Barone offers a course that aims to increase knowledge of children's literature. Students read and review an array of children's books that includes selections with a multicultural emphasis; learn to recognize, evaluate, and interpret multicultural literature; and develop the ability to select books and collections of books appropriate to children in urban schools.

In Chapter 12, "Literacy Development in the Early Years With a Focus on Children in Urban Settings: A Syllabus," Lesley Mandel Morrow and Heather Casey offer a course that reviews the research, theory, and policy issues that relate to early literacy development, as well as exemplary classroom practice in reading, writing, oral language, listening, and viewing. The course also explores the importance of integrating literacy development throughout the school day and across subject areas; the value of using a variety of teaching strategies and instructional models to organize and manage literacy instruction; and the way quality literacy instruction takes into account children's cultural background, language, socioeconomic status, and exceptionalities.

In Chapter 13, "Classroom Language and Literacy Learning Focusing on the Teaching of Culturally, Linguistically, and Ethnically Diverse Students: A Syllabus," M. Kristiina Montero offers a course designed to investigate the theories, research, practices, pedagogies, issues, perspectives, and complexities of literacy acquisition from the point of view of mainstream teachers teaching in an ethnically, culturally, and linguistically diverse classroom. The course encourages depth of focus and personal investment, as students are asked to examine their current beliefs about teaching and learning language and literacy and to document the ways those beliefs have changed over time.

We have designed this volume to be used either in its entirety as a textbook or with each chapter serving as a stand-alone reading. Consequently, we deliberately discuss some key issues in multiple chapters. Further, all the authors have enjoyed complete academic freedom to "write it as they see it." We believe that giving the authors—each a trusted expert and leader in the field—opportunities to interpret the message of this book in their own voices is what makes this volume unique.

Members of the International Reading Association are committed to playing a role in helping make all of the schools in the United States as good as they can be, a process we believe must give high priority to urban schools. We hope our work informs that of educators and policymakers and contributes to the important, ongoing dialogue about how best to educate all of our urban students. We look forward to hearing your reactions to our work and continuing this conversation in the future.

We would like to thank all of the authors of this book, both for their remarkable contributions to this volume and for their contributions to our field. We also thank the teachers and administrators working every day to develop literacy in urban schools. Finally, we thank the International Reading Association, especially Corinne Mooney, Executive Editor of Books; Priscilla Pardini and Stacey Sharp, our Developmental Editors; and Becky Fetterolf, our Production Editor, for supporting our work.

Editor Information for Correspondence
The editors of this volume welcome your feedback. Louise can be reached at lwilkin@syr.edu. Lesley can be reached at lmorro@rci.rutgers.edu. Victoria can be reached at vchou@uic.edu.

Overview of Policy, Research, and Sociocultural Issues Affecting the Preparation of Teachers of Reading for Urban Settings

Louise C. Wilkinson
Syracuse University

Lesley Mandel Morrow
Rutgers, The State University of New Jersey

Victoria Chou
University of Illinois at Chicago

Preparing urban teachers to teach reading well must be a top priority if national and state goals for closing the reading achievement gap are to be met (International Reading Association, 2003). The literacy needs of students have increased, yet the literacy achievement of children and youth in urban areas has not kept pace (Hoffman & Pearson, 2000). Much is known about urban reading instruction (Mason & Schumm, 2003), but the way to best prepare candidates for teaching in urban settings has not been clearly defined. Moreover, the current research in teacher education indicates that the quality of teacher preparation in the United States is inconsistent (Hoffman, Edwards, O'Neal, Barnes, & Paulissen, 1986; Roskos, Vukelich, & Risko, 2001) and that the preparation of teachers for urban areas needs to address issues of social class, language development, power, and privilege (Leland & Harste, 2005; Weiner, 2006). The ways that these ideas translate into the preparation of reading teachers for urban settings is currently being studied (Morrow, Reutzel, & Casey, 2006).

Improving Literacy Achievement in Urban Schools: Critical Elements in Teacher Preparation edited by Louise C. Wilkinson, Lesley Mandel Morrow, and Victoria Chou. © 2008 by the International Reading Association.

Is There a Literacy Crisis in America?

Are American students literate? The short answer is no. More than half of all American students score below proficiency in reading (National Center for Education Statistics, 2005). Ample evidence shows a growing achievement gap in reading and math achievement, as measured by standardized test scores, between (a) minority and non-minority students, (b) students from low-income families and those from middle class or affluent families, (c) native English speakers and English-language learners, and (d) special education and regular education students.

The problem is most visible in the largest urban school districts, where a majority of minority students live. The recent release of reading achievement data from the Trial Urban District Assessment (TUDA) shows that students in most of the 11 largest districts made gains that were less consistent and more modest than those in mathematics (Lutkus, Grigg, & Dion, 2007; Lutkus, Grigg, & Donahue, 2007). In addition, large achievement gaps continue to be the pattern between racial and ethnic groups. Furthermore, the students' reported gains do not mitigate the fact that some districts are failing many of their students. Only about half of the students in the District of Columbia, for example, achieve at the basic levels in reading and mathematics. Moreover, the TUDA data do not address the achievement of students excluded from the assessments, such as English-language learners (ELLs) and special education students.

Nationally reported data (Silliman, Wilkinson, & Brea-Spahn, 2004) reveal the following four trends: (1) a racial/ethnic and socioeconomic gap in emerging literacy knowledge as early as kindergarten, (2) an even larger gap between children who enter school with multiple risk factors (e.g., children of poorly educated mothers, from single-parent families, whose families are on welfare, and whose primary language is not English) and their less disadvantaged peers, (3) a significant discrepancy in reading comprehension between Caucasian students and their African American and Hispanic peers that is evident by grade 4 and continues through high school, and (4) the existence of such gaps for more than a decade.

These patterns are long-standing; perhaps the most intractable problem in American education is the achievement gap that exists between groups of children with varying socioeconomic status, first language preference, and race and ethnicity. Research has documented stable differences over time between kindergarten and grade 7 (Tabors, Snow, & Dickinson, 2001) and between first grade and the end of high school (Cunningham & Stanovich, 1997). Furthermore, as time progresses, it becomes increasingly difficult to undo the "failing to read" syndrome (Al Otaiba & Fuchs, 2002).

Teacher Quality

The passage of the federal No Child Left Behind (NCLB) Act of 2001 has put pressure on states and school districts to guarantee a skilled teacher in every regular education classroom. The legislation requires that all teachers of core academic subjects (English, reading and language arts, math, science, foreign language, civics and government, economics, history, geography, arts, etc.) be "highly qualified." (Special education and related services are not defined in the NCLB statute as core academic subjects.) This means they must hold a state teaching license or certificate, demonstrate competency in the subject(s) they teach, and demonstrate subject matter knowledge on standardized tests.

While meeting those requirements might classify teachers as "highly qualified" under NCLB standards, it might not make them effective in the classroom. We define the effective teacher as one whose students learn. Moreover, such an individual possesses high cognitive and verbal ability, as well as the subject matter knowledge and classroom experience necessary to meet the needs of all students.

Under NCLB standards, students with effective teachers are those who achieve at the proficient level on high-stakes state assessments. Strong test scores are one valued outcome in the NCLB framework because one assumes that students must have acquired knowledge to pass the tests. Students with effective teachers will also be capable of achieving at each grade level, be ready to learn the curriculum at the next level, and eventually graduate from high school having completed the required curricula. Bransford, Brown, and Cocking (2000) emphasize the link between students' learning and effective teaching with their observation that "if teaching is conceived as constructing a bridge between the subject matter and the student, learner-centered teachers keep a constant eye on both ends of the bridge" (p. 136).

Our volume is premised on the observation that a gap exists between what teachers know and what they need to know to teach effectively. Narrowing that gap is critical to ensuring successful educational outcomes for all students. In fact, recent research by the Education Trust (Peske & Haycock, 2006) amply demonstrates that poor and minority children not only underachieve because they enter school behind their peers in terms of academic preparation. They also are shortchanged when it comes to the resource they most need to reach their potential: highly qualified teachers. The Education Trust's research has shown that when it comes to the distribution of the best prepared teachers, poor and minority students do not get their fair share. The data show that highly qualified teachers elect to teach in the same kinds of classrooms they attended as K–12 students. Moreover, even those who do choose to teach in urban settings do so with less culture-specific, context-specific teacher preparation than they need. As a result they may not be as effective as they could be when it comes to teaching the predominantly minority children living in low-income urban communities.

A major challenge when studying exemplary teachers and their teaching practices is finding a reliable and valid way to identify who, in fact, is exemplary. There have been several ways in which investigators have undertaken this task. Researchers (Block, 2001; Morrow & Casey, 2003; Pressley, Rankin, & Yokoi, 1996; Taylor, Pearson, Clark, & Walpole, 1999; Taylor, Peterson, Pearson, & Rodriguez, 2002; Wharton-McDonald, Rankin, Mistretta, Yokoi, & Ettenberger, 1997) have identified teachers as exemplary based on

- Strong student achievement test scores in literacy over a period of time
- Strong student achievement test scores by students considered "at risk" of doing poorly in school
- Administrator recommendations
- Peer recommendations
- Parent recommendations
- Student recommendations

Effective and Exemplary Teaching Practices

One reason effective teachers succeed in the classroom is because they routinely engage in teaching practices that educational research has deemed sound. Taylor, Pearson, Clark and Walpole (2002) studied the literacy practices of exemplary teachers in schools that "beat the odds." The students in these teachers' classrooms were from low-income families and considered at risk of doing poorly in school. Yet they scored well on literacy achievement tests. Two teachers in grades K–3 in each of 14 schools across the United States participated in the study. Each teacher was observed teaching reading for an hour on five separate occasions from December to April. The teachers also completed a written survey, kept a weekly log of classroom reading and writing activities, and took part in interviews. Researchers found that the effective teachers focused on small-group instruction, provided time for independent reading, monitored students' on-task behaviors, and maintained close communication with parents. The teachers focused on explicit phonics instruction to ensure that their students applied phonics concepts while reading and writing. They also asked high-level comprehension questions and asked their students to respond in writing to their reading.

In their study to determine exemplary practice, Wharton-McDonald and colleagues (1997) meticulously collected and described, through surveys and interviews, the most important literacy practices and routines of 89 regular education and 10 special education teachers. The teachers, who worked with students in grades K–3, had been identified by their administrators as exemplary. They were described by their peers and supervisors as "masterful" classroom managers who organized time, materials, and student behavior with finesse. In addition, they held high expectations for their students, and their work was directed by a strong sense of purpose and a clear set of objectives.

Yet another characteristic all the exemplary teachers had in common was that each had created a literate classroom environment—a setting designed to be especially conducive to promoting success in reading, writing, listening, and speaking. To that end, these teachers provided explicit instruction in skills, strategies, and concepts related to reading and writing. That instruction included daily doses of contextualized and isolated skill and strategy instruction and access to varied reading materials and varied ways of engaging in reading and writing. The teachers also adapted instruction to the ability levels or needs of their students, worked to motivate students to engage in reading and writing, and consistently monitored student engagement and literacy progress through systematic assessment.

Morrow, Tracey, Woo, and Pressley (1999) intensively observed six exemplary teachers from three different school districts. Teachers selected for the study were nominated by school administrators, peers, parents, and students. The selection process also included checks of the teachers' student achievement scores over the past five years to confirm the effects of their exemplary status on student achievement measures. Researchers observed each teacher for approximately 25 hours and engaged each in interviews. They concluded that all six teachers taught in literacy-rich environments in which they orchestrated a variety of instructional models. Those included whole-class, small-group, one-on-one, and teacher-directed instruction. They also gave students access to learning centers and provided opportunities for students to interact with adults and peers. A rich variety of print and print-producing materials were made available to and used by children on a daily basis. Teachers also used various types of instructional approaches such as spontaneous, authentic, explicit, direct, systematic, meaning-oriented, problem-solving, and open-ended. They engaged children on a daily basis in shared, guided, oral, silent, independent, collaborative, and performance reading and writing. They offered regular writing, word analysis, and comprehension instruction. And they made consistent efforts to connect reading and writing instruction to content taught throughout the day. Many of these same effective practices and instructional routines were reported and confirmed by Cantrell (1999a, 1999b) in her study of the effects of literacy instruction on primary students' reading and writing achievement.

Sociocultural Theory and Issues

Because no one instructional method has been found most effective for teaching reading (Cantrell, 1999a), researchers studying exemplary classroom practice looked at the question from a broad perspective. Specifically, they studied not only teaching methods but also what it was about the classroom environment that affected student achievement. Researchers studied the interactions between children and teachers, classroom routines and schedules, the physical layout of the classroom, and how the classroom community affected student growth (Coker, 1985; Duffy & Hoffman, 1999; Genishi, Ryan, & Ochsner, 2001; Roehler & Duffy, 1984). Investigators attempted to tap teachers' thought processes about their teaching. For example, teachers were asked to talk about how they planned their programs, selected their materials, and scheduled their daily routines (Clark & Peterson, 1986).

In several large-scale studies of effective teachers, students in grades K–12 were questioned about the most important characteristics of excellent reading, language arts, and English teachers in an attempt to build a universal model of effective instruction (Ruddell, 1995; Ruddell & Harris, 1989; Ruddell & Kern, 1986). As part of these studies, teachers were nominated to participate in in-depth interviews and extensive classroom observations. The results of the studies indicate that influential teachers (a) use highly motivating and effective teaching strategies,

(b) build strong affective relationships with their students, (c) create a feeling of excitement about what they are teaching, (d) adjust instruction to meet the individual needs of their students, (e) create rich physical environments to support their teaching, and (f) have strong organization and management skills (Ruddell, 1995).

Based on findings from these broader studies, investigators began to draw conclusions about the way in which excellent teachers made decisions about how and what they taught, what materials they used, how they utilized space, and how they created structures for social interaction and grouping that met students' individual needs. As part of that process, researchers considered not just specific teaching practices but also the kind of classroom environments in which teaching takes place.

Such research is based on sociocultural theory, which holds that student learning is dependent upon what a teacher knows, how students come to understand that knowledge, and on the context in which that learning takes place (Vygotsky, 1978). Schools and classrooms that operate in accordance with sociocultural theory consider themselves collaborative communities in which students are assisted by more capable adults or peers. In such settings, the act of teaching and the learning environment are inextricably linked and, as a result, the culture of the classroom is taken into account when designing instruction. A sociocultural concept of learning, then, considers multiple contexts such as (a) the relationship between the teacher and student, (b) the community of the classroom, (c) the larger community of the school, and (d) how each of these factors influences each other.

Implications for Policy and Research

Given the large numbers of low-income, minority, and non–English-speaking students who continue to score below proficiency in reading, the need for effective reading teachers, especially in urban areas, has never been greater. Research tells us that effective teachers are experienced and masterful classroom managers who demonstrate high cognitive and verbal ability and in-depth subject matter knowledge. The students of such teachers, including those at risk of doing poorly in school, succeed.

We also know that the way in which teachers choose and focus literacy activities can exert measurable influences on young children's reading and writing development. Effective teachers balance their instructional time, emphasis, and content to provide their students with a variety of literacy-learning activities based on proven educational research. Such activities are integrally linked to other parts of the school day and curriculum, have an explicit purpose, include clearly defined learning tasks, and take place across a wide variety of social settings.

A synthesis of investigations about exemplary literacy practice in the elementary grades found that exemplary literacy teachers (a) provide explicit literacy instruction; (b) engage students in constructive exchanges with the teacher; (c) create a supportive, encouraging, and friendly atmosphere; (d) weave reading and writing throughout the curriculum; (e) integrate content area themes into the teaching of reading and writing; (f) use a variety of materials to create a literacy-rich environment in their classrooms; (g) teach to individual needs in small-group settings; (h) have excellent organization and management skills; and (i) develop strong home–school connections (e.g., Allington & Johnston, 2002; Block, 2001; Cantrell, 1999a, 1999b; Morrow, 2003; Morrow & Casey, 2003; Morrow et al., 1999; Pressley et al., 1996; Taylor et al., 1999; Taylor, Peterson, et al., 2002; Wharton-McDonald et al., 1997).

Lastly, exemplary language arts classrooms are informed by sociocultural theory. According to this theory, student learning is dependent upon what a teacher knows, how students come to understand that knowledge, and the context in which the learning takes place (Vygotsky, 1978). Well-organized classrooms become collaborative communities with teachers guiding instruction and student participation.

Yet, despite the wealth of research on exemplary teachers and their practice, we still do not have reliable and valid methods for identifying such teachers and exactly what it is they do. We believe a major research effort is needed in this area. Furthermore, the research to date has been undertaken, for the most part, in the primary grades. It has been descriptive and, at best, evidence based. Scientifically based research designs that address exemplary language arts teaching with older children are the next step.

REFERENCES

Al Otaiba, S., & Fuchs, D. (2002). Characteristics of children who are unresponsive to early literacy intervention: A review of the literature. *Remedial and Special Education, 23,* 300–316.

Allington, R., & Johnston, P. (2002). *Reading to learn: Lessons from exemplary fourth-grade classrooms.* New York: Guilford.

Block, C.C. (2001, December). *Distinctions between the expertise of literacy teachers preschool through grade 5*. Paper presented at the annual meeting of the National Reading Conference, San Antonio, Texas.

Bransford, J.D., Brown, A.L., & Cocking, R.R. (Eds.) (2000). *How people learn: Brain, mind, experience, and school*. Washington, DC: National Academy Press.

Cantrell, S.C. (1999a). Effective teaching and literacy learning: A look inside primary classrooms. *The Reading Teacher, 52*, 370–378.

Cantrell, S.C. (1999b). The effects of literacy instruction on primary students' reading and writing achievement. *Reading Research and Instruction, 39*, 3–26.

Clark, C.M., & Peterson, P.L. (1986). Teachers' thought processes. In M.C. Wittrock (Ed.), *Handbook of research on teaching* (3rd ed., pp. 255–296). New York: Macmillan.

Coker, H. (1985). Consortium for the improvement of teacher evaluation. *Journal of Teacher Education, 36*(2), 12–17.

Cunningham, A.E., & Stanovich, K.E. (1997). Early reading acquisition and its relation to reading experience and ability 10 years later. *Developmental Psychology, 33*, 934–945.

Duffy, G.G., & Hoffman, J. (1999). In pursuit of an illusion: The flawed search for a perfect method. *The Reading Teacher, 53*, 10–16.

Genishi, C., Ryan, S., & Ochsner, M. (with Yarnall, M.M.) (2001). Teaching in early childhood education: Understanding practices through research and theory. In V. Richardson (Ed.), *Handbook of research on teaching* (4th ed., pp. 1175–1210). Washington, DC: American Education Research Association.

Hoffman, J., Edwards, S., O'Neal, S., Barnes, S., & Paulissen, M. (1986). A study of state-mandated beginning teacher programs. *Journal of Teacher Education, 37*(1), 16–21.

Hoffman, J., & Pearson, P.D. (2000). Reading teacher education in the next millennium: What your grandmother's teacher didn't know that your granddaughter's teacher should. *Reading Research Quarterly, 35*, 28–44.

International Reading Association. (2003). *Investment in teacher preparation in the United States* (Position statement). Newark, DE: Author.

Leland, C.H., & Harste, J.C. (2005). Doing what we want to become: Preparing new urban teachers. *Urban Education, 40*, 60–77.

Lutkus, A., Grigg, W., & Dion, G. (2007). *The nation's report card: Trial Urban District Assessment mathematics 2007* (NCES 2008-452). Washington, DC: National Center for Education Statistics, Institute of Education Sciences, U.S. Department of Education. Retrieved February 11, 2008, from nationsreport card.gov/tuda_math_2007

Lutkus, A., Grigg, W., & Donahue, P. (2007). *The nation's report card: Trial Urban District Assessment reading 2007* (NCES 2008-455). Washington, DC: National Center for Education Statistics, Institute of Education Sciences, U.S. Department of Education. Retrieved February 11, 2008, from nationsreportcard.gov/tuda_reading_2007

Mason, P.A., & Schumm, J.S. (2003). *Promising practices for urban reading instruction*. Newark, DE: International Reading Association.

Morrow, L.M. (2003). *Organizing and managing the language arts block: A professional development guide*. New York: Guilford.

Morrow, L.M., & Casey, H. (2003). A comparison of exemplary characteristics in 1st and 4th grade teachers. *The California Reader, 36,* 5–17.

Morrow, L.M., Reutzel, D.R., & Casey, H. (2006). Organization and management of language arts teaching: Classroom environments, grouping practices, and exemplary instruction. In C.M. Evertson & C.S. Weinstein (Eds.), *Handbook of classroom management* (pp. 559–581). Mahwah, NJ: Erlbaum.

Morrow, L.M., Tracey, D., Woo, D., & Pressley, M. (1999). Characteristics of exemplary first-grade literacy instruction. *The Reading Teacher, 52,* 462–476.

National Center for Education Statistics. (2005). *The nation's report card: Reading 2005.* Washington, DC: Author. Retrieved January 14, 2008, from nces.ed.gov/pubsearch/pubsinfo.asp?pubid=2006451

Peske, H.G., & Haycock, K. (2006). *Teaching inequality: How poor and minority students are shortchanged on teacher quality. A report and recommendations by the Education Trust.* Washington, DC: Education Trust. Retrieved February 11, 2008, from www2.edtrust.org/NR/rdonlyres/010DBD9F-CED8-4D2B-9E0D-91B446746ED3/0/TQReportJune2006.pdf

Pressley, M., Rankin, J., & Yokoi, L. (1996). A survey of instructional practices of primary grade teachers nominated as effective in promoting literacy. *The Elementary School Journal, 96,* 363–384.

Roehler, L.R., & Duffy, G.G. (1984). Direct explanation of the comprehension process. In G.G. Duffy, L.R. Roehler, & J. Mason (Eds.), *Comprehension instruction: Perspectives and suggestions* (pp. 265–280). New York: Longman.

Roskos, K., Vukelich, C., & Risko, V.J. (2001). Reflection and learning to teach reading: A critical review of literacy and general education studies. *Journal of Literacy Research, 39,* 595–635.

Ruddell, R.B. (1995). Those influential literacy teachers: Meaning negotiators and motivation builders. *The Reading Teacher, 48,* 454–463.

Ruddell, R.B., & Harris, P. (1989). A study of the relationship between influential teachers' prior knowledge and beliefs about teaching effectiveness: Developing higher order thinking in content areas. In S. McCormick & J. Zutell (Eds.), *Cognitive and social perspectives for literacy research and instruction* (38th yearbook of the National Reading Conference, pp. 461–472). Chicago: National Reading Conference.

Ruddell, R.B., & Kern, R.B. (1986). The development of belief systems and teaching effectiveness of influential teachers. In M.P. Douglass (Ed.), *Reading: The quest for meaning* (pp. 133–150). Claremont, CA: Claremont Reading Conference.

Silliman, E.R., Wilkinson, L.C., & Brea-Spahn, M.R. (2004). Policy and practice imperatives for language and literacy learning: Who will be left behind? In C.A. Stone, E.R. Silliman, B.J. Ehren, & K. Apel (Eds.), *Handbook of language and literacy: Development and disorders* (pp. 97–129). New York: Guilford.

Tabors, P.O., Snow, C.E., & Dickinson, D.K. (2001). Homes and schools together: Supporting language and literacy development. In D.K. Dickinson & P.O. Tabors (Eds.), *Beginning literacy with language: Young children learning at home and school* (pp. 313–334). Baltimore: Paul H. Brookes.

Taylor, B.M., Pearson, P.D., Clark, K.F., & Walpole, S. (1999). *Beating the odds in teaching all children to read* (CIERA Tech. Rep. No. 2-006). Ann Arbor, MI: Center for the Improvement of Early Reading Achievement.

Taylor, B.M., Pearson, P.D., Clark, K., & Walpole, S. (2002). Effective schools and accomplished teachers: Lessons about primary-grade reading instruction in low-income schools. In B.M. Taylor & P.D. Pearson (Eds.), *Teaching reading: Effective schools, accomplished teachers* (pp. 3–72). Mahwah, NJ: Erlbaum.

Taylor, B.M., Peterson, D.S., Pearson, P.D., & Rodriguez, M.C. (2002). Looking inside classrooms: Reflecting on the "how" as well as the "what" in effective reading instruction. *The Reading Teacher, 56,* 270–279.

Vygotsky, L.S. (1978). *Mind in society: The development of higher psychological processes* (M. Cole, V. John-Steiner, S. Scribner, & E. Souberman, Eds. & Trans.). Cambridge, MA: Harvard University Press.

Weiner, L. (2006). *Urban teaching: The essentials* (2nd ed.). New York: Teachers College Press.

Wharton-McDonald, R., Rankin, J., Mistretta, J., Yokoi, L., & Ettenberger, S. (1997). Effective primary-grades literacy instruction = Balanced literacy instruction. *The Reading Teacher, 50,* 518–521.

How Context Influences the Preparation of Teachers of Reading for Urban Settings

Legislative Context and Policy Issues Concerning the Preparation of Teachers for Urban Settings

Jill Lewis
New Jersey City University

Richard Long
International Reading Association

M s. Rizzo (pseudonym) is ready to greet her English class—a group of 10th graders, most of whom are struggling readers. They attend an urban high school with an enrollment of nearly 2,600 students, and it is easy for these students to get lost in the mix.

Ms. Rizzo's class, like most in the building, is an ethnically diverse group, and on occasion students demonstrate insensitivity toward cultures other than their own. Ms. Rizzo wonders what to do about this. She is also concerned about the nearly 30% of her students who are English-language learners (ELLs); some of these students have not had formal education beyond fifth or sixth grade in their home countries, yet they were placed in this class because of their age. Also on her mind are the four mainstreamed students who have been identified as learning disabled. Although Ms. Rizzo's teacher preparation program included discussions of multicultural literature and the needs of special education students, she feels unprepared to deal with the many challenges of this class as well as the other four similar classes she will teach today. Looking for answers, Ms. Rizzo participates in the professional development offered at her school. But, given the high teacher turnover rate, few of the initiatives take hold, let alone help bring about meaningful reform.

Some nights Ms. Rizzo spends more time worrying about her students' futures than planning for the next day's classes. How many of

Improving Literacy Achievement in Urban Schools: Critical Elements in Teacher Preparation edited by Louise C. Wilkinson, Lesley Mandel Morrow, and Victoria Chou. © 2008 by the International Reading Association.

these students will finish high school? Will any go on to college or find meaningful employment? Meanwhile, after three years at the school, Ms. Rizzo wonders if she will make this one her last. She also speculates about what incentives might be enough to keep her in this frustrating setting. She is not alone in her frustration.

Purposes of This Chapter

The public has begun to recognize the enormous task facing teachers and administrators who work in urban schools. Myriad recommendations for "fixing" the schools have been proposed, but these generally have received lukewarm reception from teachers, parents, and school leaders. As a result, few recommendations have taken hold in meaningful ways.

Some of the recommendations are difficult to implement due to cuts in state and federal funding for education that come on top of unfunded mandates, such as the assessments required by the No Child Left Behind Act (NCLB). At the local level as well, funding for schools is increasingly in jeopardy as disenchanted taxpayers, including growing numbers of senior citizens living on fixed incomes, reject public school budgets. An additional complicating factor concerns the blurring of distinctions between federal and state responsibilities for determining education policy.

In this chapter we will consider how each entity is currently addressing some of the challenges of urban schools and where those policies intersect or contradict each other. We will focus specifically on the following themes:

- Urban schools are challenged by external conditions that have an impact on learning but over which administrators and teachers have no control.

- Challenges affecting teaching and learning in urban schools include working conditions, leadership, teacher turnover, and the inability of teachers to influence curriculum.

- Federal funds support a small number of teacher education programs, most within the highly specialized areas of mathematics or science education, special education, and vocational education, but few resources are dedicated to teacher education programs in urban areas.

- States can affect teacher quality within urban schools through their certification and accreditation policies.
- Preparing teachers to work effectively in urban schools requires familiarizing them with the urban context and advocacy processes, as well as offering quality mentoring programs.

We will also recommend policies that we believe can have a positive impact on Ms. Rizzo's class and the thousands of other urban classrooms across the United States. But first we put the issue in context.

The In-School Context for Urban Teachers

We must recognize how factors within schools affect teaching and learning in the classroom and, once these factors are identified, prepare teachers to address them.

Attracting recently certified teachers to urban districts is difficult. Although per-pupil expenditures for high-poverty districts increased 26% between 1995–1996 and 2002–2003, the National Center for Education Statistics (Lee, Grigg, & Donahue, 2007) finds that the playing field is still not level. In 2002–2003, total expenditures per student were highest in low-poverty districts ($10,768), next highest in high-poverty districts ($10,191), and lowest in middle-poverty districts ($8,839). A report released by the Center on Reinventing Public Education (Roza, Miller & Hill, 2005) documents how current rules allow federal funds intended for low-income schools to be shifted—sometimes inadvertently—to affluent schools within the same district. The researchers found that

> in almost every school district, experienced teachers are not only far better paid than novice teachers, but they are far more likely to work in wealthier parts of town. However, district accounting practices typically fail to show this hidden subsidy for affluent students. Instead, most districts count costs as if salaries were the same in every school. (University of Washington Office of News and Information, 2005, n.p.)

The challenges faced by urban schools include teacher and leadership quality and commitment to the schools, school and community resources, students' family experiences, and far-reaching social and economic challenges that have an adverse effect on each other. As Prince (2002) notes,

High-poverty schools suffer from fewer resources, greater teacher and administrator shortages, fewer applications for vacancies, higher absenteeism among teachers and staff, and higher rates of teacher and administrator turnover. Problems related to working conditions and the organization of the schools are compounded by social problems related to poverty in the larger community: hunger; homelessness; crime; substance abuse; chronic health problems; parental unemployment; and low levels of parental education, literacy, and job skills. These problems, in turn, contribute to higher rates of student absenteeism and mobility, higher dropout rates, and lower levels of academic achievement. (n.p.)

Achieve, Inc., and the National Governors Association (NGA; 2005) caution,

State and local education leaders must do a better job of recruiting and preparing outstanding teachers and principals and deploying them to the schools where they are most needed. Effective teachers and principals are critical to helping all students meet higher standards and leave high school ready for college and work. (p. 12)

Corcoran, Walker, and White (1988) advise that good working conditions—even more than students' socioeconomic status—are associated with better teacher attendance, more effort, higher morale, and a greater sense of efficacy in the classroom. In their view, these conditions include

- Strong, supportive principal leadership
- Good physical working conditions
- High levels of staff collegiality
- High levels of teacher control over curriculum and instruction
- High levels of teacher influence on school decisions

If we take a look at each of these conditions, we begin to realize the complexity of issues inside the urban school that have a bearing on teachers' experiences.

Strong, supportive principal leadership. The Council of the Great City Schools (Snipes, Doolittle, & Herlihy, 2002) finds that there are 16,850 public school districts in the United States, of which 100 serve 23% of all students. Many are in urban areas and enroll 40% of the country's minority students and 30% of its economically disadvantaged students. This heavy concentration of minority and economically disadvantaged students in so few school districts puts enormous demands on school principals, who need to be model instructional leaders promoting positive staff morale and teamwork that can be focused on student achievement.

Good physical working conditions. Kozol (1991) brings to light for the general public the "savage inequalities" found in urban school facilities. And study after study has documented lower student achievement in schools housed in buildings in poor condition than those in fair or excellent condition (Baker et al., 2001).

Urban districts tend to have older school buildings that require more maintenance. However, approximately 80% of education expenditures are for personnel, primarily instructional staff, according to the National Center for Education Statistics (U.S. Department of Education, 2006). Thus, there are few dollars left for much else, including school upkeep, especially in urban schools.

The effects can be significant. A building's unkempt appearance, for example, adds to the general perception that a school lacks order and safety. In fact, the physical limitations of urban school buildings can contribute to the deterioration of safety. In their study of school violence between 1999–2000, Miller and Chandler (2003) identify six factors that contribute to increased school violence:

1. School level
2. Urbanicity
3. Academic importance
4. Number of classroom changes
5. Number of serious discipline problems
6. Number of schoolwide disruptions

The study also finds that "city schools (77%) are more likely than urban fringe schools (67%) to report an occurrence of at least one violent incident during the 1999–2000 school year, while no differences are detected among schools in other locations" (p. 9).

Teachers, too, are more subject to crime in urban schools. A study by the U.S. Department of Education Institute of Education Sciences (2004) of crimes against teachers between 1997 through 2001 reports that urban teachers are more likely to be victims of violent crimes (28 crimes per 1,000 teachers) than suburban and rural teachers (13 and 16 crimes, respectively, per 1,000 teachers). Teachers in urban areas are also more likely than those in rural areas to experience theft at school (42 crimes vs. 26 crimes per 1,000 teachers, respectively).

Technology is also more limited in poor, urban schools. The Pelavin Research Institute (1997) identifies three challenges in school technology financing: (1) funding the relatively high costs of installing school technology systems, (2) sustaining annual operating costs, and (3) securing the money to maintain and replace the system to keep it modern.

High levels of staff collegiality, high levels of teacher control over curriculum and instruction, and high levels of teacher influence on school decisions. These three features of school working conditions are closely related. Collegiality develops over time and through extended interactions. Further, control over curriculum and influence on school decisions requires sophisticated knowledge of and long-term investment in a school. However, numerous studies report that high-poverty schools tend to have high teacher turnover rates and, as a result, a less stable and qualified teaching staff. Schools with high turnover rates have difficulty planning and implementing a coherent curriculum and sustaining positive working relationships among teachers. According to Guin (2004), such schools experience a loss of organizational productivity.

Teacher turnover also contributes to the teacher gap, defined by the editors of *Education Week* as the "dearth of well-qualified teachers for those who need them most" (2003, p. 7). The National Center for Teacher Education Statistics report on the condition of education for 1998 notes that schools with 50% or more minority students experience turnover at twice the rate of schools with a lower minority population. The most frequently reported reasons for teachers leaving schools include poor salary, poor administrative support, and student discipline problems (MacDonald, 1999; Tye & O'Brien, 2002), conditions that are most likely found in low-income urban schools. In a study of teachers in New York state (Lankford, Loeb & Wyckoff, 2002), the teachers who left were also more likely to have higher skills than those who remained. Even good professional development is undermined and unsustainable given the high teacher turnover in urban districts.

Contributing also to the difficulty of including teachers in curriculum decision making is the reality that students in high-poverty schools are 77% more likely to be assigned to an out-of-field teacher than those in low-poverty schools and that students in mostly non-white schools are over 40% more likely to be assigned to an out-of-field teacher than those in mostly white schools (Jerald, 2002). As we turn our attention to federal and state policies on teacher education, we need to ask if any policies will contribute to improvements in these kinds of working conditions, which ultimately affect student achievement.

Federal Education Policy and Teacher Education With an Urban Emphasis

The federal government has a wide range of programs designed to help new teachers become better teachers and current teachers become more effective. And, although most of these programs don't have a direct focus on high-poverty or urban areas, many can have an effect on elementary and secondary classrooms in urban areas. Beyond that, there are also opportunities for school districts and teacher education programs to craft successful proposals to capture federal funds.

Large-scale programs that offer opportunities for funding include the Higher Education Act of 1965, Title II of NCLB, the Elementary and Secondary Education Act (ESEA) of 1965, and the Individuals with Disabilities Education Act (IDEA). There are also other programs that, by setting standards or by creating examples, can have an impact on how teachers are taught. The most significant is the National Board for Professional Teaching Standards.

However, the most important element of federal education policy is the role it plays in setting the national agenda for education reform. The national agenda has been slowly evolving from one with an emphasis on access to and equity in programs to one that emphasizes quality. After quality was included in the mix, the boundaries between the federal government and the curriculum (traditionally a state and local issue) changed significantly. The first shift in emphasis occurred in the 1980s with the standards movement, which became a federal push for state-based standards that made use of national models. Next came the federal emphasis on assessment and the charge that state departments of education and local school districts develop ways of measuring whether students met the standards. As NCLB became the law of the land, a federal requirement for highly qualified teachers renewed attention on the critical role teachers play both in helping students learn and in closing the achievement gap.

Another change in the federal role in teacher education has come about because of shifts in the funding of higher education. Traditionally, state governments provided funds to institutions of higher education, while the federal government provided resources to individuals in the form of student loans and grants. More recently, the federal government has become the catalyst for many changes in higher education in general and teacher education specifically by funding the efforts of individuals and institutions working to address the needs of particular groups of students. For instance, with the passage in the 1970s of the Education for All the Handicapped Act (Public Law 94-142, 1975) came a program for expanding the number of special education teachers. This approach, which saw the federal government responding to the needs of a defined group of students, was also evident in federal funding to prepare teachers to work with ELLs and in expanded funding for teacher education programs at traditionally Hispanic institutions of higher learning.

The U.S. federal government has also provided funding for specific curricular areas, including vocational education, for which funding began in 1917 and is still available today. More recently, federal funding has been provided for mathematics and science teacher education through such agencies as the U.S. Department of Education, the National Science Foundation, and the U.S. Department of Energy. Such funds have been both formula-driven and made available at the discretion of the issuing agency. For example, as part of the Dwight D. Eisenhower Mathematics and Science Education Act funds were allocated to states based on the number of children living in each and then divided between a state's institutions for higher education and its elementary and secondary systems.

In reading there have been a number of federal programs that have had an impact on curriculum; the most recent large-scale such program is Reading First, which was established in 2002. Others have included Striving Readers in 2005; the Reading Excellence Act of 1998; the Basic Skills Act established in 1978 as part of ESEA; and the Right to Read Program, which was initiated in 1969.

Reading First can be seen as an urban program because it provides funds to school districts with large numbers of low-income children. However, despite the fact that the largest numbers of low-income children live and attend school in urban areas, the program doesn't directly target urban schools. Instead, Reading First funds flow to states, which use the money to provide professional development on scientifically based reading instruction for teachers in elementary schools with large numbers of low-income children. Such an approach, not surprisingly, comes at a price. Namely, states and federal agencies can significantly influence local decisions on which reading programs are ultimately adopted.

Another example of the changing nature of federal involvement can be found in the development of the Response to Intervention (RTI) plan, a provision embedded in the 2005 amendments to IDEA. While RTI is never mentioned by name in the statute, it is considered one of IDEA's key concepts. Its intent is to reduce the number of students identified for special education services by suggesting that states and local school districts provide struggling learners in the regular education setting with a series of instructional techniques or interventions. These interventions, which are differentiated for each learner, are monitored for signs of academic improvement. Students who show progress remain in regular education; those who do not, move to special education.

Because reading achievement is one of the most frequently cited reasons a student is identified as learning disabled and recommended for special education services, RTI is expected to increase the demand for K–12 reading professionals. As a result, proposals are being discussed that would expand general IDEA teacher education funding to include support for such programs that specifically include RTI activities.

Yet another area of expected change in federal law concerns those teachers who work in schools with growing numbers of students who are ELLs, a phenomenon now affecting almost every school in the United States. While this is not a problem for teachers with a multiple-language background or speaking ability, it is greatly increasing demands on teachers without such skills who are working more and more often with students with marginal English-language ability. As a result, more teachers need more information on how to teach these students; the federal government is expected to respond by expanding funding for colleges that teach these skills.

The federal government is also thinking about changing and expanding its role in state teacher education programs by making its recommendations more powerful. Its proposal for the reauthorization of the Higher Education Act of 1965, which some expect will be enacted by the summer of 2008, is a case in point. It calls for providing federal funds to states to support expanded reading instruction for preservice teachers, professional development in reading for classroom teachers, and the recruitment of more reading teachers.

What is significant about these proposals is that they put the status of reading professionals on par with that of those in other areas that have been identified as high need: special education, mathematics, and science education. That move, in turn, gives states and teacher education institutions the opportunity to expand curricula to better address high-need areas such as urban education.

Thus, individuals who choose to teach in K–12 urban schools are increasingly benefiting from an array of federal awards and grants designed to ensure high standards and improve teacher recruitment, quality, and retention.

Implications and Recommendations

What does all of this mean? The short answer is that there is a wide range of federal attention currently being focused on teacher education, attention that will most likely expand to affect reading instruction. The impact will come largely in the form of increased federal funds. However, rarely does the federal government invest in something without also requiring some type of quality control. Although such control could be exercised by the states, one can speculate that it may well fall under the domain of some type of federal standards-setting program.

It is also important to note that the federal government plans to continue allocating funds to school districts with large numbers of high-needs—but not necessarily urban—students. Although the Title I program, for example, was originally designed to support school districts with large numbers of low-income families living in areas with little or no tax base, the assumption today is that even in higher income areas the federal government needs to provide access to high-quality programs. However, since Title I was first created, much has changed in terms of both the federal government's role in education and how that role is being defined. In December 2006, the New Commission on Skills of the American Workforce, a group made up of prominent leaders from government, industry, labor, and education, came up with an expanded notion of what it will take to be literate in the 21st century. Among the commission's recommendations is that all citizens have access to an education that emphasizes problem-solving abilities (National Center on Education and the Economy, 2007). If this also becomes a Title I goal, the result would be a significant shift in what is meant by the "basic education" outlined in the 14th Amendment to the U.S. Constitution that provides equity for all and access to property rights. In turn, this would expand the definition of what it means to teach reading in Title I (or any other high-poverty) school, as well as a new national approach to teacher education and advancement.

Given all of these elements—the need for more specialized teaching for high-need children, inequitable distribution of resources around the nation and its schools, and the push to be internationally competitive—it is clear that the federal government will continue to expand its role and responsibilities into the area of teacher education. What is unclear is how the community will respond.

The U.S. federal government has been providing support to schools and colleges of teacher education in an inconsistent pattern. While it seems to be targeting specific areas of need by expanding the number of special education teachers, mathematics teachers, reading teachers, and those in allied fields, much of this is happening on a small scale and is not directly aimed at helping K–12 schools that enroll large numbers of high-needs students. Further, the effort is not increasing the number of new teachers with such needed specialized knowledge fast enough to make a difference.

It should also be noted that many teachers who teach in urban settings come from either community colleges or historically black colleges or universities, many of which need far more support than four-year institutions when it comes to building faculty capacity. Until now, the philosophy has been to earmark available funds for individuals, mostly in the form of grants and scholarships. However, if we are going to better prepare teachers to work in urban settings and increase the number of minority teachers who work in urban schools, funding needs to go to institutions of teacher education to build their capacity to offer courses and supervised field work that are rich in urban education experiences. This would include funding for professors, instructional space, and libraries.

The federal government can further build the capacity of teacher educators committed to urban schools by providing ongoing support for them to attend specialized conferences and summer institutes similar to those sponsored by the National Science Foundation for math and science teachers in the late 1950s and 1960s. Such professional programs enable teacher educators to become familiar with current research and ideas on instruction for urban students and to learn how to apply them in their teacher education programs. As things stand now, for example, ideas for curriculum usually come from concepts developed in suburban areas. Little is specifically taught about the different curricular needs of African American learners (who make up a large percentage of the urban school population) or any other high-poverty group. This will change only as teacher educators become more knowledgeable about research findings on effective curriculum and learn more about the experiences of those they prepare to teach in urban schools.

A final consideration concerns the role of the federal government in relation to that of individual states when it comes to designing teacher education programs. It would seem that if the federal government is going to continue to emphasize quality and make demands on colleges and departments of teacher education, federal policies in this area will need to be more specific and coordination between federal agencies and state-based programs will need to be improved.

State Influences on Teacher Education Policy for Urban Schools

There are few state policies on initial teacher certification that distinguish between those preparing to teach in urban schools and those who hope to work in other communities. There are, however, several significant ways in which states influence teacher preparation in general that could be reshaped to make such distinctions or to ensure that all students are prepared to teach in urban schools.

Each state's department of education or department of public instruction establishes the criteria for every teacher certification that state offers, such as certifications in elementary or early childhood, math, bilingual/ELL, reading, biology, special education, and so on. The criteria might include requirements for courses, internships, and exams. Such criteria vary from state to state. The University of Kentucky's website (www.uky.edu/Education/TEP/usacert.html) provides access to certification requirements for each of the 50 states. Information is also available on teacher candidate pass rates on required exams (usually Praxis I or II) at some colleges and universities in some states.

Although it may seem that officials at state departments of education and institutions of higher education seldom converse with each other, state officials can influence how the curricula of teacher preparation programs are organized and delivered. What's more, such influence can extend beyond merely establishing the broad parameters of required course work. Accreditation is a case in point. Each institution offering a teacher preparation program might opt to have its programs reviewed by one or more accrediting agencies, including the National Association of

State Directors of Teacher Education and Certification (NASDTEC), the National Council for Accreditation of Teacher Education (NCATE), and the Teacher Education Accreditation Council. Accrediting agencies evaluate and then either "pass" or "fail" institutions' teacher education programs; the steps required for obtaining a seal of approval may be a major factor in the design and content of such programs. Standards from professional organizations, such as the International Reading Association, are most often used to determine program quality. It is usually in an institution's best interest to apply for accreditation because it acknowledges that the school's programs meet national standards in each licensure area. Accredited schools—and their graduates—often have greater standing in the professional community than those that are not accredited. Accreditation also is often used to establish interstate reciprocity for teaching licensure.

Sometimes a state's department of education can influence accrediting decisions. In the case of NASDTEC, for instance, state requirements for teacher preparation programs and certification carry a lot of weight. NASDTEC can withhold accreditation until an institution revises its programs and aligns them with state standards and certification requirements. For example, during the mid-1980s, nearly every college in New Jersey initially failed NASDTEC's accreditation review. In order to pass, each was required to redesign its teacher preparation program so that students majored in a content field and took no more than 36 credit hours in teacher education, including student teaching. Not every state or every university goes through the NASDTEC process, but Reading First has encouraged states to conduct oversight by reviewing teacher preparation programs, especially course work in reading, to ensure that future teachers receive preparation in phonics, phonemic awareness, vocabulary, comprehension, and fluency. NASDTEC, incidentally, also coordinates reciprocity between states with respect to teacher licensure through its interstate agreement. Thus, accreditation from NASDTEC has a bearing on whether an institution's teacher preparation program that leads to licensure in one state will be accepted by another.

We cannot overlook the fact that it is also within the power of state departments of education to specify requirements for certification in certain subject areas such as reading. If there is only a vague reference to such requirements (e.g., the certification requirement in the licensure code reads "teachers must be prepared to develop students' literacy") then it is up to each university to determine how this requirement will be met. College faculty, as well as deans of schools of education, often disagree about what should be required; if more reading courses were mandated, for instance, would other requirements need to be eliminated in order to maintain reasonable credit requirements for teacher certification and graduation? One can only imagine the turf battles that might ensue. In addition, specific requirements that address urban school issues could be set for those students preparing to teach in them, although few states appear to do so at present.

States also set policies with regard to alternative routes to initial teacher certification. These state-sanctioned, market-driven pathways may include recognizing established programs, such as Troops to Teachers or Teach for America, or designing alternative routes administered by a higher education institution—or in some cases, a school district. It is estimated that more than 200,000 people have been licensed through such programs (see the National Center for Alternative Certification website, www.teach-now.org/overview.cfm, for more information).

Needs of urban districts and teacher shortages in some specialized areas, such as special education and bilingual education, gave rise to alternative certification programs—with mixed reviews. The alternative routes usually require candidates to hold a Bachelor of Arts or Bachelor of Science degree in a content field before they enter the classroom, pass a state test for licensure, and complete an induction program and work with a mentor. However, there are states, such as South Dakota, where the teacher candidate begins teaching immediately and receives on-the-job training. Another approach that addresses teacher shortages—but not necessarily urban needs—is for states to work together as consortia offering online courses to those who wish to obtain teaching licenses. The Western Governors University, founded by the governors of 19 western states, is an example. The institution's website describes it as the only accredited university in the United States offering "competency-based, online degrees" and touts its NCATE accreditation.

Entrepreneurial efforts, such as those of the American Board for Certification of Teacher Excellence (ABCTE), offer tests to certify aspiring or current teachers. In a number of states, including Massachusetts, individuals who hold initial licenses also can become certified in an additional content area simply by taking and passing ABCTE's reading certification test.

Thus, states have considerable leverage and numerous opportunities to design teacher certification programs with an eye toward better preparing teachers for urban schools. The next section makes some specific suggestions as to how this might be accomplished.

Recommended State-Level Policies for Teacher Education

There are a number of graduate programs that focus on urban teaching or urban education but few at the initial certification level. One way that an institution can address urban needs during the initial certification period, however, is through its mission, and it is up to individual institutions to decide whether an urban focus is part of its mission. At New Jersey City University in Jersey City, New Jersey, USA, for instance, the dean of the College of Education describes the university's education programs as "committed to building a learning community and to providing a high quality of instruction to those seeking careers within an urban, multicultural and educational environment" (Banks, n.d.). One example of an institution with an urban focus is the Urban Teacher Education Center in Sacramento, California, USA, a collaborative effort between California State University–Sacramento and the Sacramento City Unified School District, wherein certification students work primarily in urban schools during the entire preparation period.

Private funding to individual institutions can sometimes provide opportunities to develop models that will yield research and subsequent policy shifts. One such model is the Urban Teaching Academy Project, funded by the MetLife Foundation "to improve the preparation and transition of new teachers into high-need urban schools" (National Commission on Teaching and America's Future [NCTAF], 2006, n.p.). In March 2006, NCTAF recognized three sites as NCTAF–MetLife Foundation Urban Teaching Academies: California State University in Long Beach, California, USA; the Academy for Urban School Leadership in Chicago, Illinois, USA; and Montclair State University in Montclair, New Jersey, USA. Each received a $50,000 grant recognizing their innovative work.

Although, as we have noted, the federal government has recently been involved in defining the highly qualified teacher, state departments of education ultimately determine the nature of teacher preparation programs as well as certification requirements. For teachers to meet the needs of urban students and to feel successful in this endeavor, there must be a comprehensive overhaul of the certification process. Revised certification requirements must address

- Knowledge of the urban context
- Acquisition of skills essential for teachers of diverse populations
- Extensive field-based, preservice experience in urban schools

- Knowledge of standards setting and alignment of standards, curriculum, and assessment
- Knowledge of the advocacy processes
- A well-designed, sophisticated mentoring program that commences immediately upon entering the profession
- Postcertification opportunities that keep effective teachers in urban schools, including a career ladder that rewards and promotes the visibility of effective urban teachers

Knowledge of the urban context. The extenuating circumstances affecting urban schools have been outlined earlier in this chapter. Those preparing to teach, even if they don't intend to teach in urban schools, should become familiar with these circumstances. Minimally, such knowledge provides a yardstick by which we can evaluate social progress and assess the measure to which we value public education for all children. This knowledge can also promote reflection and provide a reality check for those who are considering urban teaching.

Acquisition of essential skills for teachers of diverse populations. "In 2004, the total foreign-born population of the United States passed 34 million, an increase of more than 3 million people from 2000 and more than triple the figure of 10 million reported in 1970" (Capps & Fortuny, 2006, p. 2). As a result, the face of the classroom, particularly urban classrooms, has changed considerably. In fact, Van Hook and Fix (2000) report that 53% of primary school students and 31.3% of secondary school students considered limited English proficient (LEP) attend schools where more than 30% of their classmates are also LEP, creating both an ethnically and linguistically segregated school environment. Like Ms. Rizzo, with whom we introduced this chapter, all urban teachers need to be culturally responsive—and help their students develop these dispositions as well. Teachers also need to understand the process of language acquisition; the relationship between language and reading acquisition; and strategies for working with struggling readers, learning disabled students, and ELLs. In addition, they need to be able to deal with school violence and drug abuse, as these issues tend to be prevalent in urban schools.

It is odd that NCLB's highly qualified teacher requirements speak only to knowledge of a content field. The expectations of teachers that are held by school administrators, parents, the business community, and others go well beyond delivering content because schools have become the arena in which almost every effort to bring about social change plays out. These expectations result in new demands on teachers (e.g., drug education, sex education, values education, environmentalism, bus duty, data management) with no reprieve from demands of the past (Mathison & Freeman, 2003). These pressures are perhaps felt the greatest by teachers in urban schools where positive in-school influences on children compete with high rates of negative influences outside of school, such as violence and drug abuse.

Further, the NCLB requirement that all children must demonstrate adequate yearly progress in reading in grades 3–8 and for at least one year of high school should have alerted state departments of education to the need for all teachers to know how to teach reading to all children beyond the elementary grades. There is sufficient evidence to prove that after fourth grade reading test scores decline. According to the Nation's Report Card, only four jurisdictions (District of Columbia, Florida, Hawaii, and Maryland) improved reading scores at both grade 4 and grade 8 between 2005 and 2007. This continues the trend noted by Perie, Grigg, & Donahue (2005) who reported that "at grade 8, no state had a higher average score in 2005 than in 2003, and 7 states had lower scores. The percentage of students performing at or above *Basic* increased in 1 state and decreased in 6 states" (n.p.).

The picture is also dismal for those who enter college. ACT, Inc. (2004), a nonprofit, independent organization, reports that "only 22 percent of the 1.2 million high school graduates who took the ACT Assessment in 2004 achieved scores that would deem them ready for college in all three basic academic areas—English, math, and science" (n.p.). A similar report released by ACT in March 2006 (ACT, Inc., 2006) indicates that only 51% are prepared for college-level reading. Yet most states require only minimal course work (one to two courses) in reading instruction for primary or elementary teacher certification, and some require none for those seeking certification to teach in grades 6–12.

States also sanction programs that provide alternative routes to teacher certification, a move originally designed to address teacher shortages. However it is unclear whether this path to the classroom is accomplishing its goal and if those who graduate from alternative route programs remain in the teaching force, let alone commit to teaching in urban classrooms. For instance, the Teach for America program that provides teachers for urban schools through an alternative route retains fewer than 50% of the teachers placed in Chicago classrooms beyond the two years candidates are required to serve (Williams, 2004).

Extensive field-based, preservice experience in urban schools. Preservice teaching experiences are designed to give those entering the profession an opportunity to observe successful teachers using a variety of instructional strategies and to learn to apply to real-life problems the pedagogy learned in their course work. Research supports the value of connecting course content to real experiences in schools (Hoffman & Roller, 2003). Through ongoing exposure during preservice experience, beginning teachers also come to appreciate those aspects of classroom life—including its complexity and unpredictability—that cannot be sufficiently understood merely through reading course textbooks.

Most field experiences for preservice teachers provide limited exposure to diverse populations (Ladson-Billings, 1995; Zeichner, 1996). This renders many beginning teachers culturally unresponsive to urban schools, the setting in which most beginning teaching assignments can be found. While not all universities are located in close proximity to urban school districts, when possible preservice teachers should be placed in urban schools for a significant part of their field experience. This experience will give them a chance to become familiar with the stresses of urban schools, to develop coping strategies, and to clarify misconceptions they may have about such schools. It can also help minimize negative expectations preservice teachers might have of urban schools (Wolffe, 1996). Preservice course work can be organized to develop skills in kidwatching, self-reflection, and case study analysis. By engaging in these activities through experiences in urban school settings, preservice teachers will come to better understand the urban context and the critical role teachers play in the achievement of urban students.

Knowledge of standards setting and alignment of standards, curriculum, and assessment. For more than 10 years, states have been developing standards as well as benchmarks for verifying student achievement of these standards. Higher education has had only minimal involvement in this endeavor, primarily through the work of a few university faculty members who have participated on task forces engaged in developing standards for state departments of education. Preservice teachers need to become familiar with the process used to set standards and how curriculum and assessments are aligned to those standards if they are to engage in standards-based decision making in the classroom. Some aspects of standards-based instruction have proven controversial, including such issues as the amount of testing involved and its effect on curriculum and student attitudes toward school, communication with parents about the results of assessments and supplemental services, and the validity of basing decisions such as student retention or graduation on a single test score.

Knowledge of advocacy processes. Lewis, Jongsma, and Berger (2005) address the need for teachers to learn strategies they can use to advocate for change. Preservice teachers knowledgeable about advocacy can enter their initial teaching experiences feeling empowered rather than believing they have little say over what happens in their classrooms. Teachers who understand the process can become part of it. They will know how to identify shared concerns, locate relevant supportive research, and work effectively with others for change.

A well-designed, sophisticated mentoring program that commences immediately upon entering the profession. Teacher retention in urban schools is a significant problem. A national study by Ingersoll (2001) indicates that approximately 25% of all new teachers leave the profession within the first year and 39% of all beginning teachers leave the profession in their first five years of teaching. In urban areas, the percentages are nearly 50% (Ingersoll, 2001). When novice teachers have a positive, coherent mentoring experience, they are much more likely to move rapidly from focusing on classroom-management concerns to focusing on student learning (NCTAF, 1996, 2003). Such a scenario increases teachers' sense of professionalism and increases their ability to affect student achievement. The National Education Association (1999) reports that new teachers who participate in induction programs that include mentoring are nearly twice as likely to stay in their profession.

A review of the research literature on teacher recruitment and retention (Guarino, Santibañez, Daley, & Brewer, 2004) finds that "(a) schools with high proportions of minority students, students in poverty, and low-performing students tended to have higher teacher turnover rates and (b) urban school districts had higher teacher turnover rates than suburban and rural districts" (p. 64). This review also noted several studies that verified the important role mentoring was found to play in teacher retention.

In addition to reducing teacher turnover, mentoring can play a critical role in a novice teacher's quality of experience and level of job satisfaction. It can minimize the stress of the induction year and early years of teaching. Mentoring also serves to move teachers beyond mere survival mode; instead, they begin to seek out and engage in professional development opportunities designed to improve their practice.

The NGA Center for Best Practices (Koppich, 2004) outlines several features of quality mentoring programs. Such programs, according to the association, extend through the entire school year and beyond. They also ensure that novice teachers are placed in less challenging situations and in schools where they can participate in quality professional development and be observed by veteran teachers. NCTAF believes mentoring programs can be designed so as to retain the best teachers (Fulton, Yoon, & Lee, 2005). Their suggestions include a mentorship that occurs along a continuum, builds teachers' professional knowledge, includes outside network supports, encourages dialogue, and sustains the positive features of the school culture and professional community. Unfortunately, while some states have mentoring systems in place, such programs are frequently not funded or underfunded, giving experienced, successful teachers few incentives to participate.

Postcertification opportunities that keep effective teachers in urban schools. The difficulties of retaining quality teachers suggest consideration of various rewards to keep excellent teachers in schools. As Koppich (2004) explains,

> Teacher pay is not enviable, and working conditions are not always welcoming. Thus, it will take a combination of state and district incentives to recruit and retain high quality teachers. Incentives might include scholarships, and loan forgiveness programs for individuals interested in becoming teachers; low-interest housing loans so teachers can buy homes; and early contracts and signing bonuses, especially for teachers to agree to teach in hard-to-staff schools or to teach subjects in which shortages are most severe. (p. 8)

Koppich also suggests that other kinds of incentives will be required to keep teachers in the profession over the long haul, saying,

> Among those to consider are well-qualified supportive administrators; job differentiation that allows teachers to assume leadership roles without leaving teaching; and differentiated pay structures that recognize teacher performance, willingness to take on challenging positions, and leadership responsibilities. (p. 8)

Several studies have found that lack of prestige is a contributing factor to teacher turnover (Johnson & Birkeland, 2003; Shipp, 1999).

For example, career ladder compensation plans reward experienced teachers who demonstrate excellence with increased respect and promotional opportunities. "They enable teachers to earn more money, take on new roles (such as mentoring novice teachers), and gain more prestige and professional fulfillment" (Farber & Ascher, 1991, n.p.).

Conclusion

Public education in the United States is supposed to be "the great equalizer." Yet, as we look at the challenges of urban schools, we realize that inequalities between such schools and their non-urban counterparts in wealthier communities throughout the country prevail. Beyond that, it is simply amazing that with all of the research available on how to improve urban education, the preparation of teachers to work in urban schools has been largely left to chance. And, while the federal government has identified a number of areas in great need of highly qualified teachers, little is occurring to ensure that the nation has a supply of well-educated teachers with the specific knowledge requisite to teach effectively in these areas. States, responsible for setting and maintaining teacher certification standards and for providing direct support for public teacher education programs, have also done little to provide for the special needs of urban students. Indeed, there are a few states that require the completion of courses in urban education for a teaching degree, but many states do not recognize the specialized training that is needed to work in urban areas.

Thus, it is not surprising that Ms. Rizzo feels overwhelmed and highly challenged as she teaches her students. She has neither adequate preparation nor the personal, fiscal, or administrative support required to help her meet the myriad needs of her students. The federal and state officials who are determining policies for her and the others who work in public schools may not have stepped inside an urban classroom for many years—if ever. Beset with difficulties beyond her control, limited resources, and few colleagues who have taught for very long in similar environments, she wonders if she will continue at her school next year. Can anyone blame her if she leaves? And, if she does, how prepared will the teacher be who takes her place?

REFERENCES

Achieve, Inc., & National Governors Association. (2005). *An action agenda for improving America's high schools*. Retrieved February 9, 2008, from www.nga.org/Files/pdf/0502ACTIONAGENDA.pdf

ACT, Inc. (2004, October 14). *College readiness crisis spurs call for change by ACT in nation's core high school curriculum*. Iowa City: Author. Retrieved January 11, 2008, from www.act.org/news/releases/2004/10-14-04.html

ACT, Inc. (2006, March 1). *High school reading not challenging enough, says ACT*. Iowa City: Author. Retrieved January 11, 2008, from www.act.org/news/releases/2006/03-01-06.html

Baker, J.A., Derrer, R.D., Davis, S.M., Dinklage-Travis, H.E., Linder, D.S., & Nicholson, M.D. (2001). The flip side of the coin: Understanding the school's contribution to dropout and completion. *School Psychology Quarterly, 16*, 406–426.

Banks, I.W. (n.d.). *Certification programs*. Jersey City: New Jersey City University. Retrieved January 11, 2008, from www.njcu.edu/academics/cert_programs.asp

Capps, R., & Fortuny, K. (2006, January). *Immigration and child and family policy*. Washington, DC: Urban Institute. Retrieved August 10, 2007, from www.urban.org/UploadedPDF/311362_lowincome_children3.pdf

Corcoran, R., Walker, L.J., & White, J.L. (1988). *Working in urban schools*. Washington, DC: The Institute for Educational Leadership. (ERIC Document Reproduction Service No. ED299356)

Editors of *Education Week*. (2003). To close the gap, quality counts [Executive summary]. *Education Week, 22*(17), 7. Retrieved April 14, 2008, from www.edweek.org/media/ew/qc/archives/QC03full.pdf

Farber, B., & Ascher, C. (1991). *Urban school restructuring and teacher burnout*. New York: ERIC Clearinghouse on Urban Education. (ERIC Document Reproduction Service No. ED340812)

Fulton, K., Yoon, I., & Lee, C. (2005). *Induction into learning communities*. Washington, DC: National Commission on Teaching and America's Future. Retrieved January 11, 2008, from www.nctaf.org/documents/NCTAF_Induction_Paper_2005.pdf

Guarino, C., Santibañez, L., Daley, G., & Brewer, D. (2004). *A review of the literature on teacher recruitment and retention* (Technical Rep. No. TR-164-EDU). Santa Monica, CA: RAND. Retrieved January 11, 2008, from www.rand.org/pubs/technical_reports/2005/RAND_TR164.pdf

Guin, K. (2004). Chronic teacher turnover in urban elementary schools. *Education Policy Analysis Archives, 12*(42). Retrieved January 11, 2008, from epaa.asu.edu/epaa/v12n42/

Hoffman, J., & Roller, C. (2003, October). *Standards for excellence in reading teacher preparation: Building on the past and planning for the future*. Paper presented at the Minnesota Reads Conference, Minneapolis, MN.

Ingersoll, R.M. (2001). Teacher turnover and teacher shortages: An organizational analysis. *American Educational Research Journal, 38*, 499–534.

Jerald, C.D. (with Ingersoll, R.M.) (2002). *All talk, no action: Putting an end to out-of-field teaching*. Washington, DC: Education Trust. Retrieved January 11,

2008, from www2.edtrust.org/NR/rdonlyres/8DE64524-592E-4C83-A13A-6B1DF1CF8D3E/0/AllTalk.pdf

Johnson, S.M., & Birkeland, S.E. (2003). Pursuing a "sense of success": New teachers explain their career decisions. *American Educational Research Journal, 40,* 581–617.

Koppich, J.E. (2004). *Developing state policy to ensure a "highly qualified" teacher in every classroom.* Washington, DC: National Governors Association Center for Best Practices. Retrieved January 11, 2008, from www.nga.org/Files/pdf/0405 QUALIFIEDTEACHER.pdf

Kozol, J. (1991). *Savage inequalities: Children's in America's schools.* New York: Crown.

Ladson-Billings, G. (1995). Multicultural teacher education: Research, practice, and policy. In J. Banks & C.A.M. Banks (Eds.), *Handbook of research on multicultural education* (pp. 747–759). New York: Macmillan.

Lankford, H., Loeb, S., & Wyckoff, J. (2002). Teacher sorting and the plight of urban schools: A descriptive analysis. *Educational Evaluation and Policy Analysis, 24,* 37–62.

Lee, J., Grigg, W., & Donahue, P. (2007). *The nation's report card: Reading 2007* (NCES 2007-496). Washington, DC: National Center for Education Statistics, Institute of Education Sciences, U.S. Department of Education. Retrieved March 12, 2008, from nces.ed.gov/nationsreportcard/pdf/main2007/2007496.pdf

Lewis, J., Jongsma, K., & Berger, A. (2005). *Educators on the frontline: Advocacy strategies for your classroom, your school, and your profession.* Newark, DE: International Reading Association.

MacDonald, D. (1999). Teacher attrition: A review of literature. *Teaching and Teacher Education, 15,* 835–848.

Mathison, S., & Freeman, M. (2003, September 24). Constraining elementary teachers' work: Dilemmas and paradoxes created by state mandated testing. *Education Policy Analysis Archives, 11*(34). Retrieved January 11, 2008, from epaa.asu.edu/epaa/v11n34/

Miller, A.K., & Chandler, K. (2003). *Violence in U.S. public schools: 2000 School survey on crime and safety, statistical analysis report* (NCES 2004-314). Washington, DC: National Center for Education Statistics. Retrieved January 11, 2008, from nces.ed.gov/pubsearch/pubsinfo.asp?pubid=2004314

National Center for Education Statistics. (1998). *The condition of education* (NCES 98-013). Washington, DC: U.S. Government Printing Office.

National Center on Education and the Economy. (2007). *Tough choices or tough times: The report of the New Commission on the Skills of the American Workforce.* San Francisco: Jossey-Bass.

National Commission on Teaching and America's Future. (1996). *What matters most: Teaching for America's future.* New York: Author. Retrieved January 11, 2008, from www.nctaf.org/documents/WhatMattersMost.pdf

National Commission on Teaching and America's Future. (2003). *No dream denied: A pledge to America's children.* Washington, DC: Author. Retrieved January 11, 2008, from www.nctaf.org/documents/no-dream-denied_full-report.pdf

National Commission on Teaching and America's Future. (2006). *Urban teaching academies*. New York: Author. Retrieved January 15, 2008, from nctaf.org/resources/demonstration_projects/urban_teaching/index.htm

National Education Association. (1999). *Creating a teacher mentoring program*. Washington, DC: National Foundation for the Improvement of Education. Retrieved January 11, 2008, from www.neafoundation.org/publications/men toring.htm#usefulness

Pelavin Research Institute. (1997). *Investing in school technology: Strategies to meet the funding challenge*. Washington, DC: Office of Educational Technology, U.S. Department of Education. Retrieved January 11, 2008, from www.ed.gov/pubs/techinvest/index.html

Perie, M., Grigg, W.S., & Donahue, P.L. (2005). *The nation's report card: Reading 2005. Reading results: Summary for grades 4 and 8* (NCES 2006451). Washington, DC: National Center for Education Statistics. Retrieved January 11, 2008, from nationsreportcard.gov/reading_math_2005/s0002.asp?printver=

Prince, C.D. (2002, Winter). Attracting well-qualified teachers to struggling schools. *American Educator*. Retrieved January 11, 2008, from www.aft.org/pubs-reports/american_educator/winter2002/AttractingTeachers.html

Roza, M., Miller, L.P., & Hill, P. (2005). *Strengthening Title I to help high-poverty schools*. Seattle, WA: Center on Reinventing Public Education, Working Paper Series. Retrieved February 9, 2008, from www.crpe.org/workingpapers/pdf/TitleI_reportWeb.pdf

Shipp, V.H. (1999). Factors influencing the career choices of African American collegians: Implications for minority teacher recruitment. *Journal of Negro Education, 68*, 343–351.

Snipes, J., Doolittle, F., & Herlihy, C. (2002). *Foundations for success: Case studies of how urban school systems improve student achievement* (Executive summary). Washington, DC: Council of the Great City Schools. Retrieved January 11, 2008, from www.mdrc.org/publications/47/execsum.html

Tye, B.B., & O'Brien, L. (2002). Why are experienced teachers leaving the profession? *Phi Delta Kappan, 84*, 24–32.

U.S. Department of Education. (2006). *The condition of education 2000–2006. Contexts of elementary and secondary education, Finance, Indicator 41: Public elementary and secondary expenditures by district poverty* (NCES 2006-071). Washington, DC: National Center for Education Statistics. Retrieved January 11, 2008, from nces.ed.gov/pubs2006/2006071_4.pdf

U.S. Department of Education Institute of Education Sciences. (2004). *Indicators of school crime and safety, 2003*. Washington, DC: National Center for Education Statistics. Retrieved January 11, 2008, from nces.ed.gov/pubs2004/2004004.pdf

University of Washington Office of News and Information. (2005, August 18). *Study finds that school-funding loopholes leave poor children behind*. Retrieved June 18, 2006, from www.uwnews.org/article.asp?articleID=11695

Van Hook, J., & Fix, M. (2000). A profile of immigrant students in U.S. Schools. In J. Ruiz-de-Velasco & M. Fix with B.C. Clewell, *Overlooked and underserved: Immigrant students in U.S. secondary schools* (pp. 9-33). Washington, DC: The Urban Institute. Retrieved January 11, 2008, from www.urban.org/Uploaded PDF/overlooked.pdf

Williams, D. (2004, September). Teach for America on hot seat. *Catalyst Chicago*. Retrieved January 11, 2008, from www.catalyst-chicago.org/news/index .php?item=1305&cat=23

Wolffe, R. (1996, Winter). Reducing preservice teachers' negative expectations of urban students through field experience. *Teacher Education Quarterly*, 23(1), 99–106. Retrieved January 11, 2008, from www.teqjournal.org/backvols /1996/23_1/w96_wolffe.pdf

Zeichner, K. (1996). Educating teachers for cultural diversity. In K. Zeichner, S. Melnick, & M.I. Gomez (Eds.), *Currents of reform in preservice teacher education* (pp. 133–175). New York: Teachers College Press.

CHAPTER 2

The Promise of Multiliteracies for the Preparation of Urban Classroom Teachers of Reading

Diane Lapp
James Flood
San Diego State University

Victoria Chou
University of Illinois at Chicago

n their chapter, Jill Lewis and Rich Long discuss the effects of legislative context and policy issues on the preparation of teachers who will teach in urban settings where students are disproportionately poor and disproportionately members of ethnic minority groups. They highlight the specific challenges facing urban schools and pose the concern that many of the recent federal initiatives aimed at teacher quality focus neither on explicitly helping K–12 schools with the greatest proportions of poor and minority students nor on supporting the teacher education institutions that prepare the majority of teachers for urban schools. They recommend revised state-level, urban-focused, pre- and postcertification requirements.

Building on their propositions, we discuss the relationship between the characteristics of urban schools and the preservice education of those preparing to become teachers in such settings. In particular, we explore the potential of those aspects of youth culture in the 21st century sometimes referred to as "multiliteracies" to become powerful instructional alternatives for urban classroom teachers.

Improving Literacy Achievement in Urban Schools: Critical Elements in Teacher Preparation edited by Louise C. Wilkinson, Lesley Mandel Morrow, and Victoria Chou. © 2008 by the International Reading Association.

Purposes of This Chapter

The purposes of this chapter are fourfold. The first is to argue the importance of taking into account the unique local particularities of "urban" school settings when it comes to preparing teachers to teach in urban areas. The second is to recognize the ways in which multiliteracies can be called upon to improve literacy for today's urban learners in powerful and productive ways. The third is to demonstrate how rich multiliteracies can be embedded in a differentiated content lesson. The final is to offer suggestions that support the continuing study of teachers who can address the unique features of students in urban settings.

Review of Research and Theory

We begin with a set of school examples to illustrate the importance of recognizing the uniqueness of and differences among schools which, like these, are found in very different urban contexts. These examples resulted from our work in three high schools in different parts of the United States; all of the high schools are in cities and urban centers and can be described as urban high schools despite their vast and significant differences.

La Jolla High School

The first of these, La Jolla High School, is located in arguably the most affluent section of the city of San Diego, California. The majority of its student body consists of neighborhood youth who are from upper middle class families. However, some students from economically distressed sections of the city attend La Jolla High through its vibrant voluntary ethnic enrollment program (VEEP). As a result, at least 10 different languages are spoken at the school; students represent many different cultural, linguistic, and ethnic backgrounds, including Mexican American, Caucasian, African American, and Asian Pacific American.

Upon entering La Jolla High, one is immediately struck by the school's strong sense of pride and tradition, evident not only in the displays and exhibits showcasing its graduates and their accomplishments but also in its well-appointed facilities and beautifully manicured grounds.

In general, the students seem happy to be there; individual classrooms "hum" like finely tuned clocks. There is a feeling of homogeneity in goals and objectives at this school. The markings of success are apparent in the school's celebratory bulletins. Students are routinely accepted into Ivy League schools, the University of California at Berkeley, Stanford University, and the California Institute of Technology, as well as to community colleges and universities all over the country. The school's overall literacy scores are at the top of state testing levels. Despite the school's clear successes, not all students are achieving; many of those struggling are neighborhood students or minority students, including some VEEP students.

Waianae High School

The second school, Waianae High School, is located in Oahu, Hawaii, with the Pacific Ocean as a backdrop. The median household income of residents of the Waianae neighborhood is $41,679, with 25.7% of the households classified as poor. A small percentage of those families live along the ocean in a tent city. Approximately 25% of the neighborhood's residents have some college education; 9% hold college degrees. The 2,068 students attending Waianae High School are primarily of Hawaiian or part-Hawaiian ancestry (45.2%); all but 20% are of Asian or Asian Pacific Islander origin. Programs focusing on enhancing awareness of students' Hawaiian ancestry have drawn a wide audience.

Truancy is high at Waianae, where student and family motivation to attend or complete school is extremely weak. Nearly 60% of the students qualify for free or reduced-price lunch, 22% are receiving special education services, and 4.5% are English-language learners (ELLs). Approximately 65% of Waianae's students graduate, and 2% go on to complete college. Their on-time graduation rate is 60.9%.

Fewer than half of the 135 teachers at Waianae have taught five or more years at the school. Their average number of years of experience is 7.5. Although 26% of the teachers have advanced degrees, 60.7% of faculty members are teaching classes in content areas in which they are not certified. A total of 20% have provisional credentials, with many first-year teachers coming to the school from Teach for America programs.

Waianae was identified in 2006 by the U.S. Department of Education as a school in need of "restructuring" for failure to meet literacy benchmarks for several years. The teachers elected to receive professional development support from Doug Fisher, Diane Lapp, and a team of stateside educators because they realized that if math and literacy scores did not increase, Waianae would be restructured under NCLB state mandates.

Crane Technical Prep Common School

The third school, Crane Technical Prep Common School, is located on the West Side of Chicago, Illinois, near the United Center where basketball legend Michael Jordan used to play. Crane's curriculum is intended to prepare its 1,038 predominantly African American, low-income students for postsecondary education opportunities and the world of work. Roughly one-quarter to one-third of Crane's students are enrolled in an Education to Careers curriculum.

Roderick, Nagaoka, and Allensworth (2006) report that 49.5% of students from Crane's 2002 and 2003 graduating classes went on to postsecondary education. A total of 20.5% attended four-year colleges; 17.9% of those students attended nonselective or somewhat selective schools. A total of 167 seniors, Crane's largest class in recent years, graduated in June 2007. Of these, 70% are planning to enroll in some form of postsecondary education. According to the principal, 42% of black males graduated, compared with the national average of 35%.

Still, many Crane students struggle academically. A total of 22% of 11th graders met or exceeded state standards in 2006 in reading; only 7% did so in mathematics. As a result, the school is on Illinois's academic watch list and is eligible for restructuring implementation, according to federal guidelines, having not made adequate yearly progress in 2006–2007.

The neighborhood surrounding Crane is in transition; signs touting new townhouses and condominiums are visible within a block of the school. At the same time, Crane has been experiencing an extremely high student mobility rate (44.3% in 2006), the result of Mayor Richard Daley's "Plan for Transformation," under which a large number of highrise public housing buildings are being torn down and replaced with "mixed-income" developments. One result is the relocation of hundreds of low-income African American families. Crane's current dean of students links the school's high number of violent incidents requiring police intervention to the presence of four different gangs that would not otherwise have found themselves in the same school.

To address the problem, Crane was reorganized in the fall of 2007, with students clustered by grades in separate wings of the school. The move is designed to improve school safety by better nurturing the development of social trust among students from three fractured neighborhood communities. In addition, all freshmen will be expected to participate in extracurricular activities. School officials hope such efforts will also help boost student achievement.

Defining Urban Schools

Each of these three schools is technically an urban school from the standpoint of geography. However, the differences among them are so great that to render the term *urban* is uninformative for guiding literacy instruction—or for differentiating good urban literacy instruction from good literacy instruction in general. Indeed, the only similarity among them is that they are all located in urban locations.

To shed some light on what is really meant by urban, a recent survey of directors of field placement and supervision (Chou & Mayeda, 2007) reports that 34% of respondents defined *urban school* exclusively by the location or size of the community where the school is located, as in "A school within the boundaries of a city as opposed to a rural area. It seems that it has come to mean within the boundaries of a large city."

Similarly, 42% of field supervisors defined *urban school* in neutral terms such as the following: "A city school in which there is a high percentage and/or wide representation of cultures, ethnic groups, languages." Another 22% used more "deficient" language: "School with large enrollments and urban school issues such as low achievement status, gang-related problems, poor teacher retention" or "I would say public schools located in the inner city, often associated with a lack of instructional resources, well-trained teachers, and students from low SES [socioeconomic status], nonmainstream cultural backgrounds." Only 2% of these field supervisors formulated a definition of *urban school* using primarily positive language.

It is true that the term *urban* is a problematic placeholder for K–12 students whom our schools are failing. Obviously, not all students who struggle with literacy attend urban schools, just as not all urban students perform poorly in school. Nevertheless, although the term fails to address the issues of racism and classism that landed economically poor minority children and youth in segregated urban centers in the first place, *urban* provides a useful means of delineating the characteristics of schools and school districts that make educating our most vulnerable students so challenging and yet so critical.

We believe an important tension underscores most discussions of the term *urban*. The dichotomy is that all-encompassing language fails to differentiate schools that are succeeding from those that are struggling, while more deficit-laden language tends to implicate students, teachers, and schools without making explicit the etiologies of urban school distress. The more neutral or demographic definitions of *urban* that comprise 76% of survey responses are not informative enough to provide insight on how best to prepare teachers in specific urban schools and communities. At best, they validate the superficial overviews and survey courses on multicultural education that represent ways schools of education address the "diversity standard" of various state certification requirements. They engender genuinely puzzled responses from field supervisors:

> By the way, I don't completely "get" this focus on "urban settings," honestly. Don't at-risk children of migrant workers, other ELL immigrants and other students who live in low-income, disadvantaged RURAL areas have similar educational needs? The big question for us is, Are credential candidates prepared adequately to focus on the assessment of individual student needs (whether these students live in urban, suburban, or rural areas) and will they be prepared/willing/able to DIFFERENTIATE instruction for these various students? (Chou & Mayeda, 2007, slides #4–7)

Without a doubt, all high school students who are not equipped to comprehend their textbooks or who are reading at or below a sixth-grade level (National Center for Education Statistics, 2005) deserve quality differentiated instruction so that they can succeed in their classes and prepare for postsecondary life. Academic failure is an urgent challenge, or as historian Kaestle (1995) reminds us,

> Americans only periodically focus on the importance of literacy to a nation's fate. Reading is a mundane activity, and in the twentieth century, with nearly universal elementary schooling and high nominal literacy rates, we have sometimes taken literacy for granted. At other times, however, our needs for literacy have become pressing and have outdistanced the abilities of American readers. At these times, literacy has become an important policy issue and a frequent topic of social commentary. We are living in such a time. (p. 330)

Certainly, our ultimate goals lie in fostering the literacy education of all students who are not meeting national, state, and local standards.

At the same time, it is important to draw attention to three characteristics of the urban environment that do in fact exert singular and significant influence on the education of K–12 students, especially on the most vulnerable members of the student population: size, scale, and bureaucracy; cultural heterogeneity and cultural capital; and the cultural politics of urban school reform (Chou & Tozer, 2008).

Size, Scale, and Bureaucracy

The biggest school districts in the country are urban school districts; they usually dwarf all other districts in a state. The Council of the Great City Schools (CGCS), which exclusively supports big-city school districts, represents 66 school districts in cities with populations greater than 250,000 or student enrollment of more than 35,000. Together, the 66 districts comprise 7.4 million students. In these large urban districts, Weiner (2000) suggests,

> Size and bureaucracy intensify the contradiction between teaching and learning as personal, human activities, on the one hand, and the standardization that is intended to make urban schools efficient, fair, and impartial. (pp. 370–371)

The organization of curricula, instruction, assessments, and resources in general gets complicated when numbers of personnel, students, and schools are huge and when dollars are tight. In such situations, teachers and principals often need to improvise and plan for the unexpected, yet they are not often privy to the reasoning behind decisions made at the top. System leaders and politicians, on the other hand, need to invest scarce resources in facsimiles of best practice that will scale to all levels of teacher competence. This is why it is not entirely surprising that scripted curricula such as Success for All make their way into large-district strategic plans (Snipes, Doolittle, & Herlihy, 2002). When one recalls the old adage of "Too many cooks spoil the broth," one can easily understand how a huge urban school district, applying well-intentioned federal and state policies to thousands of students and school personnel, becomes utterly bureaucratized and inefficient. Lest prospective teachers suffer complete curricular shock when they encounter scripted curricula and test-preparation mandates, teacher educators must prepare teacher candidates for life in the high-stakes environments of urban school districts. Failure to respect the context is failure to prepare a teacher to succeed in that context.

Cultural Heterogeneity and Cultural Capital

Note that the 7.4 million students attending school in CGCS districts are 38% African American, 33% Hispanic, and 6% Asian/Pacific Islander. Nearly two-thirds of the students are eligible for free or reduced-price lunch, 16% are ELLs, and 13% are students with disabilities. While there exists considerable interdistrict variation in terms of these demographics, the basic point is clear: The urban children and youth whom we, as teacher educators, prepare teacher candidates to teach today come from cultural and linguistic backgrounds that may be significantly different from our own, as well as those of the candidates themselves, because the vast majority of teachers are white, middle class, and female.

Because neither we nor our teacher candidates tend to live in the same neighborhoods as urban students, we are less knowledgeable than we need to be about the precious cultural capital such students bring to school and how to draw on children's resources for literacy learning. As a result, we need to exercise all available opportunities to reduce our ignorance by steeping ourselves and our teacher candidates in the students' cultures. This means becoming involved in the very schools and communities that most desperately need good teachers. At the same time, we must provide urban K–12 students with the explicit instruction and careful explanation it takes to visibly render mainstream what Delpit (1988) refers to as "codes of power"—the ways of knowing, communicating, and doing that are rewarded in the dominant or mainstream culture.

Cultural Politics of Urban School Reform

Finally, we need to be mindful of the prevalence of cultural politics in urban school districts. That includes, not incidentally, the frequent exclusion of schools of education from decision making when it comes to school reform efforts, a move based on the view that such institutions have become increasingly irrelevant to the day-to-day lives of urban K–12 students. Yet, while teacher educators in schools of education are supporting teacher candidates in developing culturally relevant pedagogy, those in charge of urban school governance have instead embraced models of accountability and decision making that are exclusively outcome-based. And while schools of education are dedicating significant resources to state-mandated accreditation processes, they typically are included in significant discussions on the issue only when the necessary certification credentials cannot be procured via any other route. Furthermore, when it comes to alternative certification, it matters not, for example, that teacher educators protest that Teach For America candidates typically stay only two years with the very students who most need quality, long-term teachers. After all, we are told, we bear a large part of the responsibility for failing to prepare quality teachers in sufficient numbers for urban schools in the first place.

The Promise of Multiliteracies to Support Literacy Learning for Urban Youth

As we near the close of the first decade of the 21st century, a decade that has witnessed the growth of a knowledge-dominated, technologically ignited nation, we see a greater-than-ever need for an educated citizenry, inclusive of all, able to speak, read, and write well enough to fully understand and promote all aspects of a democratic society. As Paulo Freire so often reminds us in many of his works, including *Pedagogy of the Oppressed* (1993), literacy is "the practice of freedom" and the power to set one free (p. 11).

We suggest that the contemporary definition of literacy and what it means to be a literate person needs to expand to include the communicative, visual, and performing arts (Alvermann & Hagood, 2000; Alvermann, Moon, & Hagood, 1999; Bearne, 2003; Flood, Heath, & Lapp, 2008). From this perspective, each art form would be viewed as a critical component of literacy as well as a phenomenon that carries within itself a representational system designed to both contain and impart meaning. In such a context, literacy would involve the ability to manipulate and understand the full array of signs, symbols, sounds, and movements (those that exist and those not yet imagined) associated with such systems. Furthermore, these signs, symbols, sounds, and movements would be treated as important tools for advancing thinking, creating, sharing, and learning and, as such, would be embedded in classroom activities and day-to-day life. This definition of literacy assumes that the ability to create, manipulate, and use an array of representational systems is at the core of the kind of high performance required for success in today's world.

This definition of literacy is not a new idea. Most students have grown up in the world of inventive and participatory media, performance, and communication; as a result, they already possess varying degrees of these abilities. Still, the kinds of planning, attention to organizational structure, relationships between parts, and manipulation of signs and symbols demanded by this expanded definition of literacy are essential to developing students' abilities to create and communicate with others (Anstey & Bull, 2006; Bearne, 2003; Cope & Kalantzis, 2000; Luke & Elkins, 1998; New London Group, 1996).

Why Redefine Literacy?

The goal of redefining literacy in such a way is to broaden students' literacy skills and expand their attitudes, knowledge, strategies, and behaviors so that they will be able to utilize and learn from an ever-growing body of text sources, both paper and electronic. To do so will involve infiltrating schools and class environments with multiliteracy tools and activities that already occur in everyday life. Those could include iPods and software that can be used to manage online instruction as well as opportunities for students to engage in podcasting and the creation of collaborative websites known as "wikis." The new literacies take their place alongside the print world and, together, provide an array of useful activities and tools for generating, receiving, communicating, and learning. With this conceptualization of literacy education, the learning world of the student would become more unified, connecting the activities and materials in the classroom to their uses in the outside world, thereby making literacy instruction more effective and empowering. Relating urban students' out-of-school language and knowledge to their in-school learning is both a powerful and productive strategy (e.g., Lee, 2007).

We already understand the value of endorsing technology as a viable means to learning. For example, in 2006, the U.S. Congress gave approval for learners to "access" higher education via the Internet. Even without this legislative approval, however, many individuals were already taking advantage of the Internet to gain postsecondary degrees. By 2007, tens of thousands of K–12 students were receiving home schooling that blended face-to-face, experiential, and online learning. Many more young students leave school each day in search of Internet access to gain information, try out ideas, and converse with others both near and far. If these trends continue to grow, it may well be that our educational research of the future will be devoted almost entirely to learning taking place in nonschool settings. In the interim, however, we still need to look to schools and after-school programs to find opportunities for improving literacy instruction.

Related Research

In the past, we expected to find most literacy researchers and educators working in schools. Today, those who study literacy and those who wish to spread its forms, uses, and effectiveness are found most abundantly outside K–16 institutions (Flood, Heath, & Lapp, 2008). Such experts work and learn in private homes, community agencies, and through public media outlets and training and development programs, exploring practical applications of literacy and its potential as a medium for change. Such changes foreshadow even more dramatic transformation of schools as we know them. By 2020, due in large part to the continuing proliferation of technology, many may have changed their physical structure, locations, and modes of operation to such an extent as to be unrecognizable.

Many researchers have addressed the question of youth culture and have concluded that, for learning to occur, teachers must know their students, as well as what engages, energizes, and motivates them. In studying student motivation and engagement, a variety of researchers argue that in our efforts to understand youth, we need to immerse ourselves in youth culture. Sutherland, Batsakis, Moje, and Alvermann (2008) note that understanding youth culture is essential to teaching effectively in today's schools. In reviewing the literature on youth culture, Epstein (1998) documents a bias against youth/adolescence in the schools. She argues that the term *youth/adolescence* is frequently connected to educational crises including drug abuse, sexual activity, and obsession with commercialized fads. She and other researchers suggest that young people have been unfairly and inaccurately described as potentially violent (Lesko, 2001; Males, 1996).

Before the term *subculture* came into vogue, Hall and Jefferson (1975) used the term to describe rebellious and subversive students. At the time, most sociologists, like Hall and Jefferson, emphasized resistance to adults as the hallmark of subculture. General subcultures in schools included jocks, burnouts, and in-betweens (Eckert, 1989). Besley (2003) categorized students as gifted, struggling, and mainstream. Some researchers found the distinction between "adult cultures" and "student cultures" particularly useful. Youths were seen as completely different from adults, with distinctive habits, customs, idiosyncrasies, and practices that often confound adults (Epstein, 1998).

In more recent years the term *youth culture* has been reconceptualized to include aspects of popular culture. Youth culture drives the market in music and many other commodities that are a part of the "real" world of young people. Several researchers now argue that popular culture plays an even more important role in schooling than schools do (Best, 2000; Buchmann, 1989; Campbell, 2004; Savage, 2007).

It is imperative to know what students are doing outside of school to make learning in school more effective. Hull and Schultz (2002) maintain that the most important advances in literacy learning knowledge have come from studies of what students do with their time when they are not in school. Unlike Hull and Schultz, whose notion of subcultures relied heavily on negative views of students, those currently researching youth culture look at how students' multiple cultural practices reflect the different ways they demonstrate literacy (Alvermann et al., 1999).

Families, friendship groups, and community organizations now generally outpace schools and classrooms in their inclusion of "multiliteracies" as the norm. Youth in peer groups or on their own in their leisure time routinely create products such as videos, DVDs, zines, blogs, and chat room dialogues. In the process, they share their expertise with one another. Yet these kinds of efforts, clearly demonstrating the application of literacy knowledge and skills, rarely are assessed by either classroom teachers or standard assessment instruments (Goodson & Norton-Meier, 2003; Moje, 2008). School literacy, as exemplified by print-only experiences and teachers as the sole arbiters, holds little appeal as learners gain real-world literacy experience.

Best Practices: Differentiating Instruction Using Multiliteracies

Students bring many differences to their classrooms. Some read well beyond their grade level; others are striving readers who read significantly below. Some students are proficient in English; others are developing their English-language skills. Some come from homes where the power language of academic English (school talk) is the language shared at the dinner table; others find such an experience completely unfamiliar. Some students work well independently; others are fidgety and tend to "roam." Some students have special needs that require accommodation.

How can the needs of all of these students be met in individual classrooms? The simple answer is differentiated literacy instruction that does not end once students learn to decode. Such an approach continues beyond the elementary and middle schools years, ultimately focusing on literacy skills and strategies that teach students to think critically about ideas, issues, and problems that invite natural connections among and interest in all areas of the curriculum.

Regardless of their differences, all students must be taught to effectively read and evaluate high school texts and related source materials in the same way proficient readers of science, social science, mathematics, and art pursue information that will help them create, defend, research, expand, and communicate. To accomplish this, teachers must model how reading, researching, discussing, debating, and writing personal and persuasive reports on information found in multiple sources influences one's personal and public lives. They must also impress upon students that being able to read and then effectively communicate what they've read is a skill that improves only with practice, reflection, and more practice.

As students embark on this process, they can be supported by teachers who demonstrate how learning is scaffolded. Starting with an entry-level source written at their independent reading level, students begin to build the language skills, concepts, and fluency they need to gain information by accessing increasingly difficult materials, including fictional, scientific, technical, and historical texts; graphs and charts; graphic novels; magazines and news reports; and Web-based sources such as e-books, podcasts, and blogs. Students must be supported in realizing that there is no end to the informational sources that can lead from one interesting question (and insight into its answer) to yet another. This kind of discovery is magical; it represents an "aha" moment by opening up a world of adventure and challenge filled with the rewards that come from seeking out and accumulating knowledge. Instruction that utilizes new literacy tools to support students—and in particular those in urban classrooms—takes a proactive stance toward building their personal learning prowess.

Students develop metacognitive understandings by examining their individual literacy processes, while their teachers model ways to personally evaluate and develop a self-awareness of one's reading purposes, processes, and accumulated knowledge. Developing this awareness over time and across texts builds students' conceptual vocabulary and knowledge base about a topic of study as well as their cognitive processing of the information source. It is important to illustrate how one idea branches to another. Through this modeling, students can be taught to

> second guess, analyze and weigh, critique and rewrite texts, not just
> of literary culture, but of popular culture, online culture, corporate
> life and citizenship. In a culture where texts are there to position, de-

fine, sell, and, indeed manipulate and shape a population at every turn, to give students anything less than a fully critical literacy would be to abrogate our responsibility as educators. (Elkins & Luke, 1999, p. 214)

For example, a proficient reader of texts within a topical area knows how to use text and Web sources to extend topical schema and vocabulary as well as how to manage attention, text difficulty, and metacognition through self-reflection and questioning. To begin to help students act similarly as they develop the content knowledge and skills to think, talk, read, write, initiate, and solve problems like expert readers in a field, teachers must have a thorough understanding of each student's entry-level knowledge of the topic and of his or her reading, writing, and language abilities. Teachers must also be aware of their students' levels of sophistication when it comes to using new literacy tools, which is highly dependent on student access to those tools. Such access, of course, is in turn closely tied to a student's socioeconomic status.

With these understandings in place, teachers can model for students how to enter a topic at different levels depending on one's background knowledge, which expands with further research. Think-aloud protocols provide the context for teachers to model their personal thinking processes as they read and work to make sense of a text. Teachers must demonstrate how a plan for reading is built by the reader according to how much is known about the topic being read and also about the source of the information. For example, if readers are preparing to use a paper text source and an electronic source such as a podcast or PowerPoint presentation to learn about a selected topic, the text needs to be at their independent reading level. If it is not, the teacher needs to model how an easier source might be located and then how to move to more difficult texts once a base of knowledge has been built. The teacher also needs to model how to efficiently use the electronic source. This is especially critical given the socioeconomic divide that limits many students' access to computers and the Internet in school or the public library (Hoffman & Novak, 1998; Servon, 2002; U.S. Department of Commerce, 1999).

Differentiation Applied

We had the opportunity to witness this type of instruction in an urban classroom with many economically disadvantaged students at a charter high school within the San Diego Unified School District. In a 10th-grade biology class, teacher Dr. Maria Grant began a study of DNA by having her students discuss what they knew about the topic and charting their thoughts in the first column of a K-W-L chart, a strategy developed by Ogle (1986). Grant used the chart to assess what her students knew or remembered about the topic since the concept of DNA had been introduced to them in 7th grade when their teacher had addressed the following science standard: "Students know DNA (deoxyribonucleic acid) is the genetic material of living organisms and is located in the chromosomes of each cell." Now, Grant was addressing the function of DNA.

To engage her students' interest, she asked them to think about their families and friends and how much they were like or unlike them. As she pushed them to differentiate between inherited and learned behaviors and characteristics, she asked them to estimate what percentage of their DNA structure made them different from others. Grant encouraged lots of conversation because she believes that topical conversations, which are first shared through the comfortable registers of students' home languages, are expanded through discussions of new information acquired from multiple sources. As her students' topical knowledge grows, so does their academic language—the more precise, powerful language typically used in postsecondary school settings.

Following this introductory large-group activity, Grant explained that when she begins to study a topic that she doesn't know well, she likes to hear as well as read something easy about it. She modeled for them how she would begin to build this background of information and language through Internet sources, many of which contain a voice feature. Thus, Grant began to scaffold her students' learning as together they listened to and read audio and print information found at Science NetLinks (www.sciencenetlinks.com/sci_update.cfm?DOCID=164).

Grant believes that this modeling demonstrates to students that it's OK not to read a difficult text as your first source. As a result, her students talk about "growing" their knowledge. This is very important for students in urban classrooms who, after years of failing school experiences, run the risk of exhibiting classic Pygmalion behavior (Rosenthal & Jacobson, 1968) characterized by the belief that they are unable to learn.

As Grant and her students discussed the questions listed at this site, their conversation expanded to include questions about ways in which DNA offers clues to identifying sources of infectious diseases and subsequently providing a healthier quality of life. They decided to create a timeline to illustrate their findings. Grant explained that oftentimes a study in one area (science) leads to study in another (history). To create the timeline, they explored additional websites such as Family Tree DNA (www.familytreedna.com/facts_genes.asp), which was discovered after Grant modeled for them how to conduct an Internet search. She also told them that when she can't find a source that includes audio on the Internet, she goes to iTunes to find a podcast. She demonstrated for them how to search iTunes for podcasts about DNA. Her search turned up a number of sources, including some that were musical in nature. From this list she selected two for further investigation: "NPR: Health and Science" and "The Best of *National Geographic*." Several students offered to collaboratively explore these sites, both of which offer free subscriptions. Prior to beginning their personal electronic searches, Grant and the students used the following URLs to gain insights about the worth of a source:

- Finding Information on the Internet: A Tutorial (www.lib .berkeley.edu/TeachingLib/Guides/Internet/Evaluate.html)
- Kathy Schrock's Guide for Educators: Critical Evaluation Information (school.discovery.com/schrockguide/eval.html)

Reminding her students that to get "smart" about something they had to start with what they knew, Grant next modeled for them how they could use children's books written at their independent reading levels as sources of information on DNA. She specifically showed them how she skimmed the books to get an overview—or general picture—of their content.

She demonstrated various literacy strategies, such as varying her speed in different sections, depending on the material's level of difficulty; predicting which sources would have the information she needed; and changing her predictions based on the inferences she drew from the material. She showed them how she kept growing her knowledge by synthesizing new information with previously discovered facts. She pointed out how her understanding of the topical vocabulary grew as she skimmed and read from multiple sources. Because her students exhibited a wide range of reading ability, Grant made a point of integrating these kinds of strategies into her content instruction. Such detailed modeling may not be necessary in more affluent schools, but it is a definite must in this urban high school attended by economically deprived students.

Grant always secures lots of related, relevant books that are not as difficult to read as the class text. Her goal is to have her students increase

Table 2.1. Books Used During Classroom Study of DNA

Asimov, I., & Wool, D. (1985). *How did we find out about DNA?* New York: Walker & Company.

Balkwill, F.R. (1994). *Cells are us.* Ill. M. Rolph. Minneapolis, MN: Carolrhoda.

Balkwill, F.R. (1994). *Cell wars.* Ill. M. Rolph. Minneapolis, MN: Carolrhoda.

Balkwill, F.R. (1994). *DNA is here to stay.* Ill. M. Rolph. Minneapolis, MN: Carolrhoda.

Balkwill, F.R. (2002). *Have a nice DNA.* Ill. M. Rolph. Minneapolis, MN: Carolrhoda.

Claybourne, A., Brooks, F., & Seay, C.A. (2003). *Usborne Internet-linked introduction to genes and DNA.* Ill. S. Moncrieff. London: Usborne.

Fridell, R. (2001). *DNA fingerprinting: The ultimate identity.* Danbury, CT: Franklin Watts.

Phelan, G. (2006). *Double helix: The quest to uncover the structure of DNA.* Washington, DC: National Geographic Children's Books.

Rainis, K.G. (2006). *Blood and DNA evidence: Crime-solving experiments.* Berkeley Heights, NJ: Enslow.

Snedden, R. (2002). *DNA & genetic engineering.* Portsmouth, NH: Heinemann.

Stille, D.R. (2006). *DNA: The master molecule of life.* Ill. E. Hoffmann. Mankato, MN: Compass Point.

Walker, R.W. (2003). *Genes and DNA.* Boston: Kingfisher.

Woodard, K. (2002). *My first book about DNA.* Tinicum, PA: Xlibris.

their academic and topical language and content knowledge by accessing the topic through paper and electronic sources that support their interests and provide a personal scaffold, or link, to the knowledge they need to acquire.

The books that Grant borrowed from the public and school library for this study are listed in Table 2.1. Notice that the array of sources Grant uses presents information at different difficulty levels. Grant believes that her students, like all readers, enter any topic of study with varying degrees of knowledge and that this kind of differentiated approach supports each student's learning. Dr. Grant's classroom was a model of differentiated instruction that focused on students' individual differences by supporting the study of a topic through varied materials that accommodated learning differences.

Summary of Main Ideas

To summarize, we argue that salient characteristics of urban schools and school districts influence and therefore must inform the preparation of teachers of reading.

As demonstrated by the instructional example in Grant's class, instruction must address the uniqueness of every student. Instruction of this type exemplifies the following principles that support students as they develop knowledge and know-how about how to continue to learn individually and collaboratively in an ever-growing world of new multiliteracies:

- All students are unique, and their differences do not necessarily remain constant. Their strengths and needs change as their literacy skills develop and they grow in their knowledge.
- Instruction that attempts to meet the needs of all students must be flexible and adaptable to each individual.
- Assessment of students' strengths and needs must be continual to ensure that students learn all they can.
- Instruction must be multisensory with learning opportunities that rely on all of the senses, and it must be scaffolded for each student's learning level.
- Instruction with multimedia enhances the probability of each student's learning.

The use of multiliteracies offers powerful instructional alternatives for urban classroom teachers who oftentimes teach in extremely challenging instructional environments. Multiliteracies offer teachers routes to differentiated instruction in supersized school districts that tend to focus on "scaling up" and "one size fits all" instructional solutions. Multiliteracies offer teachers the means to access the cultural capital and assets of K–12 students who typically are more attuned to alternative literacies than prior generations. Finally, multiliteracies enable teacher educators to create literacy pedagogy that not only supports important yet narrow achievement outcomes but that also provides all urban students with intellectually rich and engaging learning opportunities.

Implications for Research, Practice, and Policy

More needs to be learned about the specific influences of the urban context on the practice of urban classroom teachers. One example, the Teacher Pathways Project (www.teacherpolicyresearch.org), an extensive and ongoing study of teacher preparation routes to teaching in New York City schools, provides important starting points for study.

This is a vastly understudied arena with enormous implications for the preparation of urban teachers in general and, more specifically, urban teachers of reading. For instance, we typically do not differentiate instruction in our college classrooms for those teacher candidates who are members of the communities in which they will be teaching and those who are not. Yet should we not differentiate our curricula for those candidates who are learning to teach in communities radically different from those in which they grew up?

Beyond that, how shall we arrange for well-mentored field experiences that develop candidates' resilience, adaptability, and perseverance in underfunded, highly bureaucratized urban school settings? And to what extent can the promise of multiliteracies be brought to bear on teacher preparation in service of student learning in urban environments? Finally, it is clear that further study is needed to better understand how to improve literacy for today's urban learners in powerful and productive ways that support differentiated lesson design for high school as well as elementary and middle school students.

REFERENCES

Alvermann, D.E., & Hagood, M.C. (2000). Critical media literacy: Research, theory, and practice in new times. *Journal of Educational Research, 93*, 193–205.

Alvermann, D.E., Moon, J.S., & Hagood, M.C. (1999). *Popular culture in the classroom: Teaching and researching critical media literacy*. Newark, DE: International Reading Association.

Anstey, M., & Bull, G. (2006). *Teaching and learning multiliteracies: Changing times, changing literacies*. Newark, DE: International Reading Association.

Bearne, E. (2003). Rethinking literacy: Communication, representation and text. *Literacy, 37*, 98–103.

Besley, A.C. (2003). Hybridized and globalized: Youth cultures in the postmodern era. *The Review of Education, Pedagogy & Cultural Studies, 25*, 153–177.

Best, A.L. (2000). *Prom night: Youth, schools, and popular culture*. New York: Routledge.

Buchmann, M. (1989). *The script of life in modern society: Entry into adulthood in a changing world*. Chicago: University of Chicago Press.

Campbell, N. (2004). *American youth cultures*. New York: Routledge.

Chou, V., & Mayeda, S. (2007, May). *Literacy Leaders for Urban Teacher Education (LLUTE) survey results analysis: Director of field placements and supervision survey* (slides #4–7). Symposium conducted at the 52nd annual convention of the International Reading Association, Toronto, ON.

Chou, V., & Tozer, S. (2008). What's urban got to do with it?: The meanings of *urban* in urban teacher preparation and development. In F.P. Peterman (Ed.),

Partnering to prepare urban teachers: A call to activism (pp. 1–20). New York: Peter Lang.

Cope, B., & Kalantzis, M. (2000). *Multiliteracies: Literacy learning and the design of social futures*. New York: Routledge.

Delpit, L. (1988). The silenced dialogue: Power and pedagogy in educating other people's children. *Harvard Educational Review, 58*, 280–298.

Eckert, P. (1989). *Jocks and burnouts: Social categories and identity in the high school*. New York: Teachers College Press.

Elkins, J., & Luke, A. (1999). Redefining adolescent literacies. *Journal of Adolescent & Adult Literacy, 43*, 212–215.

Epstein, J.S. (1998). Introduction: Generation X, youth culture, and identity. In J.S. Epstein (Ed.), *Youth culture: Identity in a postmodern world* (pp. 1–23). Oxford, England: Blackwell.

Flood, J., Heath, S.B., & Lapp, D. (2008). *Handbook of research on teaching literacy through the communicative and visual arts* (Vol. 2). Mahwah, NJ: Erlbaum.

Freire, P. (1993). *Pedagogy of the oppressed*. New York: Continuum.

Goodson, F.T., & Norton-Meier, L. (2003). Motor oil, civil disobedience, and media literacy. *Journal of Adolescent & Adult Literacy, 47*, 258–262.

Hall, S., & Jefferson, T. (Eds.). (1975). *Resistance through rituals: Youth subcultures in post-war Britain*. London: Hutchinson.

Hoffman, D.L., & Novak, T.P. (1998). *Bridging the digital divide: The impact of race on computer access and Internet use*. Nashville, TN: Vanderbilt University.

Hull, G., & Schultz, K. (Eds.). (2002). *School's out! Bridging out-of-school literacies with classroom practice*. New York: Teachers College Press.

Kaestle, C.F. (1995). Literate America: High-level adult literacy goals. In D. Ravitch & M.A. Vinovskis (Eds.), *Historical perspectives on the current education reforms* (pp. 329–354). Baltimore: The Johns Hopkins University Press.

Lee, C.D. (2007). *The role of culture in academic literacies: Conducting our blooming in the midst of the whirlwind*. New York: Teachers College Press.

Lesko, N. (2001). *Act your age! A cultural construction of adolescence*. New York: Routledge.

Luke, A., & Elkins, J. (1998). Reinventing literacy in "new times." *Journal of Adolescent & Adult Literacy, 42*, 4–7.

Males, M.A. (1996). *The scapegoat generation: America's war on adolescents*. Monroe, ME: Common Courage Press.

Moje, E.B. (2008). Youth cultures, literacies, and identities in and out of school. In J. Flood, S.B. Heath, & D. Lapp (Eds.), *Handbook of research on teaching literacy through communicative and visual arts* (Vol. 2, pp. 207–220). Mahwah, NJ: Erlbaum.

National Center for Education Statistics. (2005). The condition of education, 2005. *Education Statistics Quarterly, 7*(1–2).

New London Group. (1996). A pedagogy of multiliteracies: Designing social futures. *Harvard Educational Review, 66*, 60–92.

Ogle, D. (1986). K-W-L: A teaching model that develops active reading of expository text. *The Reading Teacher, 39*, 564–570.

Roderick, M., Nagaoka, J., & Allensworth, E. (with Coca, V., Correa, M., & Stoker, G.). (2006, April). *From high school to the future: A first look at Chicago Public*

School graduates' college enrollment, college preparation, and graduation from four-year colleges. Chicago: Consortium on Chicago School Research. Retrieved January 15, 2008, from ccsr.uchicago.edu/publications/Postsecondary.pdf

Rosenthal, R., & Jacobson, L. (1968). *Pygmalion in the classroom: Teacher expectation and pupils' intellectual development*. New York: Rinehart and Winston.

Savage, J. (2007). *Teenage: The creation of youth culture*. New York: Viking.

Servon, L.J. (2002). *Bridging the digital divide: Technology, community, and public policy*. Oxford, England: Blackwell Publishing.

Snipes, J., Doolittle, F., & Herlihy, C. (2002). *Foundations for success: Case studies of how urban school systems improve student achievement*. Washington, DC: Manpower Demonstration Research Corporation for the Council of the Great City Schools. Retrieved January 15, 2008, from www.mdrc.org/publications/47/full.pdf

Sutherland, L., Batsakis, S., Moje, E., & Alvermann, D. (2008). Drawing on youth cultures in content learning and literacy. In D. Lapp, J. Flood, & N. Farnan (Eds.), *Content area reading and learning: Instructional strategies* (3rd ed., pp. 133–156). Mahwah, NJ: Erlbaum.

U.S. Department of Commerce. (1999). *Falling through the net: Defining the digital divide*. Washington, DC: National Telecommunications and Information Administration. Retrieved January 15, 2008, from www.ntia.doc.gov/ntiahome/fttn99

Weiner, L. (2000). Research in the 90s: Implications for teacher preparation. *Review of Educational Research, 70*, 369–406.

CHAPTER 3

Critical Elements for Literacy Instruction of Teacher Candidates for Urban Settings

Susan Lenski
Carol L. Mack
Julie Esparza Brown
Portland State University

S tudents in urban settings may have different language and cultural experiences, may encounter different types of environmental print, and may speak a language other than Standard
American English. As a result, teacher preparation programs have a responsibility to help teacher candidates understand cultures different
from their own, creatively work with students' families, and advocate for
their students' literacy development.

Although there is a relatively strong research base on the teaching
of reading (e.g., National Institute of Child Health and Human Development, 2000; three volumes of the *Handbook of Reading Research*—Barr,
Kamil, Mosenthal, & Pearson, 1991; Kamil, Mosenthal, Pearson, & Barr,
2000; Pearson, Barr, Kamil, & Mosenthal, 1984) and a growing research
base on teacher preparation (Cochran-Smith & Zeichner, 2005), the research base on the preparation of literacy teachers in urban settings is
modest (Lenski, Grisham, & Wold, 2006). Two books about teaching
reading in urban settings have been written by commissions of the
International Reading Association: The Urban Diversity Initiatives
Commission developed an edited book *Promising Practices for Urban
Reading Instruction* (Mason & Schumm, 2003), and the Urban Partnership Committee edited a book *Literacy Development of Students in
Urban Schools* (Flood & Anders, 2005). Missing from the literature are

Improving Literacy Achievement in Urban Schools: Critical Elements in Teacher Preparation
edited by Louise C. Wilkinson, Lesley Mandel Morrow, and Victoria Chou. © 2008 by the
International Reading Association.

recommendations for teacher preparation that can be extrapolated from this research base.

Purpose of This Chapter

The purpose of this chapter is to describe the critical elements in literacy teacher preparation that are essential for the literacy learning of students in urban settings, elements that take into account the students' distinct cultural and language experiences and needs. The chapter begins with a review of the pertinent research on urban literacy practices and goes on to put forth a set of recommendations for practice, policy, and further research on teacher preparation programs that target successful practices in urban settings.

Review of Research and Theory

No two urban areas are alike, but all have large numbers of students who have distinct literacy needs. Most urban areas have high numbers of students who do not speak or read English, students who live in generational poverty, and immigrants with little or no formal education. To further complicate matters, urban public schools tend to have students with high mobility rates, inadequate resources, and special literacy needs (Strickland & Alvermann, 2004). All urban areas face major issues related to the literacy learning of students, one of which is socioeconomic status (SES).

Socioeconomic Status

The SES of students plays a big role in their literacy development. According to Snow, Burns, and Griffin (1998), low SES is both an individual risk factor and a group risk factor for literacy learning. Low SES students who attend the same schools as students from a higher SES are more likely to have trouble learning to read. Further, groups of students from low SES communities are more likely to have difficulty reading than students from wealthier families. Because most urban areas have large numbers of low SES students, literacy problems are often intense and difficult to solve. Among the barriers to literacy instruction found in low SES areas are the delayed language development of many children and the kinds of environmental print available for children to read.

Language development. The language development of young children is a significant predictor of success in school (Snow, 1991). According to the U.S. Department of Education's Early Childhood Longitudinal Study (2001), children come to school with disparate levels of language exposure, ability, and knowledge, a situation that contributes to the beginning of an ever-widening achievement gap. Exacerbating the situation is the fact that many children in urban areas exhibit significant language delays that hinder them from making typical gains in language learning.

A related predictor of literacy achievement in American classrooms is the number and type of verbal interactions within families. Heath's (1983) classic study found differences between the types and number of interactions between low and middle SES families. Within each of the communities Heath studied, the communicative value of differing interaction patterns was not significant. What was significant for predicting later success in school was how closely each community's interactional patterns resembled those the children would later encounter in school. The closer the match, the less difficult the transition from home to school. The more teachers know about varying communication patterns, the better able they will be to help students make the transition to the patterns of the school context.

Although students' experiences with language during their developmental years can either promote or hinder reading success, Hayward (2004) reminds us that all communication, verbal and nonverbal, is culturally determined. Children experience problems in school when the interactional style of the teacher does not match the interactional style of the student. Heath found that this disparity poses problems for students from some cultures who may value nonverbal communication and listening more than the kinds of verbal fluency that is often valued in schools.

Environmental print. One of the ways children learn about language is by seeing print in their environment. Most children in the United States are surrounded by print. They see print in books and other written materials at home; on television; in stores; on food items; on trucks, buildings, and billboards; and in school. The print in children's environment supports their development as literacy learners (e.g., Clay, 1979; Teale & Sulzby, 1986).

Children who are surrounded with print have what Duke (2000) terms *semiotic capital*, an understanding of signs and symbols within their environment. Urban children also have semiotic capital, but it is different from that of middle class suburban children. Children from middle-income suburban neighborhoods, for example, tend to have access to print in public spaces in the form of billboards, street signs, and business signs. There tend to be many more stores, strip malls, and businesses in middle-income neighborhoods. Children from lower-income urban neighborhoods typically have access to fewer business signs but more community murals and graffiti (Aguilar, 2000). This print is meant to communicate messages for specific audiences and members of the community.

Children from urban areas, therefore, may actually experience multiple literacies (McPherson, 2004) because they may have the ability to convey and recover meaning from a variety of different symbol systems. This print, however, is different from the print that is typically seen in schools.

The availability of print material also plays an important role in helping children learn to read. In a study of two low-income and two middle-income neighborhoods, Neuman and Celano (2001) found that resources such as books and magazines are much more available in the homes and schools of children living in middle-income neighborhoods than in the homes and schools of those living in the low-income areas. Children in lower economic settings have to rely more heavily on public institutions such as libraries for access to these materials.

Teaching Diverse Groups of Students

Approximately 90% of the current teacher workforce is white, middle class, and female, and teacher candidates reflect this same pattern (Center on Education Policy, 2006). As a result, the majority of teacher candidates have inadequate experience with students from backgrounds that are not middle class and white. What's more, research indicates that many teacher candidates view students from diverse backgrounds from a deficit model (Banks et al., 2005).

The differences between the life experiences of teacher candidates and the students in urban areas have an impact on the way candidates approach instruction (Lazar, 2004). According to Lenski, Crawford, Crumpler, and Stallworth (2006), "The meeting of cultures in schools can result in a cultural clash when the culture of students is different from that of the teacher" (p. 3). Although we have a long way to go before the teaching workforce mirrors the diverse student population, all teachers—urban, suburban, and rural—can learn how to effectively work across the cultural spectrum of their students.

Language Issues of Minority Students

Language—whether it is a first, second, or third language—develops in a sequential manner, is experientially based (Cummins, 1984), and is inextricably linked with cultural and community. Yet Standard American English is not the language spoken in the homes of many students in urban schools. Students may come from homes where they hear Spanish, Russian, or other languages; African American Language (AAL); English dialects that are different from Standard American English; or combinations of heritage languages and English.

Linguistic minority students are referred to by many terms, including *limited English proficient, English as a second language, bilingual, English-language learners* (ELL), and *English learners*. These terms describe children who live within two language systems and who may or may not have been born in the United States. All of these students have one or more languages that are connected with their homes, families, communities, and personal identities (Delpit, 2005). Some of these children have two underdeveloped language systems (Kohnert, Yim, Nett, Kan, & Duran, 2005). (In this chapter, we use the term *English-language learner* or ELL when describing students whose primary language is not English because that term focuses on students' potential for learning.)

According to Hollie (2005), more than 80% of African Americans speak AAL, which refers to the distinct language patterns used by many African Americans. Students who have grown up hearing and speaking AAL face challenges similar to other linguistic minorities, and yet they are rarely recognized as language-minority students. According to experts on teaching African Americans, AAL should be recognized and valued as a distinct language that is different from Standard American English, the dialect of English currently used by those in power.

Like other second-language students, students who speak AAL must learn when to use Standard American English and when to use AAL. This type of code-switching (or dialect-shifting) requires that teachers understand how AAL is different from Standard American English and how to scaffold students' learning so that they can be proficient in both languages (Harris-Wright, 2005).

Mastering two languages. As students struggle to learn a second language, first-language functions and opportunities are often truncated. The contexts for developing a complete language system is taken for granted in middle class homes but may be absent in working class and linguistic-minority communities when families struggling to make ends meet have little time for extended discourse (Macedo, Dendrinos, & Gounari, 2003). Therefore, a large number of linguistic-minority students in the United States are what Valdés and Figueroa (1994) call *circumstantial bilinguals* because they must acquire some degree of proficiency in the societal language (i.e., English) prior to developing full proficiency in their primary language.

Students lacking a complete primary language have a weak first-language foundation on which to build a second language (Harper & de Jong, 2004). They are "bilingual" in the sense that they are exposed to two languages—one at home and one at school. However, they may not be truly bilingual in terms of linguistic proficiency in either or both languages. Many students will experience further attrition of their primary language when they acquire English because they enter predominantly English environments that do not foster maintenance of their heritage language (Oller, Pearson, Umbel, Fernández, & Navarro, 1997). An individual's degree of bilingualism, therefore, is dependent upon linguistic, social, emotional, political, demographic, and cultural factors; general ability level; age; occupation; opportunities for contact with speakers of English; exposure to media in English; the nature of interactions with members of her or his own linguistic community; and exposure to and explicit instruction in the second language.

Children who undergo language loss in their primary language may exhibit language patterns that resemble errors typically seen in children who exhibit language disorders solely due to their circumstantial bilingual status (Artiles & Ortiz, 2002). Therefore, it is important for educators to be knowledgeable about the second-language acquisition process but also aware of their students' native-language experiences and backgrounds (Case & Taylor, 2005). It is even more crucial, however, to understand that the language each child brings to school is a valuable and precious linguistic resource that ties that child to her or his family and community.

Consider the example of a family with which one of the authors worked. The family, which included two boys, emigrated from Mexico. The older brother had been born in Mexico and moved with the family to the United States when he was 4 years old. As a result, he had a good foundation in Spanish, his first language, before entering an English-only classroom. This child retained the ability to communicate in Spanish. His younger brother was born in the United States, and although he heard some Spanish at home he was exposed to English through television, neighbors, and his brother. He became proficient in English but not in Spanish, which made communicating with his family very difficult.

Cultural determinations of text structures. In a recent study about informational texts, Pappas (2006) asserts that "genres are social acts. They occur because these acts, as texts, are recurring activities in the culture" (p. 229). Thus, text structures are culturally determined. Hayward (2004) describes ways in which writings from different cultures may vary through organization, sentence style, and informality. For example, the organization of North American writing is typically inductive and direct, whereas writers from Spanish, Arabic, and some European cultures value deductive reasoning as their organizational framework. The sentence style of North Americans, influenced by Strunk and White's (1999) *The Elements of Style*, has become increasingly short and direct, while writers from Spanish cultures prefer longer sentences. North American writing is becoming increasingly informal, while writing from South America and Asia retains a more formal approach.

In a typical public school setting, teachers promote stories organized in linear, chronological patterns typical of those found in middle class contexts (Gee, 2002). Once again, this style may not be typically intuitive to many urban school children because "different cultures and social groups organize language within stanzas in different and culturally distinctive ways" (Gee, 2002, p. 16).

Below is a translation of a story written by an ELL student receiving literacy instruction in his native language, Spanish.

> "Is this the first rainbow you have seen?" asked my cousins while it was raining with the sun out. They said, "The rainbow shines in the sunshine." I said, "Of course it shines in the sun," and I continued to ask them about the rainbow. It rained very hard. The sun shone so much that we could not even see the rainbow. It stopped raining so hard. The sun stopped shining and we could once again see the resplendent rainbow. After that I asked a question. "Is this the first rainbow you have ever seen?" "Yes, we are looking at it right now," they answered. We watched the resplendent and beautiful rainbow all day.

This story is an example of a culturally divergent writing style where the focus is on the object rather than on a story with a clear beginning, middle, and end. The student carefully chose vocabulary to describe the beauty of the rainbow, and he captures a magical moment in time. The style of this story, however, does not match the preferred story style that is common in North America.

Family and Community Influences

Families are an important influence on children's attitudes toward and achievement in school (Sheldon & Epstein, 2005). According to the U.S. Department of Education (2001), children from homes with more books and those whose parents value reading tend to perform higher on achievement tests than children from homes where less reading takes place. Reading, however, is not the only family practice that supports literacy. Many parents come from families with rich oral language traditions that are highly valued and passed down from generation to generation. Telling family or cultural stories, usually in the home language, and engaging in post-storytelling discussions can also support children's school achievement and cognition.

Cultural Differences and Family Involvement

Parents from different cultural groups may have different expectations of schools and show different types of involvement. For example, Lee and Bowen (2006) find that European Americans report more involvement in schools than both Hispanic and African American parents. European Americans support their children in the traditional ways expected by the school systems, such as engaging in educational discussions and helping their children with homework.

Although all parents foster their children's learning, some parents teach their children things that relate directly to school learning (as defined in American schools) while others do not (Purcell-Gates, 2000). In some cultures, for example, parents believe that their job is to teach their children life skills, values, and manners and the school's job to academically educate their children (Faltis, 2001; Rodríguez-Brown, 2001). These families consider it disrespectful to the teacher to teach their children academic skills at home. To many educators, however, such cultural beliefs could be misconstrued as lack of interest on the part of parents in their child's academic progress.

Cultural Capital and Family Involvement

According to McNeal (1999), the cultural capital parents possess influences the degree to which they are likely to get involved in their children's schools in traditional ways. *Cultural capital* is a term used to describe the advantages individuals or groups possess that result in their life experiences being congruent with institutions such as schools (Bourdieu & Passeron, 1977). Middle and upper class cultural capital is respected and reproduced in schooling. For example, Standard American English is valued and expected in American schools. Those students whose home cultures are steeped in Standard American English have an advantage over students who speak another language or a different dialect of English at home and who, as a result, do not have as firm a grasp on the subtleties of the English language. Not all students, therefore, possess equal amounts of cultural capital.

Parents with cultural capital are able to converse in Standard American English and are comfortable in school settings; their cultural capital makes it easier for them to become involved in schools than parents from diverse backgrounds, who may view their roles differently (Rodríguez-Brown, 2001). Parents from cultural backgrounds that are different from the cultures valued by schools may participate in schools differently because they have different predispositions toward certain types of behaviors, attitudes, and perceptions (Rodríguez-Brown, 2001). These predispositions are called *habitus*. For example, the father of a child attending an inner-city school volunteered to help care for the school grounds even though he would not attend parent–teacher conferences. Teachers, however, can misinterpret this kind of predisposition as a lack of caring on the part of parents about their children's academic achievement.

Promising Practices

Students in urban areas have unique literacy needs. Because urban areas are densely populated regions that are often immigrants' first homes, the language and literacy needs of these students often center on language acquisition and development. Students who live in urban areas are also in greatest need of understanding the role education plays in their lives. Many students from urban areas often question the relevance of school learning as they watch their families face the daily struggle to survive in sometimes hostile environments. There are, however, several promising practices that can help teacher candidates facilitate the literacy needs of students from urban areas.

Help Teacher Candidates Identify Their Own Cultural Beliefs

Teacher candidates often have a difficult time understanding that they, too, have cultural beliefs, values, and prejudices. When asked to discuss their personal cultures, middle class, white candidates frequently respond by saying they have no culture (Lenski, Crawford et al., 2006). Such a response points out the need for teacher candidates to explore their own identity, biases, stereotypes, and cultural beliefs as well as the cultural beliefs and values of students in urban schools (Howard, 1999; Lazar, 2006). Through the process of comparing and contrasting their own life experiences and cultural values with those of their students, teacher candidates can develop a framework to use throughout their careers to get to truly know each of their students and to connect school learning to their lives.

Describe How Teacher Candidates Can Learn About Students' Cultures

Darling-Hammond and Garcia-Lopez (2002) state, "It is impossible to prepare tomorrow's teachers to succeed with all of the students they will meet without exploring how students' learning experiences are influenced by their home languages, cultures, and contexts" (p. 9). There are many ways in which teacher preparation programs can help teacher candidates learn about the cultures of students in urban areas. Lynch and Hanson (2004) suggest four:

1. Learning through books, the arts, and technology
2. Talking, socializing, and working with individuals from the cultures who can act as cultural guides or mediators
3. Participating in the daily life of another culture
4. Learning the language of other cultures

One of the most promising practices is to help teacher candidates learn how to use children's and young adult books to approach literature from a critical literacy perspective. When candidates read from a critical literacy perspective, they read, analyze, and evaluate books within a sociocultural framework and they teach students in schools to read books to understand the social realities of the world (Lenski, 2008).

Leland and Harste (2005), for example, use text sets as a vehicle to discuss with teacher candidates the social issues that confront students from diverse backgrounds. Teachers can also use literature written by authors representing the cultural groups of their students and find themes that resonate with urban children. All children need opportunities to see themselves reflected in books and the curriculum.

Caution Teacher Candidates Against Overgeneralizing Cultural Understandings

Once teacher candidates learn about the cultures of their students, they tend to overgeneralize cultural experiences and apply them to students regardless of a student's background. Garcia (2002) writes about herself, "I felt that I was losing my voice because of my status as a 'minority' student and that some people viewed me as part of a cultural framework I had not claimed" (p. 23). Teacher candidates need to think about the differences *within* a culture as well as the differences *between* cultures. Some students, for example, are socialized into the culture of their family, while other students from the same background may be socialized into the culture that they see around them. Lynch and Hanson (2004) believe that

> assumptions about an individual's behavior based on a cultural label or a stereotype may result in inaccurate, inappropriate, or harmful generalizations. Although individuals may identify with a given cultural, ethnic, or racial group by way of birthplace, skin color, language, or religious practices, these factors will not determine the degree to which individuals see themselves as members of a group. (p. 15)

Teacher candidates should be encouraged to use their assumptions as a hypothesis and then test these assumptions in order to ascertain how accurate they are.

Teacher candidates also need to learn about the dynamic nature of all cultures and ways in which immigrants change as a result of living in the United States. Culture is not static. As students attend school, they begin to incorporate the cultural practices of North American schooling into their lifestyles and worldviews. For example, some cultures have a fluid notion of time, but North Americans tend to place great importance on time as indicated by the number of expressions about time in the United States (Hayward, 2004). Immigrant students and their families may begin to adopt the cultural practice of being sensitive to time. Although students may not be as aware of time as teachers, they may no longer approach time in the same way as others from their home culture. Such a cultural shift places these students and families outside the accepted notions of either culture, illustrating a small way in which students and families make cultural changes. Thus, teacher candidates need to understand not only the benefits but also the possible pitfalls of learning about students' cultural backgrounds, and they should be cautioned not to overgeneralize their knowledge about cultures to all students.

Help Teacher Candidates Situate Standard American English as the Dialect of Power

"As educators, we must resist the tendency to equate the use of language other than Standard English with incompetence or lack of intelligence" (Strickland, Ganske, & Monroe, 2002, p. 9). Many students in urban schools speak dialects or languages other than Standard English. Teacher candidates need to learn how to teach in ways that do not denigrate a student's home language yet teach students when and how to use Standard English, the accepted language of academia, business, and politics (Delpit, 1986, 1988). Teacher candidates can encourage students to use code-switching that builds on their home-language experiences. For example, students can use their home language in small-group discussions to develop their ideas and then switch to English when bringing their ideas to the entire group. This type of scaffolding encourages students to use more than one language as they develop their English-speaking abilities (Wheeler & Swords, 2006).

Show Teacher Candidates How to Find and Use Print Available in Urban Areas

Teacher candidates need to be aware of the different challenges urban settings present for young readers just learning about print in their world. Orellana and Hernández (2003) find that children in Los Angeles are surrounded by multilingual signs and exposed to a variety of different types of environmental print, both in their home languages and in English. Children in other urban areas might see signs in languages and alphabets that are different from their own. Teacher preparation programs need to make teacher candidates aware of the environmental print available locally and how best to use that material to help young children become readers and writers.

One type of print found in many urban areas is graffiti, defined as "writings or drawings made in public places" (Harris & Hodges, 1995, p. 98). Because graffiti is so prevalent in urban areas, it is a primary source of environmental print for children who live there. Yet children in some urban areas have difficulty making the connection between the stylized fonts typical of the graffiti they see in their communities and the more standard kind of print used in books. As a result, teacher candidates need to think about how to use local graffiti to help students learn the alphabet and make other kinds of connections between environmental and other kinds of print. This helps students better understand that all types of reading and writing represent ways to communicate.

Teacher preparation programs, therefore, need to expand their teaching on environmental print to take into account the very real exposure to letters, words, and meanings that children find in their world. That could mean teaching teachers appropriate ways of using graffiti in the classroom.

Help Teacher Candidates Understand Multiple Ways to Organize Texts

Teacher candidates need to learn that text patterns are cultural representations. Before teaching story structure, for example, teacher candidates should learn about the cultural roots of written texts, including the ways in which text structure varies from culture to culture. Further, they need to learn not only how narrative or informational texts are organized in North American culture but also how such text patterns are organized in other cultures. That way, stories from other cultures can be appreciated for their vivid descriptions rather than viewed as poorly organized.

Help Teacher Candidates Consider Creative Approaches to Parental Involvement

Moll and Gonzalez (1994) suggest discovering the "funds of knowledge" parents have to offer schools. Funds of knowledge are those areas of life in which individuals are competent and knowledgeable. For example, parents who emigrated from Laos may have special skills in embroidery. A school that values this knowledge, even though it is in an area not traditionally valued by schools, might invite the parents to share examples of their embroidery work with their child's classmates. Such an invitation might encourage the parents, in turn, to learn about the school's culture.

Another way to think about parental involvement is to adopt a flexible approach. Too often teachers define *parental involvement* as attending parent conferences and volunteering to help with school projects. A flexible approach implies that parents should be offered various levels of school participation depending on their interests, availability, and degree of comfort. The levels of involvement can range from attendance at school functions to serving on advisory boards. Teacher candidates need to learn how to make appropriate opportunities for parental involvement available to the parents in their unique school community.

Help Teacher Candidates Learn How to Advocate for Students

Many students in urban areas face daunting family and social situations that have an impact on their learning. Weiner (2006) writes, "Urban teachers need to understand the way conditions outside classrooms influence the ways teachers and students act" (p. 21). Because schools have long been considered one agent for social change in the United States (Cremin, 1961), it is appropriate for teacher candidates to learn how to advocate effectively for their students.

Catapano (2006) suggests that teacher candidates can learn to become student advocates by conducting service-learning projects in school communities. For example, candidates who are bilingual can conduct home visits to talk with parents or to translate documents. Home visits can also result in teacher candidates' gaining new understandings of families, their resources, and lives. Other options include having teacher candidates organize book clubs for families or spend time serving meals at a local homeless shelter. These activities can help teacher candidates formulate a vision of what is possible for their students, increasing the likelihood they will begin advocating on their behalf (Knight, 2004).

Summary of Main Ideas

Students in urban areas have different needs from students in small cities, suburban areas, and rural settings. Students in large urban areas live in densely populated areas, are more likely to speak languages or dialects other than Standard American English, and often live in poverty. Students of color make up more than 90% of the student population in the districts of several of the largest U.S. cities (Center on Education Policy, 2006), and the school systems of urban centers are often steeped in bureaucracy.

The literacy needs of urban students are unique, and teacher preparation programs need to address these needs through literacy programs or courses that are adapted to prepare teacher candidates for urban settings. The content of these programs and courses should encompass at least three different areas: addressing the unique literacy needs of urban students, working with families in urban settings, and navigating urban school systems. A variety of promising practices currently exists, such as redefining literacy and print environments that are appropriate for urban education, helping teacher candidates learn about cultural differences, and finding creative ways to work with families. These promising practices are just a few of the ways literacy teacher preparation programs can focus on urban education. As more research on how to successfully prepare new teachers for urban settings is conducted, literacy programs and courses need to be revised to incorporate new findings.

Implications for Research, Practice, and Policy

Schools of education, in general, and teacher preparation programs, specifically, are facing challenges of accountability. Questions of the value of a university preparation are coming not only from the general public but also from policymakers and legislative decision makers. It is becoming increasingly important to address these concerns through active participation in these discussions. More important, it is crucial that we, as teacher educators, address the following questions, not just for legislators and the general public but for ourselves, professionals who know how to ask the right research questions, implement research studies, gather data, and draw conclusions from these data. Policy and research questions drawn from this chapter include the following:

- How are practicing teachers modifying their approach to teaching in a way that includes the language and cultural patterns of students? What is the impact of their practices on students' learning?
- What are the successful teaching methods of those who systematically raise the achievement of students, regardless of language, culture, ability, and socioeconomic differences?
- How are teacher preparation programs preparing students for working in urban settings? Is this preparation distinct in its form and function?
- What assessment methods are teacher preparation programs using to monitor their effectiveness?
- How are teacher preparation programs helping teacher candidates prepare to teach in ways that will result in closing the achievement gap?
- Are there existing policies or licensure requirements that conflict with what we know about preparing teachers for urban settings?
- What policies should we advocate for that will make a difference in the preparation of teachers to work effectively in urban settings?

Clearly, a thorough self-examination of our own practices as educators in teacher preparation institutions is needed. That work begins with each of us asking some of the same questions we ask of our students: Do we understand the varying literacy needs of urban students? What makes working with diverse groups of students different from working with groups that look like the majority? What are our own biases about the reasons for the achievement gap? Are we willing to work to close the achievement gap by examining those biases as well as our own assumptions about diversity? It is only through an ongoing conversation about these issues that we will make a difference in the way we prepare teachers to teach literacy in urban schools and ultimately improve the literacy skills of urban students.

REFERENCES

Aguilar, J.A. (2000, April). *Chicano street signs: Graffiti as public literacy practice.* Paper presented at the annual meeting of the American Educational Research Association, New Orleans, LA.

Artiles, A.J., & Ortiz, A.A. (Eds.). (2002). *English language learners with special education needs: Identification, assessment, and instruction.* Washington, DC: Center for Applied Linguistics.

Banks, J., Cochran-Smith, M., Moll, L., Richert, A., Zeichner, K., LePage, R., et al. (2005). Teaching diverse learners. In L. Darling-Hammond & J. Bransford (Eds.), *Preparing teachers for a changing world: What teachers should learn and be able to do* (pp. 232–274). San Francisco: Jossey-Bass.

Barr, R., Kamil, M.L., Mosenthal, P., & Pearson, P.D. (Eds.). (1991). *Handbook of reading research* (Vol. 2). White Plains, NY: Longman.

Bourdieu, P., & Passeron, J.C. (1977). *Reproduction in education, society and culture.* Thousand Oaks, CA: Sage.

Case, R.E., & Taylor, S.S. (2005). Language difference or learning disability? Answers from a linguistic perspective. *Clearing House, 78*(3), 127–131.

Catapano, S. (2006). Teaching in urban schools: Mentoring pre-service teachers to apply advocacy strategies. *Mentoring & Tutoring, 14*(1), 81–96.

Center on Education Policy. (2006). *A public education primer.* Washington, DC: Author.

Clay, M.M. (1979). *The early detection of reading difficulties: A diagnostic survey with recovery procedures.* London: Heinemann.

Cochran-Smith, M., & Zeichner, K.M. (Eds.). (2005). *Studying teacher education: The report of the AERA panel on research and teacher education.* Mahwah, NJ: Erlbaum.

Cremin, L. (1961). *The transformation of the school: Progressivism in American education, 1876–1957.* New York: Vintage.

Cummins, J. (1984). *Bilingualism and special education: Issues in assessment and pedagogy.* Clevedon, England: Multilingual Matters.

Darling-Hammond, L., & Garcia-Lopez, S.P. (2002). What is diversity? In L. Darling-Hammond, J. French, & S.P. Garcia-Lopez (Eds.), *Learning to teach for social justice* (pp. 9–12). New York: Teachers College Press.

Delpit, L.D. (1986). Skills and other dilemmas of a progressive black educator. *Harvard Educational Review, 56,* 379–385.

Delpit, L.D. (1988). The silenced dialogue: Power and pedagogy in educating other people's children. *Harvard Educational Review, 58,* 280–298.

Delpit, L.D. (2005). Ebonics and culturally responsive instruction: What should teachers do? In B. Hammond, M.E.R. Hoover, & I.P. McPhail (Eds.), *Teaching African American learners to read: Perspectives and practices* (pp. 164–172). Newark, DE: International Reading Association.

Duke, N.L. (2000). For the rich it's richer: Print experiences and environments offered to children in very low- and very high-socioeconomic status first-grade classrooms. *American Educational Research Journal, 37,* 441–478.

Faltis, C. (2001). *Joinfostering: Teaching and learning in multilingual classrooms* (3rd ed.). Upper Saddle River, NJ: Merrill.

Flood, J., & Anders, P.L. (Eds.). (2005). *Literacy development of students in urban schools: Research and policy.* Newark, DE: International Reading Association.

Garcia, K. (2002). Swimming against the mainstream: Examining cultural assumptions in the classroom. In L. Darling-Hammond, J. French, & S.P. Garcia-Lopez

(Eds.), *Learning to teach for social justice* (pp. 22–29). New York: Teachers College Press.

Gee, J. (2002). Discourses at school. In D. Li (Ed.), *Discourses in search of members: In honor of Ron Scollon* (pp. 79–101). Lanham, MD: University Press of America.

Harper, C., & de Jong, E. (2004). Misconceptions about teaching English-language learners. *Journal of Adolescent & Adult Literacy, 48,* 152–162.

Harris, T.L., & Hodges, R.E. (Eds.). (1995). *The literacy dictionary: The vocabulary of reading and writing.* Newark, DE: International Reading Association.

Harris-Wright, K. (2005). Building blocks for literacy development: Oral language. In B. Hammond, M.E.R. Hoover, & I.P. McPhail (Eds.), *Teaching African American learners to read: Perspectives and practices* (pp. 173–188). Newark, DE: International Reading Association.

Hayward, N. (2004). Insights into cultural divides. In S. Bruce & B. Rafoth (Eds.), *ESL writers: A guide for writing center tutors* (pp. 1–15). Portsmouth, NH: Boynton/Cook.

Heath, S.B. (1983). *Ways with words: Language, life, and work in communities and classrooms.* New York: Cambridge University Press.

Hollie, S. (2005). Acknowledging the language of African American students: Instruction that works. In B. Hammond, M.E.R. Hoover, & I.P. McPhail (Eds.), *Teaching African American learners to read: Perspectives and practices* (pp. 189–199). Newark, DE: International Reading Association.

Howard, G.R. (1999). *We can't teach what we don't know: White teachers, multiracial schools.* New York: Teachers College Press.

Kamil, M.L., Mosenthal, P., Pearson, P.D., & Barr, R. (Eds.). (2000). *Handbook of reading research* (Vol. 3). Mahwah, NJ: Erlbaum.

Knight, M.G. (2004). Sensing to the urgency: Envisioning a black humanist vision of care in teacher education. *Race Ethnicity and Education, 7*(3), 211–227.

Kohnert, K., Yim, D., Nett, K., Kan, P.F., & Duran, L. (2005). Intervention with linguistically diverse preschool children: A focus on developing home language(s). *Language, Speech, and Hearing Services in Schools, 36,* 251–263.

Lazar, A.M. (2004). *Learning to be literacy teachers in urban schools: Stories of growth and change.* Newark, DE: International Reading Association.

Lazar, A.M. (2006). Literacy teachers making a difference in urban schools: A context-specific look at effective literacy teaching. *Journal of Reading Education, 32*(1), 13–21.

Lee, J.-S., & Bowen, N.K. (2006). Parent involvement, cultural capital, and the achievement gap among elementary school children. *American Educational Research Journal, 43,* 193–218.

Leland, C.H., & Harste, J.C. (2005). Doing what we want to become: Preparing new urban teachers. *Urban Education, 40*(1), 60–77.

Lenski, S. (2008). Teaching from a critical literacy perspective and encouraging social action. In S. Lenski & J. Lewis (Eds.), *Reading success for struggling adolescent learners* (pp. 227–245). New York: Guilford.

Lenski, S.D., Crawford, K., Crumpler, T., & Stallworth, C. (2006). Preparing preservice teachers in a diverse world. *Action in Teacher Education, 27*(3), 3–12.

Lenski, S.D., Grisham, D.L., & Wold, L.S. (Eds.). (2006). *Literacy teacher preparation: Ten truths teacher educators need to know*. Newark, DE: International Reading Association.

Lynch, E.W., & Hanson, M.J. (2004). *Developing cross-cultural competence: A guide for working with children and their families* (3rd ed.). Baltimore: Brookes.

Macedo, D., Dendrinos, B., & Gounari, P. (2003). *The hegemony of English*. Boulder, CO: Paradigm.

Mason, P.A., & Schumm, J.S. (2003). *Promising practices for urban reading instruction*. Newark, DE: International Reading Association.

McNeal, R.B. (1999). Parental involvement as social capital: Differential effectiveness on science achievement, truancy, and dropping out. *Social Forces, 78*, 117–144.

McPherson, K. (2004). Multiplying literacies in school libraries. *Teacher Librarian, 32*(1), 60-62.

Moll, L.C., & Gonzalez, N. (1994). Lessons from research with language-minority children. *Journal of Reading Behavior, 26*, 439–456.

National Institute of Child Health and Human Development. (2000). *Report of the National Reading Panel. Teaching children to read: An evidence-based assessment of the scientific research literature on reading and its implications for reading instruction* (NIH Publication No. 00-4769). Washington, DC: U.S. Government Printing Office.

Neuman, S.B., & Celano, D.C. (2001). Access to print in low-income and middle-income communities: An ecological study of four neighborhoods. *Reading Research Quarterly, 36*, 8–26.

Oller, D.K., Pearson, B., Umbel, V., Fernández, M., & Navarro, A. (1997, February). *Educational implications of early bilingualism: A review of recent results*. Paper presented at the annual meeting of the American Association for the Advancement of Science, Atlanta, GA.

Orellana, M.F., & Hernández, A. (2003). Talking the walk: Children reading urban environmental print. In P.A. Mason & J.S. Schumm (Eds.), *Promising practices for urban reading instruction* (pp. 25–36). Newark, DE: International Reading Association.

Pappas, C.C. (2006). The information book genre: Its role in integrated science literacy research and practice. *Reading Research Quarterly, 41*, 226–250.

Pearson, P.D., Barr, R., Kamil, M.L., & Mosenthal, P. (Eds.). (1984). *Handbook of reading research*. New York: Longman.

Purcell-Gates, V. (2000). Family literacy. In M.L. Kamil, P. Mosenthal, P.D. Pearson, & R. Barr (Eds.), *Handbook of reading research* (Vol. 3, pp. 853–870). Mahwah, NJ: Erlbaum.

Rodríguez-Brown, F.V. (2001). Home–school connections in a community where English is the second language: Project FLAME. In V.J. Risko & K. Bromley (Eds.), *Collaboration for diverse learners: Viewpoints and practices* (pp. 273–289). Newark, DE: International Reading Association.

Sheldon, S.B., & Epstein, J.L. (2005). School programs of family and community involvement to support children's reading and literacy development across the grades. In J. Flood & P.L. Anders (Eds.), *Literacy development of students in urban schools: Research and policy* (pp. 107–138). Newark, DE: International Reading Association.

Snow, C. (1991). The theoretical basis for relationships between language and literacy in development. *Journal of Research in Childhood Education, 6*(1), 5–10.

Snow, C.E., Burns, M.S., & Griffin, P. (Eds.). (1998). *Preventing reading difficulties in young children.* Washington, DC: National Academy Press.

Strickland, D.S., & Alvermann, D.E. (2004). Learning and teaching literacy in grades 4–12: Issues and challenges. In D.S. Strickland & D.E. Alvermann (Eds.), *Bridging the literacy achievement gap grades 4–12* (pp. 1–13). New York: Teachers College Press.

Strickland, D.S., Ganske, K., & Monroe, J.K. (2002). *Supporting struggling readers and writers: Strategies for classroom intervention 3–6.* Newark, DE: International Reading Association.

Strunk, W., & White, E.B. (1999). *The elements of style* (4th ed.). Boston: Allyn & Bacon.

Teale, W.H., & Sulzby, E. (Eds.). (1986). *Emergent literacy: Writing and reading.* Norwood, NJ: Ablex.

U.S. Department of Education, Office of the Deputy Secretary, Planning and Evaluation Sevice. (2001). *The longitudinal evaluation of school change and performance in Title I schools, Volume 1: Executive summary.* Retrieved January 8, 2007, from www.ed.gov/offices/OUS/PES/esed/lescp_vol1.pdf

Valdés, G., & Figueroa, R.A. (1994). *Bilingualism and testing: A special case of bias.* Norwood, NJ: Ablex.

Weiner, L. (2006). *Urban teaching: The essentials.* New York: Teachers College Press.

Wheeler, R.S., & Swords, R. (2006). *Code-switching: Teaching standard English in urban classrooms.* Urbana, IL: National Council of Teachers of English.

Effective Preparation of Teachers of Reading for Urban Settings

CHAPTER 4

Preparing Expert Teachers of Reading for Urban Schools: Models and Variations in the Literature

Amy D. Broemmel
Wendy B. Meller
Richard L. Allington
University of Tennessee

Our urban schools increasingly reflect the melting pot in which we live, yet the U.S. teaching force is becoming increasingly white. Since 1990, the population of African American, Hispanic, and Asian teachers has been declining, due in part to increasing interest on the part of these student populations in pursuing business degrees instead of enrolling in teacher education programs (Hodgkinson, 2002). This concern extends beyond the elementary and secondary school doors; minorities are also found in small numbers among teaching faculty and administrators in higher education. Scholars indicate that this cultural/racial mismatch often results in a significant detachment of white teacher educators and white teacher education students from children of color (Cross, 2003). What does that say for our recruitment and retention of the 79.6% white teachers teaching in our urban districts, districts that enroll mostly nonwhite and often multilingual immigrants (Shakespear, Beardsley, & Newton, 2003)? Moreover, what drives preservice teachers to choose this seemingly more complicated path?

In an early report of a longitudinal study examining the perspectives of new professionals on teaching in urban settings, preservice teachers in an urban multicultural program described their reasons for selecting such settings. Their reasons included the desire to have a

Improving Literacy Achievement in Urban Schools: Critical Elements in Teacher Preparation
edited by Louise C. Wilkinson, Lesley Mandel Morrow, and Victoria Chou. © 2008 by the
International Reading Association.

positive influence, the need to fulfill a moral imperative, the attraction of meeting a challenge, the desire to teach in familiar surroundings, and the attraction of the positive attributes associated with urban schools (Hatch, 2006). In Lazar's (2004) research, preservice teachers report more pragmatic reasons for selecting urban placements, including the belief that experiences in urban settings will help them become better teachers, look good on a résumé, and satisfy their curiosity about urban schools. These varying perspectives can help provide a sense of what preservice teachers anticipate they will learn from their experiences and achieve in their careers. However, if we expect beginning teachers to remain in urban classrooms for the long term, we need to look at how their desires, expectations, and goals match the needs of the student populations in urban settings.

Purposes of This Chapter

The U.S. Department of Education estimates that by 2010, 2.2 million teachers will be needed to fill vacancies, and 330,000 of these new teachers will be needed in urban schools in large cities with large minority populations (Gimbert, Cristol, Wallace, & Sene, 2005). Every year, many low-income and minority children enter these urban schools without the knowledge and skills associated with successful early literacy learning. We know that these children are often assigned teachers with less experience, education, and skill than those who teach other children (Peske & Haycock, 2006). In order to stop this unsettling trend, we need urban teacher education programs that will prepare highly qualified teachers to fill these anticipated vacancies. The purpose of this chapter is to identify what we know about preparing expert teachers of reading, describe the current status of reading achievement in urban settings, examine specific models of urban teacher preparation and identify the common strengths of their literacy components, and establish a vision of what is needed to effectively meet the literacy needs of urban students.

Review of Research and Theory

Research focused on preservice reading education is scarce, accounting for less than 1% of reading research over the past 30 years (Anders, Hoffman, & Duffy, 2000). The available research has typically focused on two sources of information: teacher educators and recent graduates. However, after the publication of the National Reading Panel's report (National Institute of Child Health and Human Development, 2000) indicating that "because of the small number of studies that constituted the final sample, the panel could not answer the question of how research can be used to improve teacher education in specific ways" (p. 5-2), preservice reading education has garnered more attention.

In fact, a number of recent reports have brought preservice reading education to the forefront of education policy. Both the National Council on Teacher Quality (NCTQ) and the International Reading Association (IRA) have initiated reading teacher education research initiatives in recent years. In addition, the National Assessment of Educational Progress (NAEP) initiated the Trial Urban District Assessment (TUDA) to compare student scores in large, urban districts with those of the nation. All three efforts have informed our understanding of the educational needs of teachers and students in urban settings.

Preservice Reading Education Research

The NCTQ study (Walsh, Glaser, & Wilcox, 2006) examines what aspiring elementary teachers learn about reading instruction during their formal undergraduate training through a controversial methodology that analyzes course syllabi chosen from a random sample of 72 elementary education programs. Grounded in the belief that about a third of all kindergarteners require explicit, systematic instruction in order to learn how to read, researchers examine required reading course syllabi to assess the degree to which they include the five components of effective reading instruction: phonemic awareness, phonics, fluency, vocabulary, and comprehension. The researchers conclude that not only were most education schools not teaching the science of reading but even courses claiming to provide a "balanced" approach ignore the science of reading (Walsh et al., 2006). Controversial methodology aside, this report received much coverage in the popular press (e.g., *USA Today*, *New York Times*, *Washington Post*, *Education Week*) and in the professional press (e.g., *AACTE News*, *Chronicle of Higher Education*). As a result, the report increased scrutiny of preservice programs for reading teachers (Allington, 2007).

In 1999 IRA convened the National Commission on Excellence in Elementary Teacher Preparation for Reading Instruction to conduct a national survey of almost 950 reading teacher educators. The goal was to examine current practices in reading teacher education; to identify common characteristics of excellent reading teacher preparation programs; and to conduct a major, comparative study of the effectiveness of the graduates of excellent reading teacher preparation programs. After receiving applications from 28 colleges and universities, 8 institutions were invited to participate in the project, which would last for more than three years and become the most comprehensive longitudinal research study on reading teacher preparation ever conducted. The study followed 101 graduates as they progressed through their first three years in the classroom, assessing their attitudes and effectiveness. Participants were identified according to which of three different tracks their teacher education program followed: (1) programs with a reading specialty, (2) programs that infused literacy teaching into general education courses, or (3) programs of a general education nature that lacked an emphasis on literacy (IRA, 2003).

Findings showed that teachers prepared in quality reading teacher education programs were more successful and confident than other beginning teachers in making the transition into the profession. They were well grounded in their vision of literacy and their ability to enrich programs, utilizing multiple strategies to help struggling readers.

The commission's research findings provided evidence that served as a basis for identifying critical features of high-quality teacher preparation programs (Hoffman & Roller, 2001; IRA, 2003). There are eight features:

1. Content
2. Apprenticeship
3. Vision
4. Resources and mission
5. Personalized teaching
6. Autonomy
7. Community
8. Assessment

These features, listed in random order, together form a comprehensive, integrated outline to guide the identification or creation of an excellent reading teacher education program (IRA, 2003). Subsequent research indicates that high-quality reading teacher education programs do indeed positively influence beginning teachers, specifically when it comes to establishing a literacy-rich classroom environment and ensuring student engagement (Hoffman et al., 2005).

Urban Teacher Education Research

Twenty-five years of research have led us to understand that urban teachers need more than typical instructional methods to meet the demands presented by their students (Watson, Charner-Laird, Kirkpatrick, Szczesiul, & Gordon, 2006); they need to understand the community's culture, political economy, and social support network (Oakes, Franke, Quartz, & Rogers, 2002). Watson et al. (2006) interviewed beginning teachers who had just completed an urban education program and found that participants noted the differences in the skills necessary for teaching in urban settings versus non-urban settings. In a second series of interviews, two-thirds of the teachers referenced concepts related to culturally responsive teaching as they attempted to describe effective urban instruction. In a sense, they realized their responsibility to be agents of change, implementing culturally responsive teaching practices in order to meet both the academic and social needs of culturally diverse students (Gay, 2000; Ladson-Billings, 1994).

Because of the unique demands of urban teaching, effectively preparing preservice teachers for these settings must take on a different look. Peske and Haycock (2006) identify five indicators of teachers' abilities to produce gains in student learning, particularly in regard to poor and minority students:

1. Academic skills and knowledge
2. Mastery of content
3. Experience
4. Pedagogical skill
5. Effective use of first four indicators in combination

By including the fifth indicator, as measured by the "Combined Index of Teacher Quality" (p. 8), the authors suggest that the first four abilities in isolation are not sufficient to characterize teacher quality. It is critical as well that they be used effectively in combination.

Watson and colleagues (2006) go one step further by suggesting three critical focal points in creating effective teacher preparation programs in urban education. They indicate programs must be designed so that students are forced to grapple with inherent issues of race and inequity throughout the program; programs must help preservice teachers take an antiracist stance, not only in terms of curriculum and classroom management issues but also in a way that "helps prospective teachers learn to recognize, expose, and eradicate racism both in themselves and in society" (p. 407). They continue, indicating that faculty members must have a deep understanding of and be committed to this type of teaching philosophy and that course work and fieldwork must be designed in ways that prompt students to make the critical connections required to effectively combat racism and meet the needs of their students.

Urban Student Data

The NAEP launched TUDA in six selected large urban districts in 2002. The project, which assessed reading and writing achievement, was continued and expanded in 2003 and 2005 with a focus on reading and mathematics (Lutkus, Rampey, & Donahue, 2006). Project reports compared national results of U.S. public school students' performance overall to that of those living in large cities, where applicable. The 2005 average score for fourth-grade students was lower than the national average; however, scores for the 11 participating districts varied from higher-than-average showings in Austin, Texas; Charlotte, North Carolina; Houston, Texas; and New York City, New York; to lower-than-average in Atlanta, Georgia; Chicago, Illinois; Cleveland, Ohio; the District of Columbia; and Los Angeles, California. The average eighth-grade reading scores for each district were lower than the national scores, except in Austin and Charlotte where again there was no significant difference from the national average. However, when trends were examined over time, it became evident that between 2003 and 2005 no district showed a significant change in its average score or in the percentage of students scoring at or above the basic level of proficiency at grade 4, although the percentage of students performing above proficient did increase in Los Angeles during the same time frame. Eighth-grade scores were similar, with only two of the districts reporting an increased percentage of students performing at or above basic from 2002–2005.

The possibility of such trends continuing and expanding to other urban districts makes clear the critical need to prepare highly qualified teachers to work in big-city schools. The Executive Summary of IRA's

(2003) Commission on Excellence in Elementary Teacher Preparation for Reading Instruction notes,

> Policy concerns center on low-performing schools that serve minority and economically disadvantaged students—schools that are struggling to improve despite significant investments. Many children in these schools lack basic reading, language, and English literacy skills. But the fundamental issues facing educators and policymakers are more complicated. Schools with the most challenging students have the most difficult time attracting and retaining qualified teachers. (p. 1)

The reading achievement gap between the "have" and the "have-not" districts will likely continue to widen without increased investments in the quality of teaching. As it stands now, there is tremendous variation in the content and experiences provided within the 1,150 teacher preparation programs across the United States (IRA, 2003).

Best Practices

What might high-quality preparation for urban teachers look like? In an attempt to answer this question, a thorough investigation of peer-reviewed professional research literature was undertaken on the premise that discussion of high-quality urban literacy education programs would likely be present. Both the Education Full Text and PsycInfo databases were used to conduct searches of the literature using search terms such as *urban teacher preparation*, *urban teacher education*, and *urban teacher education programs*. Results were first limited to peer-reviewed journals and then examined more closely to identify those that contained programmatic descriptions of urban teacher education programs. The search revealed only eight references to specific preservice urban teacher education programs, one of which did not provide the name of the affiliated university and was therefore excluded from further investigation. In an attempt to verify each program's existence and investigate the literacy requirements of the programs, we further searched the website of each university and school associated with a program. If references to the program could not be found, the programs were not included. Two programs were eliminated for this reason, and the final five programs were divided into two categories: urban teacher education programs and alternative urban teacher education programs. Table 4.1 compares key components of the programs, and detailed explanations of each program follow.

Table 4.1. Key Components of Selected Urban Teacher Education Programs

University Program	Program Name	Program Focus	Cohort	Recruitment Strategy	Commitment	Partnership	Literacy Elements	Reference
Urban								
Tufts University	Urban Teacher Training Collaborative (UTTC)	School culture	Yes	Systematic recruitment of a racially diverse cohort of interns in conjunction with the Institute for Recruiting Teachers, Community Institute for Teachers, and Morehouse College and other traditionally African American colleges (Beardsley, 2004)	N/A	Two Boston high schools	N/A	Beardsley, L.V., & Teitel, L. (2004). Learning to see color in teacher education: An example framed by the professional development school standard for diversity and equity. *The Teacher Educator, 40*(2), 91–115.
University of California, Los Angeles (UCLA)	Center X	Promoting social justice for urban schools	Yes	School paraprofessionals who showed promise of attaining teacher certification	N/A	N/A	Exploration of urban youth literacies across the academic content areas Literacy-related courses such as Methods for English Language Development, Principles and	Oakes, J., Franke, M.L., Quartz, K.H., & Rogers, J. (2002). Research for high-quality urban teaching: Defining it, developing it, assessing it. *Journal of Teacher Education, 53,* 228–234.

University Program	Program Name	Program Focus	Cohort	Recruitment Strategy	Commitment	Partnership	Literacy Elements	Reference
							Methods for Teaching Reading, Language Structure, Acquisition, and Development, Methodology for Primary Language Instruction, and Language and Culture	
Washington State University (WSU)	CO-TEACH (Collaboration for Teacher Education Accountable to Children with High Needs)	Experiences with diverse students in high-needs schools	No	N/A	N/A	Schools identified as in "need" based on free- and reduced-price lunch rates of at least 50%	Literacy-based courses, including Developing Literacy in a Multicultural Setting, Literacy Development 1, and Teaching Literacy in a Multicultural Setting—each appears to be integrated into one of three blocks of course work	Shinew, D.M., & Sodorff, C. (2003). Partnerships at a distance: Redesigning a teacher education program to prepare educators for diverse, high-needs classrooms. *Action in Teacher Education, 25*(3), 24–29.

(continued)

Table 4.1. Key Components of Selected Urban Teacher Education Programs (continued)

University Program	Program Name	Program Focus	Cohort	Recruitment Strategy	Commitment	Partnership	Literacy Elements	Reference
Alternative Urban								
Old Dominion University	Transition to Teaching (T2T)	Addressing critical teacher shortage areas	No	Career switchers, recent college graduates, substitute teachers, and paraprofessionals with classroom experience	Teach three years in the same urban district where trained	Newport News Public Schools	Master's degree option in reading education	Gimbert, B., Cristol, D., Wallace, D., & Sene, A.M. (2005). A case study of a competency-driven alternative route to teacher licensure in an urban "hard to staff" school system. *Action in Teacher Education, 27*(1), 53–71.
Wayne State University	Limited License to Instruct (LLI)	Affecting teacher shortage in urban schools	Yes	Individuals interested in teaching in high-need areas	Teach full-time in the Detroit Public Schools.	The Detroit Public Schools, the Michigan Department of Education, and the Detroit Federation of Teachers	Two required reading courses and two additional methods courses. The methods courses are chosen from among four options, two of which are literacy-related	Ilmer, S., Nahan, N., Elliott, S., Colombo, M., & Snyder, J. (2005). Analysis of urban teachers' first-year experiences in an alternative certification program. *Action in Teacher Education, 27*(1), 3–14.

N/A = This information was available neither in the professional literature nor on the institutions' websites.

Urban Teacher Education Programs

Concern over the lack of qualified teachers available to educate public school students has been growing (Gimbert et al., 2005). That concern becomes even more pronounced when urban schools are considered; there are clear differences between the qualifications of teachers working in schools with the highest concentration of poor and minority students and those working in schools with few minority and low-income students (Peske & Haycock, 2006).

Oakes and colleagues (2002) suggest that "the shortage of qualified urban teachers is fueled at least as much by high rates of teacher turnover and attrition as it is by insufficient numbers of qualified people being attracted to teaching" (p. 228). They continue, stating that "career satisfaction and longevity lies in creating cadres of urban teachers who have the technical, collegial, and political support required to have an impact on the quality of students' lives in classrooms and communities" (p. 228). Peske and Haycock (2006) concur, indicating that "the simple truth is that public education cannot fulfill its mission if students growing up in poverty, students of color, and low-performing students continue to be disproportionately taught by inexperienced, under-qualified teachers" (p. 15). In order to determine what is being done to counteract these challenges, we examined three teacher education programs designed to prepare teachers for these underserved communities.

Tufts University–Boston

The Tufts Master of Arts in Teaching (MAT) program has made a commitment to prepare teachers to teach effectively in urban schools through a partnership between the Tufts Department of Education and two small public high schools in Boston. The partnership, created in 1999 and known as the Urban Teacher Training Collaborative (UTTC), is built on the systematic recruitment of a racially diverse cohort of teacher candidates and focuses on the understanding of the impact of race on teaching and learning. In fact, the curriculum was designed to prepare teachers to explore their own racial and cultural identities as well as those of their students.

Prior to 1999, Tufts' MAT students participated in field placements in mostly white, middle class, suburban communities in the Boston area and were required to complete one course in multicultural education. The new UTTC curriculum requires a full-time, year-long internship in one of the partnership schools; weekly onsite seminars; and course work related to effective urban education (Beardsley & Teitel, 2004). UTTC interns serve on curriculum development teams, participate in faculty meetings, engage with families, provide support services, tutor students, organize field trips and college visitation days, and work as members of school committees. Interns coteach with their mentors and are supervised by both an on-site program coordinator and a Tufts professor (Beardsley & Teitel, 2004). In addition, one of the program's required courses is offered on-site at one of the participating schools. UTTC believes its program reflects the five professional development standards established by the National Council for Accreditation of Teacher Education:

1. Learning community
2. Accountability and quality assurance
3. Collaboration
4. Diversity and equity
5. Structures, resources, and roles

The program places a special emphasis on standard four—diversity and equity (Beardsley & Teitel, 2004).

Each year, UTTC interns are asked to complete a survey at the midpoint and again at the end of their program on their experiences in both its site-based and academic components. An outside evaluator reviews the surveys and interviews a number of the interns. These evaluations have indicated that "the presence of interns of color promoted deep, authentic discussions about the influence of race and ethnicity in educational issues throughout the academic courses" (Beardsley & Teitel, 2004, p. 96). Minority participation in UTTC has increased from 2% in 1998 to 26% in 2003, in part due to support from the Institute for Recruiting Teachers, Community Institute for Teachers, and Morehouse College and other traditionally African American colleges (Beardsley & Teitel). As a result of the growing number of minority participants with strong academic records, scholarship support for interns has grown to nearly $600,000.

University of California, Los Angeles (UCLA)

UCLA created its Center X teacher education program explicitly to promote social justice in urban schools and to help preserve teachers understand local cultures, the urban political economy, the bureaucratic structure of urban schools, and the community and social service support networks serving urban centers. Recruitment efforts target promising school paraprofessionals who show interest in attaining teacher certification. The goal of the program is to train teachers to draw on urban youth literacies across academic content areas (Oakes et al., 2002). It also prepares teachers to become agents of fundamental change who can help shape the urban educational context. UCLA's approach to teacher learning is based on five principles:

1. Learning occurs as novices participate with each other and experts on meaningful tasks.
2. Learning unfolds as individuals participate in groups.
3. Learning emerges in and through dialogue.
4. Learning involves the emerging identities of participants.
5. Learning through mutual engagement in a joint enterprise enables participants to develop socially valued work products.

The program encourages students to join activist groups, participate in community initiatives, and collaborate with faculty members on urban research projects (Oakes et al., 2002).

Once in the program, which encompasses the dual perspectives of theory and practice, students become part of a cohort, completing work as part of a community of learners. They take a series of courses related to literacy, including Methods for English Language Development; Principles and Methods for Teaching Reading; Language and Culture; Language Structure, Acquisition, and Development; and Methodology for Primary Language Instruction (UCLA Center X Teacher Education Program, n.d.).

Interestingly, fewer than 5% of the students entering the program fail to complete it; those who do earn a Master's of Education go on to teach in low-income, predominantly minority schools. According to spring 2001 data (Oakes et al., 2002) 90% of the 326 students who had graduated from the program in the previous five years were still teaching, and most were teaching in urban schools.

Washington State University (WSU)

The main campus of WSU is located in Pullman, Washington, a small rural community in the eastern part of the state. With little racial, linguistic, and socioeconomic diversity and only five public schools, Pullman could not provide the 700 students enrolled in WSU's College of Education (COE) with the kind of field experience placements that would prepare them to teach in urban settings. In the fall of 1999, WSU-COE was awarded a $9.67 million, five-year, Title II Teacher Quality Enhancement grant from the U.S. Department of Education to fund the Collaboration for Teacher Education Accountable to Children with High Needs (CO-TEACH). The project focuses on six major goals:

1. Collaboration
2. Partnerships
3. Revised programs
4. Professional development
5. Education forums
6. Recruitment and retention of Native American teachers (Shinew & Sodorff, 2003)

A total of 13 schools across the state of Washington participated in the project during the first year. The schools were selected on the basis of documented rates of free and reduced-price lunch eligibility that met or exceeded 50%. The program quickly grew to include 28 schools, with each school receiving CO-TEACH funds for professional development, materials, technology, and travel.

Data collected in annual student surveys conducted by the WSU field experiences office showed a disconnect between students' field experience and their courses, especially in the area of literacy. Responses of many graduates of the program showed they left feeling ill-prepared to work in high-needs schools with multiethnic, multilingual students (Shinew & Sodorff, 2003). The faculty of WSU's Elementary Education program therefore made changes, reorganizing most of the required courses into three major blocks: a 12-credit block on literacy and instructional planning; a 10-credit block on the integration of math, science, social studies, and literacy; and a final block dedicated to understanding the needs of diverse learners that included a new course on English as a second language (Shinew & Sodorff, 2003). There are currently three courses related to literacy listed on the CO-TEACH website: Developing Literacy in a Multicultural Setting, Literacy Development 1, and Teaching Literacy in a Multicultural Setting. (WSU Masters in Training, n.d.).

Evaluations indicate that 83% of the program's first graduates secured positions as either long-term substitutes or full-time teachers and that 80% of those students stayed in the same urban district where they did their fieldwork. Approximately 30% of subsequent graduates have remained in the Tacoma School District—one of the districts across the state whose schools serve as CO-TEACH field placement sites—while an equally impressive 60% have taken positions in other high-needs districts. Shinew and Sodorff (2003) indicate that "ninety-two percent of the graduates of this program successfully completed student teaching and continued in the profession" (p. 27).

Alternative Urban Teacher Education Programs

In the early 1980s in response to teacher shortages in poor urban schools, the alternative certification movement began (National Association of State Boards of Education, 1998). Today, at least 46 states and the District of Columbia have such programs, which are run by school districts, educational service agencies, universities, and collaborative partnerships (Gimbert et al., 2005). The major goal of these programs is to solve the school staffing crisis in high-needs urban and rural schools.

There is little consensus about the effectiveness of alternative routes to certification. Laczko-Kerr and Berliner (2003) indicate that these types of programs negatively affect student achievement, while a study conducted by Miller, McKenna, and McKenna (1998) found no effect on student achievement in either reading or math based on the type of training teachers receive. Darling-Hammond (2005) argues that due at least in part to alternative certification programs, "students' access to well-qualified teachers is more unequal than ever before" (p. 238), especially in high-needs schools. However, others argue that alternative certification programs attract more ethnically and culturally diverse educators as well as male teacher candidates. They also cite studies that show alternatively certified teachers are just as highly qualified as those who complete traditional teacher preparation programs (Gimbert et al., 2005). In search of answers, we investigated two alternative urban education certification programs.

Old Dominion University

Old Dominion University's partnership with the Newport News Public Schools in Virginia was initially funded by a five-year (2002–2007)

Transition to Teaching (T2T) grant that the school district received from the U.S. Department of Education. The grant has since been extended to run until fall 2008. According to Gimbert and colleagues (2005), the partnership adopted Haberman's five standards of excellence for alternative certification programs. The standards call for such programs to: (1) implement a highly selective approach to selecting participants, (2) define a process to attract the best teacher educators to teach and mentor new teachers, (3) enact a standards-based curriculum for prospective teachers, (4) offer effective teaching methods that focus on pedagogy, and (5) evaluate the program's effectiveness (Haberman, 1991).

The partnership seeks to recruit career switchers, recent college graduates, substitute teachers, and paraprofessionals with classroom experience. Entry requirements include a bachelor's degree with course work or experience related to English, mathematics, social studies, or science; a minimum GPA of 2.5; and a qualifying score on the Praxis I and II. Applicants must also fulfill all requirements for employment as a public school teacher in Virginia and teach in the Newport News schools for the three years they are enrolled in the T2T program.

T2T participants are required to (a) participate in a content-specific cohort; (b) take part in an intensive mentoring program; (c) engage in professional growth experiences; (d) participate in classroom-based research; (e) attend the Newport News New Teacher Academy; (f) complete college credits for professional development; and (g) create an electronic portfolio. Eligible participants receive financial support. Those who complete the program successfully receive master's degrees in literacy education or special education from Old Dominion University (Gimbert et al., 2005).

Wayne State University

Wayne State University, the Detroit Public Schools (DPS), the Michigan Department of Education, and the Detroit Federation of Teachers collaborated to create the Limited License to Instruct (LLI) alternative certification program, which began in 2001. The program was designed to increase the number of qualified, certified teachers employed in the DPS. A total of 625 candidates, each of whom was simultaneously hired as a full-time DPS teacher, have participated in the program since its inception.

Through LLI, participants teach in high-needs areas such as secondary science and mathematics, special education, bilingual education, early childhood education, and elementary education. The teachers work with mentors, participate in induction activities, and complete 10 credit hours of online instruction. According to the program website, students are required to take four methods courses in literacy, including two on teaching reading (Wayne State University, n.d.).

The students in this year-long program work toward a Master of Arts in Teaching (MAT) degree in cohort groups that meet for approximately 90–120 minutes a week. These on-site meetings are led by a cohort leader-instructor, usually a former DPS teacher, curriculum leader, or principal and are designed to allow participants to discuss course work, talk about issues affecting their classrooms, and build learning communities (Ilmer, Nahan, Elliott, Colombo, & Snyder, 2005). Results of participant interviews indicate that the majority (88%) felt positively about the experiences they associated with the cohort model.

Summary of Main Ideas

IRA is leading the effort to generate a growing body of research that can be used to effectively influence the widely varying models of preservice reading teacher education currently in place (Hoffman et al., 2005). In a qualitative study of first-year teachers, Maloch and colleagues (2003) find clear differences between graduates of teacher education programs IRA (2003) deems excellent in undergraduate reading teacher preparation and graduates of general teacher education programs housed at some of the same institutions. The first-year teachers whose course work specifically emphasized literacy reported basing their instructional decisions on student needs rather than on mandated curriculum and say they had sought out learning communities for professional development. They are also significantly more likely to report that they valued their teacher preparation programs than their counterparts from general teacher education programs. Such findings suggest that these first-year teachers were able to withstand the pressure to conform to their schools' standards of practice, standards that can often threaten novice teachers' pedagogical practices (Puk & Haines, 1999).

Because we know that urban schools are often filled with novice teachers and students in need of literacy support, wouldn't it make sense to design urban education programs that included a research-supported emphasis on literacy? Yet most of the urban teacher education programs we reviewed provided limited or in some cases no information on how preparation for literacy teaching was addressed. Our quest became somewhat akin to a scavenger hunt. We searched program databases and read and reread program websites, some of which in turn led us to course lists that indicated the inclusion (or not) of literacy courses. Hence, although urban teacher education models have developed some consistency in terms of their framework, often structuring programs around long-term goals or principles of social justice and multiculturalism, most of those we reviewed did not reflect the sorts of preparation for the teaching of reading that IRA researchers identified as effective. In fact, of the programs that identified specific literacy courses, most seemed only to require the same minimum number of reading methods courses as students in traditional teacher education programs. UCLA's Center X is a notable exception, requiring five literacy-related courses for their teacher education students. UCLA's program is unique in that it is the only option the school offers for elementary certification and has embedded within its social justice framework an emphasis on literacy. Given the concerns that have been raised about the adequacy of the preparation of teachers of reading in general, we remain concerned that so few urban teacher education programs have clearly set excellence in reading instruction as one of the primary goals of their efforts.

Implications for Research, Practice, and Policy

There appears to be little overlap between urban teacher education and literacy teacher education despite the clear indications that students in urban settings have the greatest need for effective teachers of literacy. The mismatch between the research on exemplary preparation of teachers of reading and what appears to be an absence of attention to the preparation for teaching reading in urban teacher education programs indicates that such preparation has not been emphasized in these programs. When we know that student reading achievement in the highest poverty schools routinely falls below the achievement of students in nonpoor, non-urban schools, one could argue that a focus on teaching reading is critical in urban teacher education programs. Likewise, when students in urban schools are almost twice as likely to be assigned to a novice teacher than their peers at low-poverty schools, and children who so clearly need expert instruction more often end up being taught by "teachers with less experience, less education, and less skill" (Peske & Haycock, 2006, p. 2), we must ask ourselves why a literacy component that could significantly improve those teachers' practice has not been given higher priority in urban teacher education programs.

It is clear that urban teacher education programs share many important characteristics. They consistently group students in cohorts, provide opportunities for reflection on teaching practice, and require both course work and other activities focusing on cultural diversity. University partnerships with local schools, organizations, and businesses often help fund preservice teacher preparation. Perhaps these programs' focus on collaboration and community is a sign that it takes more than a straightforward program of academic study to educate an effective urban teacher. Perhaps such programs rely on collaborative communities to provide strong mentors and professional development during their field experience components. However, without documentation of the need for such specific instructional support, particularly in the area of literacy, we simply cannot know if such assumptions are true.

Moreover, if we cannot establish that urban teacher education programs are providing their students with at least minimal course work in literacy combined with exposure to literacy best practices in their field experience settings, how can we be sure that their graduates will be able to meet the literacy needs of the children who fill our urban schools?

Au's (2002) work may provide a starting point for discussion between educators specializing in literacy instruction and those specializing in urban teacher preparation. She points to the effectiveness of constructivist approaches in meeting the needs of and promoting achievement among diverse students, going so far as to identify five steps to provide these students with opportunities for literacy growth. She advocates

1. Addressing issues of motivation by building positive relationships with students and demonstrating the power and rewards that come with literacy
2. Providing rich instruction in a workshop setting
3. Striving to get beyond the surface level in understanding the needs of second-language learners
4. Learning to teach in a culturally responsive manner
5. Implementing multiple assessments to provide information on students' progress and to inform instruction

These steps clearly fall in line with both the content of effective literacy instruction and Watson et al.'s (2006) focal points for creating quality urban teacher education programs.

Children from urban settings often come to school without the background experiences and literacy tools that form the foundation for future literacy. These children need "teachers who are capable of accelerating the learning of students who experience the greatest difficulty acquiring literacy" (Dozier, Johnston, & Rogers, 2006, p. 11). In terms of developing children as readers and writers, the quality of classroom instruction is the most powerful feature of schools. Therefore, in order to make a difference in urban schools, we must continue to search for innovative ways that not only familiarize preservice teachers with the unique contexts associated with urban schools but also provide them with extensive course work in best practices in literacy (Allington, 2006). Furthermore, we must look beyond the minimum requirements if we want to prepare teachers who are equipped to face the challenges of urban settings. Only those prepared for cultural and linguistic diversity and armed with a strong understanding of how to teach students of all ages to read will be ready to make a difference in the lives of our neediest students. We have a responsibility to develop teacher education programs that do both.

REFERENCES

Allington, R.L. (2006). *What really matters for struggling readers: Designing research-based programs* (2nd ed.). Upper Saddle River, NJ: Pearson Education.

Allington, R.L. (2007). What education schools, maybe, aren't teaching about reading. Or maybe not. *Journal of Reading Education, 32*(2), 5–9.

Anders, P.L., Hoffman, J.V., & Duffy, G.G. (2000). Teaching teachers to teach reading: Paradigm shifts, persistent problems, and challenges. In M.L. Kamil, P. Mosenthal, P.D. Pearson, & R. Barr (Eds.), *Handbook of reading research* (Vol. 3, pp. 719–742). Mahwah, NJ: Erlbaum.

Au, K.H. (2002). Multicultural factors and the effective instruction of students of diverse backgrounds. In A.E. Farstrup & S.J. Samuels (Eds.), *What research has to say about reading instruction* (3rd ed., pp. 392–413). Newark, DE: International Reading Association.

Beardsley, L.V., & Teitel, L. (2004). Learning to see color in teacher education: An example framed by the professional development school standard for diversity and equity. *The Teacher Educator, 40*(2), 91–115.

Cross, B.E. (2003). Learning or unlearning racism: Transferring teacher education curriculum to classroom practices. *Theory Into Practice, 42*, 203–209.

Darling-Hammond, L. (2005). Teaching as a profession: Lessons in teacher preparation and professional development. *Phi Delta Kappan, 87*, 237–240.

Dozier, C., Johnston, P., & Rogers, R. (2006). *Critical literacy/critical teaching*. New York: Teachers College Press.

Gay, G. (2000). *Culturally responsive teaching: Theory , research, & practice*. New York: Teachers College Press.

Gimbert, B., Cristol, D., Wallace, D., & Sene, A.M. (2005). A case study of a competency-driven alternative route to teacher licensure in an urban "hard to staff" school system. *Action in Teacher Education, 27*(1), 53–71.

Haberman, M. (1991). The rationale for training adults as teachers. In C. Sleeter (Ed.), *Empowerment through multicultural education* (pp. 275–286). Albany: State University of New York Press.

Hatch, J.A. (2006). Pre-service teachers' reasons for selecting urban teaching. In A. Louque (Ed.), *2006 e-yearbook: Urban learning, teaching, and research* (pp. 4–10). Los Angeles, CA: Urban Learning, Teaching, and Research Special Interest Group. Retrieved October 10, 2006, from www.aera-ultr.org/2006_eYearbook_final.pdf

Hodgkinson, H. (2002). Demographics and teacher education. *Journal of Teacher Education, 53*, 102–105.

Hoffman, J.V., Roller, C.M., Maloch, B., Sailors, M., Duffy, G. & Beretvas, S.N. (2005). Teachers' preparation to teach reading and their experiences and practices in the first three years of teaching. *The Elementary School Journal, 105*, 267–287.

Ilmer, S., Nahan, N., Elliott, S., Colombo, M., & Snyder, J. (2005). Analysis of urban teachers' first-year experiences in an alternative certification program. *Action in Teacher Education, 27*(1), 3–14.

International Reading Association. (2003). *Prepared to make a difference: An executive summary of the National Commission on Excellence in Elementary Teacher Preparation for Reading Instruction*. Newark, DE: Author.

Laczko-Kerr, I., & Berliner, D. (2003). In harm's way: How undercertified teachers hurt their students. *Educational Leadership, 60*(8), 34–39.

Ladson-Billings, G. (1994). *The dreamkeepers: Successful teachers for African-American children*. San Francisco: Jossey-Bass.

Lazar, A.M. (2004). *Learning to be literacy teachers in urban schools: Stories of growth and change*. Newark, DE: International Reading Association.

Lutkus, A.D., Rampey, B.D., & Donahue, P. (2006). *The nation's report card: Trial urban district assessment reading 2005*. Washington DC: National Center for Education Statistics.

Maloch, B., Flint, A.S., Eldridge, D., Harmon, J., Loven, R., Fine, J.C., et al. (2003). Understanding, beliefs, and reported decision making of first year teachers from different reading teacher preparation programs. *The Elementary School Journal, 103*, 431–457.

Miller, J.W., McKenna, M.C., & McKenna, B.A. (1998). A comparison of alternatively and traditionally prepared teachers. *Journal of Teacher Education, 49*, 165–176.

National Association of State Boards of Education. (1998). *The numbers game: Ensuring quantity and quality in the teaching workforce. Report of the NASBE Study Group on Teacher Development, Supply, and Demand*. Alexandria, VA: Author.

National Institute of Child Health and Human Development. (2000). *Report of the National Reading Panel. Teaching children to read: An evidence-based assessment of the scientific research literature on reading and its implications for reading instruction: Reports of the subgroups* (NIH Publication No. 00-4754). Washington, DC: U.S. Government Printing Office.

Oakes, J., Franke, M.L., Quartz, K.H., & Rogers, J. (2002). Research for high-quality urban teaching: Defining it, developing it, assessing it. *Journal of Teacher Education, 53,* 228–234.

Peske, H.G., & Haycock, K. (2006). *Teaching inequality: How poor and minority students are shortchanged on teacher quality.* Washington, DC: The Joyce Foundation.

Puk, T.G., & Haines, J.M. (1999). Are schools prepared to allow beginning teachers to re-conceptualize instruction? *Teaching and Teacher Education, 15,* 541–553.

Shakespear, E., Beardsley, L., & Newton, A. (2003). *Preparing urban teachers: Uncovering communities. A community curriculum for interns and new teachers.* Boston, MA: Jobs for the Future.

Shinew, D.M., & Sodorff, C. (2003). Partnerships at a distance: Redesigning a teacher education program to prepare educators for diverse, high-needs classrooms. *Action in Teacher Education, 25*(3), 24–29.

UCLA Center X Teacher Education Program. (n.d.). Retrieved October 10, 2006, from centerx.gseis.ucla.edu/TEP/Program/overview.php

Walsh, K., Glaser, D., & Wilcox, D.D. (2006). *What education schools aren't teaching about reading and what elementary teachers aren't learning: Executive summary.* Washington, DC: National Council on Teacher Quality.

Washington State University Masters in Teaching. (n.d.). Retrieved October 10, 2006, from www.tricity.wsu.edu/tricity/catalog/MITProgram.htm

Watson, D., Charner-Laird, M., Kirkpatrick, C.L., Szczesiul, S.A., & Gordon, P.J. (2006). Effective teaching/effective urban teaching: Grappling with definitions, grappling with difference. *Journal of Teacher Education, 57,* 395–409.

Wayne State University: Limited License to Instruct. (n.d.). Retrieved October 10, 2006, from ted.coe.wayne.edu/brochures/lli.pdf

Essential Fieldwork for the Preparation of Teachers of Reading for Urban Settings

Cynthia Hynd Shanahan
University of Illinois at Chicago

Fieldwork is one of the key elements of teacher preparation programs. During the most intense field experience—student teaching—teacher candidates get the opportunity to apply the theory and practice of pedagogy to the day-to-day task of teaching, melding the "why" and the "what" with the "how to." They also learn how to operate in the context of a professional setting under the guidance of a cooperating teacher and a university field instructor who support their development as professionals.

Teaching their students reading is a large part of the task, and the work is challenging for most candidates. And for those who student teach in settings unlike those that they remember from their own schooling, the experience can be especially daunting. It is vitally important that all teacher candidates be well prepared to practice teach reading, not only in such settings but also to students from ethnic, racial, and socioeconomic groups that are different from their own. This chapter focuses on that preparation.

Purposes of This Chapter

This chapter focuses on a very specific and critically important aspect of preparing teachers to teach reading in urban environments—fieldwork. The chapter explores a review of the research on various fieldwork models and discusses the unique challenges that exist in connection with

Improving Literacy Achievement in Urban Schools: Critical Elements in Teacher Preparation edited by Louise C. Wilkinson, Lesley Mandel Morrow, and Victoria Chou. © 2008 by the International Reading Association.

fieldwork in urban settings. It also proposes a number of elements essential to effective fieldwork and implications for future research, practice, and policy.

Setting the Scene: The University of Illinois at Chicago

The University of Illinois at Chicago (UIC), located in the heart of Chicago, is committed to serving its urban constituency. The College of Education and Council on Teacher Education at UIC focus specific efforts on schools located in low-income, culturally diverse neighborhoods south and west of campus. Most programs confine student teaching and other field experiences to schools in the Chicago Public Schools (CPS) and concentrate most field experiences in these southern and western areas.

CPS is run by a large, centralized administration that oversees 481 elementary schools, 115 high schools, and 27 charter schools. The total student enrollment in 2006 was 420,982. In terms of race, 48.6% of the students are African American, 37.6% are Hispanic, 8.1% are white, 3.2% are Asian/Pacific Islander, 2.4% are multiracial, and 0.1% are Native American. The schools on the south and west sides of the city, for the most part, enroll either African American or Hispanic students, rather than a mix of students of different races. Overall, 85.6% of CPS students are from low-income families; this percentage is even higher in the schools served by UIC. Districtwide, 14% of students are limited English proficient.

The district employs 24,664 teachers, including 47.3% of whom are Caucasian, 35.8% of whom are African American, and 13.2% of whom are Hispanic. At UIC, 56.1% of our teacher candidates are Caucasian, 12% are African American, 14.5% are Hispanic, 9.0% are Asian/Pacific Islander, and 6.9% are of some other race. Thus, UIC prepares mostly white (and middle class) teachers to teach in African American and Hispanic low-income environments (research.cps.k12.il.us/cps/accountweb).

Statewide, 70–74% of elementary school students met or exceeded state reading standards on the Prairie State Achievement Exam in 2006. At one of the schools we work with, Benito Juarez Community Academy High School, only 18% of the largely Hispanic population met or exceeded state reading standards. At two largely African American high schools, Crane Tech and Hugh Manley Career Academy, only 21.6% and 8.9%, respectively, met or exceeded standards. Statewide, 58.4% of students met the standards. The picture looks somewhat better at the elementary (K–8) level. At James Shields School, 62.5% of the largely Hispanic population met or exceeded state standards. But this is not true of all schools. At the largely African American National Teachers Academy, for example, approximately 11% of the students met or exceeded state standards in reading.

Schools such as these need and deserve excellent teachers who are committed to raising student reading achievement levels and who know how to work with students who bring to the classroom diverse cultural experiences that may differ from their own. They also deserve school leadership that places a high priority on increasing reading achievement and leaders who know how to enlist community and district resources to make that happen. UIC doesn't have a lock on how to prepare teachers to meet the literacy needs of urban schools. However, like other teacher preparation institutions in big cities, we are deeply enmeshed in this endeavor.

Review of Research and Theory

Most of the research regarding preservice teachers and their fieldwork focuses on general teacher preparation rather than reading teacher preparation. Yet these data are relevant in that many of the issues are the same.

One strategy to prepare educators to teach in schools with large minority populations is to recruit candidates with similar ethnic or racial backgrounds. Indeed, UIC's internally collected data show that candidates who are Hispanic or African American are more likely to seek employment in Hispanic or African American schools upon graduation. Numerous examples of such recruitment efforts exist, most of which increase the number of minority students brought into teacher education programs (e.g., Becket, 1998; Brennan & Bliss, 1998). Yet few institutions have studied the impact on schools.

Another strategy is to accept only teacher candidates with particular attributes tied to successful urban teaching. Haberman (1996), for example, argues in favor of individuals of color between the ages of 30 and 50 who have urban experiences and successful ways of dealing with both students and bureaucracy. His research suggests that one can predict the success of future teachers based on the degree to which their attributes match those of star urban teachers. Yet many teacher preparation institutions prepare undergraduates and graduates who are typically much younger than and without the experience suggested by Haberman.

Yet another strategy is to provide field placements that provide teacher candidates with relevant experiences teaching in urban environments. The research findings on field experiences, even when tied to multicultural curriculum, are mixed. For example, Sleeter's (2001) review of the literature finds four studies (Bondy, Schmitz, & Johnson, 1993; Grottkau & Nickolai-Mays, 1989; Mason, 1997; Wiggins & Follo, 1999) that showed a positive outcome when teacher candidates completed multicultural course work and took part in tutoring or other field experience, and two studies (Haberman & Post, 1992; Reed, 1993) that found such a combination actually reinforced candidates' stereotypes. Sleeter (2001) also finds little more than anecdotal evidence to suggest that school–university collaborations are effective in preparing teachers to teach in diverse urban environments.

A final strategy is immersion. In immersion programs, teacher candidates live in the urban environments in which they teach. Very few immersion programs in urban areas have been the focus of research and even the studies done on immersion programs in non-urban areas (the American Indian Reservation Project, for example) have been mainly anecdotal. However, these reports attest to the power of such experiences (Mahan, 1982). Leland and Harste (2005), for example, provide case studies showing the ultimate success of an urban immersion program that improved teacher candidates' attitudes about teaching in urban environments. They attribute the change in attitude, in part, to the candidates' participation in seminars on critical literacy. Most educators eschew programs that prepare preservice teachers for urban teaching by merely adding curricular and field experience elements to their existing programs. Ladson-Billings (1999), using critical race theory, calls for more dramatic programmatic changes in teacher education focused on five elements:

1. Content integration
2. Knowledge construction
3. Prejudice reduction
4. Equity pedagogy
5. Empowering school culture

She also references Bennett's (1995) list of five key components of successful programs:

1. Selection
2. Understanding cultural, historical perspectives
3. Developing intercultural competence
4. Combating racism
5. Teacher decision making

The idea that cultural responsiveness must be infused throughout the teacher preparation curriculum is echoed in other publications as well. Villegas and Lucas (2002), for example, call for a preservice curriculum that prepares culturally responsive teachers who (a) are socioculturally conscious, (b) have affirming views of students from diverse backgrounds, (c) see themselves as responsible for and capable of bringing about change to make schools more equitable, (d) understand how learners construct knowledge and are capable of promoting knowledge construction, (e) know about the lives of their students, and (f) design instruction that builds on what their students already know while stretching them beyond the familiar.

These foci are echoed in the ideas of those who prepare reading teachers. Rogers, Marshall, and Tyson (2006) say that "immersing students in community-based environments and providing spaces for dialogue are promising strategies for complicating and deepening preservice teachers' understandings of language and literacy, particularly in relation to issues of cultural diversity and social justice" (p. 202). To specifically focus on literacy, these educators added an internship to their already urban curriculum that required teacher candidates to work in one of three community-based sites. The teacher candidates grappled with issues of social justice as they engaged in seminar readings and literacy teaching within a community setting. This study suggests that preservice teachers who focus on literacy in diverse environments can improve their understanding of both literacy and diversity.

Ladson-Billings (1992) discusses the literacy practices of two successful teachers of African American students in low-achieving schools. Her study is of practicing teachers, yet she provides us with a picture of what urban literacy instruction might focus on for preservice teachers as well. Although the two teachers used different approaches to teaching literacy (one a whole-language approach and one a basal reader approach), there were similarities in their practices.

Neither teacher shied away from issues of race and culture, and both made students' culture a reference for instruction. Students were allowed to use nonstandard American English without reprimand or correction, and both teachers modeled how one moves between Standard American English and African American Language. Both teachers also maintained a critical perspective of knowledge, recognizing that knowledge is privileged and positioned within power relationships and engaging their students in adopting this perspective. For example, they helped students question the texts they were reading regarding whose voice was being heard.

Both teachers spent an extended amount of time early in the year establishing a community of trust and respect with students and parents that was clearly focused on student achievement. They created literate environments filled with books and refused to accept failure. And finally, both teachers, along with their students, examined the question "Why become literate?" emphasizing in particular the liberating effect of literacy. This glimpse into the lives of successful teachers gives us a view of the kind of teachers we would like to prepare.

In summary, the research and theory regarding urban teacher preparation and field instruction suggests that a program completely focused on urban experiences, both in terms of course work and field placement, is likely to be more effective than a program with a compartmentalized treatment of urban teaching. In addition, literacy teaching in urban environments needs to take into account the cultural capital of urban students while building an environment that is supportive of new learning.

Best Practice in Field Instruction

At UIC, the mostly Caucasian group of teacher candidates generally have not had previous experiences working in diverse urban schools, which are sometimes chaotic and lack effective leadership. What's more, they may have had limited contact with low-income, minority students or students whose primary language is not Standard American English. Yet these students bring to school many rich, cultural experiences and limitless potential. If teacher candidates fail to realize that, and view these students simply from a deficit perspective, they are bound to fail at meeting these students' needs. All students, including those in our urban schools deserve high-quality, culturally responsive reading education, and it is within the purview of teacher preparation institutions to ensure that they get it, despite the institutional challenges endemic to large school systems such as Chicago's.

In choosing sites for candidate fieldwork, UIC struggles with a central question—is it better to place teacher candidates in a typical urban school that is struggling to meet student needs or in one that, against the odds, is succeeding? Although we want our candidates to be exposed to and prepared to work in challenging settings, we also want them to be exposed to the kind of positive teaching models they need to become effective reading teachers. Yet we've found that teacher candidates who experience fieldwork in struggling schools are more likely to take jobs in such settings. Our position, then, is to place candidates in challenging settings but also to work to ensure that they receive adequate support.

UIC educators believe that the entire experience of a teacher candidate—the application and selection process, course work, field experiences, readings, and so on—must focus on diversity and be aligned with what research and theory say about teaching in an urban setting. Thus, candidates are clearly told at the time of application that UIC's mission is to serve its urban constituency. Early on, candidates are asked to refer to our conceptual framework and dispositions, which focus on succeeding in urban environments. For example, we believe that a candidate for certification must (a) commit to the democratic ideal of developing all students' potential, (b) seek remedies to educational inequalities, (c) recognize and make use of the human and cultural resources of local communities, and (d) create collaborative environments. In course work, candidates reflect on issues of positionality, that is, an individual's position in a social/political/racial context. They learn about culturally responsive pedagogy, and they begin to engage in the practice of teaching in urban settings through their pre–student-teaching fieldwork.

There is also a focus on the teaching of reading. For example, undergraduate students planning to teach at the elementary level take three reading courses. These courses complement the CPS Reading Initiative, a P–12 approach to improving reading that among other things asks each of the district's elementary teachers to devote at least two hours—and more if their students are reading significantly below grade level—to the teaching of reading, with an equal emphasis on word knowledge, comprehension, fluency, and writing. The courses also complement UIC's Partnership Read, a professional development project under the direction of Taffy Raphael, faculty member at UIC, which helps 10 local schools use assessment data in planning reading instruction.

In addition, field experiences at UIC have been designed to focus on the teaching of literacy in urban environments, as evidenced by the following 10 beliefs.

1. *Sites must provide opportunities to teach all aspects of reading.* It is important that our teacher candidates practice teaching reading in schools where reading instruction is a focus. Moreover, such instruction should be comprehensive, focusing on multiple aspects of reading, and it should be grade-appropriate. In the primary grades, instruction must focus on phonemic awareness, phonics, fluency, vocabulary, comprehension, and writing. In later grades, instruction in phonemic awareness and phonics diminishes, with vocabulary instruction becoming a higher priority. In secondary schools, students who struggle with reading take special courses; instruction in how to read in various content areas is provided by regular classroom teachers. Because the CPS Reading Initiative focuses on all these aspects of reading instruction, we seek to send our teacher candidates to schools that have enthusiastically worked with this initiative.

2. *Sites must provide opportunities to observe and engage in reading instruction in one-on-one, small-group, and whole-class settings.* At UIC, student teaching and other field experiences begin by giving preservice teachers a chance to observe other teachers and to work with individual students and in small-group settings. In such settings, it is easier for practiced teachers to pay attention to how their students are responding to instruction, one of the biggest challenges new teachers face. Once teacher candidates master this skill in small groups, they are more likely to be able to put it to use when teaching the whole class.

3. *Sites must provide opportunities to differentiate instruction for English-language learners (ELLs), bilingual students, and special needs students.* T. Shanahan (personal communication, April 10, 2007) has argued that instruction can be differentiated in four ways: through changes in the content, amount, intensity, and level of instruction. Varying the *content of instruction* might mean providing students with different background information, vocabulary instruction, or reading material based on their familiarity with the subject and ability level.

Varying the *amount of instruction* may mean giving some students extra time to learn and practice new skills. In our view, a change in the content of instruction is often not enough to bring lower achieving students up to speed. It takes extra time. This extra time could be provided in before- or after-school programs, in content area classes, or in other creative ways throughout the school day.

Varying the *intensity* of instruction requires teachers to provide struggling students with more support, which might mean scaffolding instruction or drilling down into more complex understandings of instruction, perhaps by providing students with more work on vocabulary. Teachers can also increase the intensity of their instruction with more frequent assessment. Such assessment could involve something as simple as sitting more often with struggling students during seatwork to evaluate their understanding of a concept. Often, increasing the intensity of instruction also requires extra time. For example, in order for students to learn not only how to use a reading strategy but also how to use it with a variety of different kinds of texts, more intense and more time-consuming instruction would both be required.

Varying the *level* of instruction means ensuring that each student is taught at his or her own instructional level. For example, a struggling reader may need an easier version of the text than other, more proficient readers.

If teacher candidates are to become successful reading teachers in challenging urban environments, they must have opportunities to practice strategies that allow them to differentiate instruction to meet individual student needs. Fieldwork and student teaching sites need to provide such opportunities.

4. *Sites must provide opportunities for teacher candidates to create and use reading lessons and units that are likely to succeed.* Such reading lessons state clear goals, spell out ways to teach to those goals, and include assessment measures that determine whether or not the goals have been met. They also include strategies designed to ensure student engagement, promote mutual respect between student and teacher, help students use their existing knowledge or cultural capital as a basis for learning new information, give students the explicit instruction they need to learn new concepts and skills, and stress all aspects of reading.

5. *Sites must provide opportunities for teacher candidates to understand and use assessment data.* In this age of screening, diagnostic, progress-monitoring, and summative high-stakes assessments, it is important that teacher candidates have the opportunity to observe the use of different kinds of assessments, participate in the administration of classroom assessments, and learn to interpret the results of high-stakes tests. Because many urban schools are under intense pressure to demonstrate student achievement high enough to keep them off state academic "watch" lists, test preparation often becomes the focus of ins-truction, especially in the months preceding high-stakes testing. I argue that this focus on test

preparation is counterproductive. Yet my view isn't necessarily shared by struggling schools that feel as though they are under pressure. It is important, then, that teacher candidates spend time in schools where test preparation is kept to a minimum and the focus of instruction is on reading, not passing the reading test.

However, our teacher candidates will likely be employed in schools where test preparation is emphasized. For that reason, they need to engage in conversations with teachers, seminar instructors, and field instructors that focus on the fact that the best way to prepare students to do well on such tests is to truly teach them to read.

Schools in which teachers use assessments in varied and reasoned ways create and maintain a positive assessment environment. Our teacher preparation programs stress the importance of using informal classroom assessment data, for example, to sequence instruction. Such a skill is considered so important that it is the focus of an overarching assignment called the Teaching and Assessment Event that all teacher candidates complete during their student teaching semester. To complete the assignment, teacher candidates prepare a lesson or unit plan that includes assessments designed to measure whether the goals of their lesson or unit were met. Next, they teach the lesson or unit and give the assessments. After that, they discuss the results of the assessments and the next instructional steps needed, both for the class as a whole and for any student whose assessment data indicate a need for extra attention. In order to complete this assignment with optimal support from field instructors and cooperating teachers, teacher candidates need to be in schools where assessment data are used to guide instruction.

6. *Sites need to provide positive classroom environments.* In the best classrooms, cooperating teachers have created environments of mutual respect where students feel safe and can focus on reading and learning. These classrooms most optimally exist within a larger school context that is also safe and respectful. Positive learning environments often take quite a bit of effort to establish, especially if classrooms are filled with students who come from more than one culture or if the students have little experience in such environments. We want teacher candidates to observe how cooperating teachers create these environments and then maintain them throughout the year.

Teacher candidates also benefit from placement in classrooms that are well organized. That's because it's only within such a setting they can learn to handle their own classroom management challenges in positive ways, develop routines that are conducive to effective reading instruction, and learn how to set up and manage the flexible grouping that is necessary to provide differentiated reading instruction. When teacher candidates are placed in chaotic classrooms, such practices are virtually impossible to carry out.

7. *Fieldwork should be accompanied by appropriate amounts of support.* Teacher candidates can feel overwhelmed during urban field and student teaching experiences. Thus, they need the university to provide them with opportunities to debrief and engage in collaborative problem solving. These debriefing experiences should not shy away from—but in fact should encourage—conversations about issues of race and ethnicity, class, and culture and the ways in which these issues intersect with instruction. In cases where teaching candidates are placed in classrooms filled with students who are not like them in terms of those characteristics, they need to feel supported in their efforts to cope yet challenged to take on new perspectives.

Universities can provide this support in several ways. One way is to tie field experiences with particular classes that encourage discussion. For example, at the same time secondary teacher candidates are learning about adolescent development and curriculum theory, they are observing instruction in high school classrooms and attending colloquia on diversity. They engage in online discussion board conversations that help them tie the instruction they see to the content of the courses and colloquia they are attending. During student teaching, all teacher candidates attend a weekly seminar where they get opportunities to engage in discussions about their experiences.

UIC also tries to find ways to help cooperating teachers become better mentors. This semester, we are teaching a course for cooperating teachers that requires them to engage in conversations with their student teachers about issues such as race and ethnicity, class, and gender. The cooperating teachers also share with student teachers the ways in which they learn about their students and how they can create positive environments for learning.

8. *Teacher candidates should have opportunities to understand the environments in which they teach.* At UIC, we ask teacher candidates to learn about the neighborhoods of the schools they work in. One assignment, for example, requires teacher candidates to attend a neighborhood event and observe and reflect on the literacy practices they witness at the event. Later, they complete a study of the neighborhood in which their field experience school is located. They also must interview different groups of people who take part in the life of the school, such as students,

principals, librarians, lunchroom staff, and so on. In addition, they use technology to find census data, take virtual tours, read neighborhood histories, and uncover other information that will help them learn more about and better understand their students. Our hope is that they will engage in similar studies of the schools in which they eventually become employed.

9. Sites need strong leaders who focus on achievement. Strong leaders help create strong schools; principals of the strongest schools, for example, have found ways to focus on achievement. Although many of the schools we work with at UIC report low student achievement, we try to partner with schools that are on the move—schools where faculty and administration are working together to make a difference.

Some of these schools have especially close relationships with UIC. Several, for example, are Partnership Read schools and benefit from the professional development in reading they receive from UIC faculty. Others work with us on federal Teacher Quality Grant funds. In these schools, UIC supports deeper levels of mentoring, matching not only teacher candidates but also new teachers with mentors.

UIC has also begun to explore ways for candidates in its teacher preparation and educational leadership programs to work together. Candidates in the EdD program in Urban Educational Leadership, for example, complete three-year internships in urban schools where they are required to create and implement school-improvement plans. Because of that kind of focus on school reform, we believe these schools make excellent field experience sites for our teacher candidates.

10. Field experiences need to be part of a larger, consistent message about urban teaching. We want students who are considering becoming teachers in urban environments to come to UIC and, thus, in the past several years, have clarified the message potential students receive about our urban mission. This mission is spelled out in all of our documents, on our websites, in strategic planning, in recruitment materials, and so on. It is also shared by the faculty, through syllabi, assignments, discussions, and assessments. But perhaps no aspect of our program better reflects our commitment to urban environments than the sites we've chosen to provide our teacher candidates with field experience in urban literacy teaching—schools where they can engage in service projects, meaningful research, and supervised instructional practice that will truly prepare them to work in challenging urban environments.

Finally, the International Reading Association has recently developed a Certificate of Distinction for the Reading Preparation of Elementary and Secondary Teachers. Teacher preparation institutions can earn this certificate by demonstrating that they meet six standards, including standards on field instruction and diversity. Although the field instruction and diversity standards are not specifically focused on urban experiences, many of the rubric categories used to evaluate institutions are also pertinent for teaching reading in diverse urban settings. The standards can be found at www.reading.org/downloads/resources/quester_standards_rubrics.pdf.

Summary of Main Ideas

Some of the characteristics of ideal field sites and experiences designed to help teacher candidates learn to teach reading in diverse urban environments focus on reading instruction specifically, some on the kinds of environments conducive to successful reading instruction, and others on the kind of supports and messages teacher preparation institutions should provide.

At UIC, we struggle to take into account these characteristics, and we often fall short. For example, sometimes we have too many candidates to place, and so we put a teacher candidate in an unknown site upon the recommendation of the placement staff at the school, only to find out that the site is problematic—for example, the classroom is chaotic, the cooperating teacher is struggling as much as the teacher candidate, or the school is unsupportive. Alternatively, we find at times that teacher candidates fail to fully develop the dispositions that are necessary for successful urban teaching. There are tensions in urban teaching, and these tensions sometimes exist at the expense of the individuals for whom we feel an immense sense of responsibility, the teacher candidate, the student, and the cooperating teacher. At least once each semester, a field instructor will pull a teacher candidate from a particular urban setting and create an action plan aimed at ameliorating a difficult situation.

Yet, despite the occasional setback, UIC continues to aggressively pursue its mission. Our faculty engages in frequent conversations about tough issues. We look at our data. We see where our teacher candidates go when they graduate, and we assess how well prepared they feel. We see how they fare on assessments such as the Teaching and Assessment Event and their student teaching evaluations. We discuss curricular changes and frequently revise our programs. We work hard to develop stronger ties with our partner schools, implementing service projects, holding joint "summit" meetings and workshops, and teaching courses for cooperating teachers. We encourage our teacher graduates to take on their own teacher candidates. It's an ongoing process. The urban landscape changes quickly: Schools close, others open, administrative changes are made, and gentrification causes poor families to move to other neighborhoods. Such changes all have a bearing on where we send teacher candidates for their field experiences.

Implications for Research, Practice, and Policy

One thing that may be evident from this chapter is the dearth of research on the preparation of urban reading teachers. Although I strongly believe that the issues I discuss in this chapter are central to the development of effective teachers of reading, my conclusions are based largely on anecdotal evidence and are not research-based. To determine if those conclusions are valid would require controlled studies on the effectiveness of teacher candidates vis-à-vis the reading achievement of the students they encounter both during field experiences and as beginning teachers. At present, however, only a few states are tying achievement data to teacher preparation programs; Illinois is not one of them. Yet, even with access to such data, there are numerous variables that are difficult to control. The difficulty of engaging in such research, however, doesn't mean that it's not warranted.

Regarding implications for practice, we know that preparing teachers to meet the specific challenges and reap the unique rewards of urban teaching is vital. At present, many of our largest cities are failing to provide their students with the reading education they deserve. In many cases the neediest schools have the most difficult time getting and keeping competent faculty. We know, however, that teacher candidates who have taken part in student teaching and other field experiences in urban settings are more likely to become employed in those settings. Thus, we can make a difference in urban schools if we get our best teacher candidates to effectively engage in instruction at those sites.

National, state, and local policy should focus on preparing talented reading teachers to teach in urban settings. Policy is often accompanied by monetary support, and monetary support promotes greater effort. Policy focused on urban reading teacher preparation would mean that urban teacher preparation programs would be larger; the elements of those programs would be more carefully created, implemented, and studied; and findings about promising practices would receive wider distribution.

REFERENCES

Becket, D.R. (1998). Increasing the number of Latino and Navajo teachers in hard-to-staff schools. *Journal of Teacher Education*, *49*, 196–205.

Bennett, C.I. (1995). Preparing teachers for cultural diversity and national standards of academic excellence. *Journal of Teacher Education*, *46*, 259–265.

Bondy, E., Schmitz, S., & Johnson, M. (1993). The impact of coursework and fieldwork on student teachers' reported beliefs about teaching poor and minority students. *Action in Teacher Education*, *15*(2), 55–62.

Brennan, S., & Bliss, T. (1998). Increasing minority representation in the teaching profession through alternative certification: A case study. *Teacher Educator*, *34*(1), 1–11.

Grottkau, B.J., & Nickolai-Mays, S. (1989). An empirical analysis of a multicultural education paradigm for preservice teachers. *Educational Research Quarterly*, *13*(4), 27–33.

Haberman, M. (1996). Selecting and preparing culturally competent teachers for urban schools. In J. Sikula (Eds.), *Handbook of research on teacher education* (2nd ed., pp. 747–760). New York: MacMillan.

Haberman, M., & Post, L. (1992). Does direct experience change education students' perceptions of low-income minority students? *Midwest Educational Researcher*, *5*(2), 29–31.

Ladson-Billings, G. (1992). Reading between the lines and beyond the pages: A culturally relevant approach to literacy teaching. *Theory Into Practice*, *31*, 312–320.

Ladson-Billings, G. (1999). Preparing teachers for diverse student populations: A critical race theory perspective. *Review of Research in Education*, *24*, 211–247.

Leland, C.H., & Harste, J.C. (2005). Doing what we want to become: Preparing new urban teachers. *Urban Education*, *40*(1), 60–77.

Mahan, J.M. (1982). Native Americans as teacher trainers: Anatomy and outcomes of a cultural immersion project. *Journal of Educational Equity and Leadership*, *2*, 100–110.

Mason, T.C. (1997). Urban field experiences and prospective teachers' attitudes toward inner-city schools. *Teacher Education Quarterly*, *24*(3), 29–40.

Reed, D.F. (1993). Multicultural education for preservice students. *Action in Teacher Education*, *15*(3), 27–34.

Rogers, T., Marshall, E., & Tyson, C. (2006). Dialogic narratives of literacy, teaching, and schooling: Preparing literacy teachers for diverse settings. *Reading Research Quarterly*, *41*, 202–224.

Sleeter, C.E. (2001). Preparing teachers for culturally diverse schools. *Journal of Teacher Education*, *52*, 94–106.

Wiggins, R.A., & Follo, E.J. (1999). Development of knowledge, attitudes, and commitment to teach diverse student populations. *Journal of Teacher Education*, *50*, 94–105.

Villegas, A.M., & Lucas, T. (2002). Preparing culturally responsive teachers: Rethinking the curriculum. *Journal of Teacher Education*, *53*, 20–32.

CHAPTER 6

Academic Language Proficiency and Literacy Instruction in Urban Settings

Louise C. Wilkinson
Syracuse University

Elaine R. Silliman
University of South Florida

A major goal of education is for all students to develop academic language proficiency sufficient to meet the increasingly complex academic discourse requirements of schooling. Academic language proficiency, in turn, allows access to the oral and written registers of schooling, the discourse medium through which children engage with literacy concepts, processes, and content—"the stuff of schooling" (Cummins, 2000, p. 12).

Increasingly, American teachers encounter students who are English-language learners (ELLs). For these students, in particular, linguistic systems, coupled with sociocultural norms, collectively function as the conceptual engine for students' development of academic language proficiency. Yet whether English is the first or second language, academic language proficiency is a critical competence for students in that it enables them to engage in language-based classroom activities designed to deliver curriculum.

Purposes of This Chapter

One of the purposes of this chapter is to define academic language proficiency and academic discourse requirements and to describe their importance to students' achievement in school. This chapter reviews the

Improving Literacy Achievement in Urban Schools: Critical Elements in Teacher Preparation edited by Louise C. Wilkinson, Lesley Mandel Morrow, and Victoria Chou. © 2008 by the International Reading Association.

research on academic language proficiency and its relationship to successful participation in the academic discourse requirements across disciplines and in specific content areas such as science. It also discusses the best evidence-based practices in academic language instruction, particularly as it pertains to the education of ELLs in urban settings. Recommendations are also presented on practice, policy, and further research on literacy and language learning.

This chapter includes a special focus on children who are Spanish-speaking ELLs. As a group, the Hispanic population is now 14.8% of the total United States population and, in several states (e.g., California, New Mexico, and Texas), constitute the new "majority-minority" (U.S. Census Bureau, 2007, n.p.). Currently, 18% of the school-age population is of Hispanic heritage, up from 9% in 1970. That figure is expected to continue growing over the next two decades because of higher-than-average birth rates and continued immigration (U.S. Census Bureau, 2005). Many students of Hispanic heritage are enrolled in high proportions in urban schools.

More than 31 million United States residents five years of age and older report that they speak Spanish at home; more than 50% of those same residents also report that they speak English very well (U.S. Census Bureau, 2006). Therefore, although in many cases ELLs entering school may indeed have adequate everyday, social, conversational abilities, they may not have the necessary oral language underpinnings for entering into academic discourse. That's particularly true in content areas such as science and social studies, each of which involves unique ways of thinking and communicating.

Academic Language

Academic Language Proficiency: Definition and Significance

Students' school achievement depends upon their being proficient in academic language, the language of classroom instruction and textbooks. For ELL students, who are still in the process of acquiring English, developing full academic language proficiency can take many years and may be a daunting experience. Yet mastery of advanced oral and written English-language skills that enable students to formulate and express their ideas well enough to participate fully in classroom activities is the *sine qua non* of success in American schools. Cummins (2000) states that academic language proficiency

> refers not to any absolute notion of expertise in using language but the degree to which an individual has access to and expertise in understanding and using the specific kind of language that is employed in educational contexts and is required to complete academic tasks [and] to function effectively in the discourse domain of the school. (pp. 66–67)

Three negative outcomes are likely when students lack proficiency in understanding and using academic language: First, students are less likely to learn from daily classroom experiences skills, such as how to use reading and writing to engage in new ways of thinking. Second, because their participation in classroom activities is significantly reduced, they do not benefit as they should from interactions with peers and teachers. Third, this reduction in participation subsequently interferes with the development of their social identities as competent members of a learning community (Christian & Bloome, 2004; Danzak & Silliman, 2005; Riley, 2006).

This exchange between a researcher and a 7-year-old Mexican American boy named Steve points out the social effects of insufficient proficiency in academic language ability (Martínez-Roldán & Malavé, 2004, p. 156):

Researcher: And what happens when a person speaks Spanish? (Pause) Does that mean the person is not smart?

Steve: I speak in English and I can't speak Spanish and I'm not smart 'cause I don't know what they're saying.

As Steve's comments imply, the lack of status and prestige that results from poor academic language can affect a student's self-concept, overall adjustment to school, and academic achievement (Silliman, Wilkinson, & Brea-Spahn, 2004; Wilkinson & Silliman, in press).

Three decades of research have established that the requirements of the multiparty structure typical of school talk differ functionally from those of the two-party structure of face-to-face conversation (Fisher, 2005; Wilkinson & Silliman, 2000). The research literature is sparse, however, regarding the connection between student academic language proficiency and mastery of academic material in content areas.

The distinction between one's everyday oral language register and the more specialized register of academic language is a critical one (see Table 6.1). These two registers, each of which is characterized by its own vocabulary, syntax, degree of formality, and social context, are simultaneously interdependent and independent (Cummins, 2000). In other words, while it is possible to "code switch" from one register to the other in a relatively seamless manner (the interdependent dimension), each register can be used separately (the independent dimension) in both the oral and print domains. For example, in talking with close friends, one probably would use a more oral, or informal register; one is more likely to activate the academic language register when giving a class presentation or writing a research report on global warming.

Thus, developing academic language proficiency is similar, in some respects, to learning a second language. Young, normally developing children acquire a first language that allows them to become competent and cooperative conversationalists in their social interactions with family, peers, and others. Primary-language ability means knowing "how to talk" in the situations of everyday life; as such, it encompasses the language socialization processes of a child's culture.

No causal relationship has been found between specific Spanish- or English-language systems and English reading comprehension (Cain & Oakhill, 2007). However, research has determined that a robust everyday oral language register predicts subsequent proficiency in reading

Table 6.1. General Characteristics of the Everyday Oral Language Register Compared With Those of Specialized Classroom Registers

Everyday Oral Language Register (Home Register)	Academic Language Registers (School Registers)
• Vernacular varieties that are more oral	• Specialized varieties that are more literate
• Describes primary language abilities	• Describes advanced literacy-related language abilities and advanced literacy-related language abilities
• Typical of face-to-face conversation	• Typical of the language of schooling, including the language of textbooks and composition
• Insufficient for academic achievement	• Necessary for academic achievement

Modified from Cummins, 2000; Gee, 1999.

comprehension (National Institute of Child Health and Human Development Early Child Care Research Network, 2005), including that of ELLs (Roberts & Neal, 2004). Berman (2007) contends there is a difference between being a fluent native speaker of a language, as indicated by command of the everyday oral language register, and becoming a proficient user of language for school learning, which is intertwined with literacy learning well into adolescence and beyond. In contrast to the oral language register, the academic language register represents a new tool for thinking and communicating in more literate ways.

The Academic Discourse Demands of Content Areas

Each content area, whether it be literature, math, history, science, or social studies, uses its own specialized academic language register. Each calls on students to learn new ways of communicating. One content area currently receiving special attention in the elementary grades is science. Here's why: First, from a big-picture perspective, the development of a scientific attitude should be interconnected with the processes of "inquiry and investigation at all educational levels" (Zimmerman, 2007, p. 173). To that end, children have to learn the language of science and develop the ability to discuss, read, and write about scientific concepts. A second reason is entwined with literacy learning and the transition to an academic language register—that is, explicitly guiding students to build scientific schemas by integrating scientific discourse with expository text experiences. Such a process can promote the creation of an academic register for communicating scientific concepts via the tools of speaking, reading, and writing (Pappas, Varelas, Barry, & Rife, 2002; Purcell-Gates, Duke, & Martineau, 2007; Varelas & Pappas, 2006). The final reason is a highly pragmatic one. Under No Child Left Behind (NCLB) legislation, states must administer science assessments at least once by 2007–2008 in three grade ranges: 3–5, 6–9, and 10–12. However, science instruction may be receiving the short end of the educational stick. Because of the time teachers now spend with elementary students on reading and math to meet the adequate yearly progress standard of NCLB, only minimal instructional time may be given to hands-on science experiences (Wallis & Steptoe, 2007).

Recent longitudinal data from a study of a small group of monolingual, English-speaking preschoolers found that an oral bridge to scientific concepts emerges around three years of age, as evidenced by the children's questions about biological phenomena such as the lives of

Figure 6.1. Second-Grader Mike's PowerPoint Presentation on the Anatomy of the Praying Mantis

I will tell you about the anatomy of the praying mantis and what their body parts are called. Praying mantises have a very big compound eye. A Praying mantises eyes change color at night. A praying mantis is green, tan, brown and yellow-green when they're not trying to catch prey and their color depends on their body temperature. When they are trying to catch pray, their color changes to match their surroundings and that is called camouflage. Praying mantises have a head, thorax, abdomen and wings. Praying mantis can see 360 degrees so it can see in the back of its head and the sides. The wings are attached to the thorax. Praying mantises have antennae that are connected to their head. The praying mantis grows up to 2 and a half inches long. Praying mantis have front legs that have spikes that catches its pray. Their spikes are made of chitin. Praying mantises find their prey by blending into gardens and brushy fields. Then they catch their prey with their spikes then they eat them.

animals (Chouinard, 2007). These questions can relate to the life cycle ("Why is he sleeping"), death ("Is he dead?"), and reproduction ("How do bees grow their babies?"). There is little research, however, on the development of children's expository skills as they move into and through the elementary grades (Berman & Nir-Sagiv, 2007).

Figure 6.1 shows an example of budding above-average ability in the application of expository knowledge to scientific investigation combined with an emerging scientific discourse register in Mike, a second grader who is an English-only speaker from a middle class family. As part of a class research project on insects, Mike's responsibility was to investigate the anatomy of the praying mantis and then to independently synthesize his findings with a PowerPoint presentation.

Mike's research report is consistent with the features of what is called *science information text*, a type of expository discourse. The following list outlines examples of academic language features distinguishing information texts from other expository texts (Berman & Nir-Sagiv, 2007; Purcell-Gates et al., 2007), accompanied by examples from Mike's presentation:

- Descriptions of attributes or components (e.g., "a very big compound eye," "have front legs that have spikes")
- Identifications of a characteristic event (e.g., "Praying mantises find their prey by blending into gardens and brushy fields")

- The use of present tense (or timeless) verb constructions (e.g., "A preying mantis is green, tan, brown, and yellow-green")
- The use of a few vocabulary meanings that are specific to scientific concepts (e.g., "Praying mantises have antennae," "Their spikes are made of chitin")
- The use of generic, impersonal noun references—as opposed to the personal references of personal experience narratives (e.g., "Praying mantises have a very big compound eye")

Only a few classroom-based studies have been conducted on ELLs' acquisition of scientific knowledge and their development of a scientific discourse register. These studies aimed to examine the effects of introducing an integrated, scaffolded approach to doing science experiments and talking about science concepts in more literate ways in first- and fourth-grade classrooms (Varelas & Pappas, 2006; Westby, Dezale, Fradd, & Lee, 1999).

On a larger educational scale, Bailey and Butler (2007) make the case that the wide range of variations in academic discourse expectations across teachers, grade levels, content areas, and textbooks have created obstacles for the development of national and state content standards for ELL students.

Bailey, Butler, Stevens, and Lord (2007) investigate the academic language register of typical fifth-grade science, social science, and math textbooks in terms of their lexical/semantic, grammatical, and global discourse organizational features. The science textbooks (a) include the highest proportion of general academic vocabulary, suggesting the need for a higher baseline of "must know" material, and (b) are more likely to be written in the passive voice and use more complex clauses and coordinating conjunctions such as *when*, *if*, and *but*. The three types of textbooks tended to overlap in terms of their core features of discourse organization, which included comparison, description, enumeration, paraphrase, and sequencing. This finding suggests the importance of an ELL curriculum that focuses on instruction related to these concepts.

Table 6.2 lists examples of the lexical/semantic, grammatical, and global discourse organizational features of the academic language register. It also compares how each might be used in a science text or article with Mike's beginning efforts to use each in a PowerPoint presentation. The examples indicate that by second grade, Mike is well on his way to recruiting the academic language register of science for the analysis, synthesis, and interpretation of the natural world.

Table 6.2. Use of Academic Language Features Typical of Academic Works as Used in Mike's Report

	Academic Language Features	Examples Typical of Academic Works	Examples From Mike's Work
Lexical/Semantic Features	General academic meanings	*Introduce, presume, consequence, inadequate*	*Compound, temperature, camouflage, blending*
	Specialized academic meanings Derivations	*Species, denominator, nymphs, historical Predicament (predict), disagreeable (disagree), geometric (geometry), fusion (fuse)*	*Prey, thorax, chitin Temperature (temper), brushy (brush)*
Grammatical Features	Independent clause only	"The ice on the river melts quickly under the warm sun."	"Then they catch their prey with their spikes."
	Coordinate clause	"Some deserts are very hot in the daytime, but temperatures can drop below freezing at night."	"Preying mantis can see 360 degrees so it can see in the back of its head and the sides."
	Dependent clause	"Although human beings don't notice the noises of nature, a lot of animals react to the sounds around them."	"When they are trying to catch pray, their color changes to match their surroundings and that is called camouflage."
	Complex (elaborated) noun phrases	"Our planet looks like a big, beautiful marble from a distance."	"A praying mantis is green, tan, brown, and yellow-green when they're not trying to catch prey."

Academic Language Features		Examples Typical of Academic Works	Examples From Mike's Work
Global Discourse Organizational Features	Comparison	"A praying mantis is like a chameleon."	"A praying mantis is green, tan, brown, and yellow-green when they're not trying to catch prey."
	Description	"The praying mantis is an environmentally friendly insect."	Note: The overall structure of the composition is primarily descriptive or informational (Purcell-Gates et al., 2007).
	Enumeration	"Most mantis vary in colors from light green to pink, pea green, and brown."	"Praying mantises have a <u>head, thorax, abdomen and wings</u>."
	Paraphrase	"There are multiple species of the praying mantis, most of whom reside in tropical areas."	"Praying mantis have front legs that have spikes that catches its pray."
	Sequencing	"Laying in wait, the praying mantis grabs its prey with its forelegs, and then paralyzes and consumes it."	"Then they catch their prey with their spikes then they eat them."

Features compiled from Bailey et al., 2007.

The remainder of this chapter focuses on the central role of general academic vocabulary for ELL students in their development of academic language proficiency and the best practices that emerge from the research literature.

General Academic Vocabulary Knowledge: A Key to School Success for ELLs

General Vocabulary Knowledge

Consider this statement made during a science lesson by a fourth-grade teacher: "Flowers have mechanisms of attractions like whales have echolocation" (Bailey et al., 2007, p. 122). This nine-word sentence contains different layers of vocabulary knowledge, which in turn carry various levels of meaning. ELLs learn basic vocabulary in their first language as part of their everyday oral language register. Examples include words such as *flowers, whales, baby, clock, walk, eyes, happy,* and *sad.* Beck, McKeown, and Kucan (2002) define such words as Tier 1 words. More complex words, including many associated with more literate academic use across content areas, are classified as Tier 2. Some examples are *mechanisms, attractions, predict, sinister, mention, detest, timid, absurd,* and *compose.* Many Tier 2 words are derivations—that is, root words to which prefixes and suffixes have been added. These additions can change the meaning, pronunciation, and spelling of the root word, as well as the derived word's syntax. Examples include *mechanic-mechanical-mechanism-mechanistically, predict-prediction, mention-unmentionable, detest-detestable,* and *compose-decompose.* Tier 3 words are content-specific words that make up the specialized vocabulary of a particular discipline, such as math, history, geology, or art. Tier 3 words include *echolocation, entomology-entomologist, geometry-geometric, carnivore-carnivorous, raptor-raptorial.* These domain-specific vocabulary words, such as *echolocation* as used in the example cited above, are rarely part of everyday conversations or text such as that found in daily newspapers. Nevertheless, they represent new concepts that function as important building blocks for students' content knowledge (Beck & McKeown, 2007).

Knowledge of Tier 2 and Tier 3 words, combined with an understanding of word formation, constitutes an essential aspect of academic language proficiency (Nagy, Berninger, & Abbott, 2006). However, Bailey and colleagues (2007) found that teachers often introduced new Tier 2 and Tier 3 words without giving students sufficient contextual support to infer their meanings. When supports were provided, they occurred in the form of definitions, synonyms, examples, and repetitions that did not necessarily inform students' knowledge of subject matter content.

Some research substantiates the claim that, during the preschool years, vocabulary is the element of the oral language register most closely associated with establishing a foundation for academic language proficiency (Foorman, Anthony, Seals, & Mouzaki, 2002). That's due to the interplay among three facets of vocabulary: (1) breadth—the number of words with which someone is somewhat familiar and that aspect of vocabulary measured by standardized tests; (2) diversity—the number of different, familiar words someone is able to produce, such as those a student would use in writing a story; and (3) depth (or density)—characterized by one's ability, for example, to understand multiple and figurative meanings (Silliman & Scott, in press). Vocabulary breadth, diversity, and depth are all involved in decoding and, subsequently, in reading comprehension (Foorman & Nixon, 2006). Moreover, the depth of students' vocabulary in the early grades has been shown to predict their future reading comprehension (Berman, 2007; Snow & Kim, 2007; Snow, Porche, Tabors, & Harris, 2007).

An unresolved issue concerns the nature of any *causal* link between early vocabulary knowledge and later reading comprehension. Some research suggests there may be nonlanguage processes, such as working memory capacity (Swanson, Howard, & Sáez, 2007) or the ability to process information quickly and efficiently (Cain & Oakhill, 2007), that affect the relationship between vocabulary and comprehension. Others (e.g., Berninger, in press) contend it is language processes, such as verbal working memory, that are responsible for the vocabulary–reading comprehension link. It may also be the case that different factors, both language and nonlanguage in nature, contribute to reading comprehension at different points in time (Cain & Oakhill, 2007).

Nevertheless, longitudinal data show that proficient reading comprehension does not guarantee academic success for adolescents from low-income families. Factors such as adequate motivation, planfulness about school, and maintenance of long-term goals (Snow et al., 2007, p. 111) strongly influence positive educational outcomes for this group of adolescents.

General Vocabulary Knowledge and ELLs

Bilingual vocabulary learning is complex because there are multiple linguistic, sociocultural, educational, and individual factors influencing vocabulary acquisition. A comprehensive review of bilingual instructional research by the National Literacy Panel (August & Shanahan, 2006) identifies only three studies on vocabulary instruction with Spanish-speaking children that met empirical criteria for inclusion (Shanahan & Beck, 2006). Nevertheless, those three studies confirm that family values and attitudes toward second-language learning combined with the quality of second-language instruction, can significantly affect students' motivation to switch from the oral to academic language register.

In a large-scale, cross-sectional study, Duursma and colleagues (2007) interviewed low-income Hispanic parents whose fifth-grade children had experienced either (a) reading instruction in Spanish during grades 1 and 2, followed by a transition into English reading instruction, or (b) reading instruction in English only. The study finds three language-specific predictors of performance on English vocabulary measures at grade 5: (1) paternal preference for English use in the home; (2) the extent to which parents assist the child, in English, with homework or learning; and (3) sibling interaction in English. The third predictor proved to produce a much larger influence on English (vocabulary) proficiency than parental language preference.

Perhaps because developing academic language is a complex process, Snow and Kim (2007) find little evidence that vocabulary transfer from everyday conversational Spanish to everyday conversational English is a significant mechanism for increasing the depth of English vocabulary knowledge (see also Carlo et al., 2004; Ordonez, Carlo, Snow, & McLaughlin, 2002; Ouelette, 2006.) In practice, the literate vocabulary (Tiers 2 and 3) needed to process and understand content area texts at a deep level most likely originates from the frequency and quality of engagement in meaningful experiences across a range of literacy contexts (Fuste-Herrmann, Silliman, Bahr, Fasnacht, & Federico, 2006). A final point in regard to language transfer in the typical ELL student is that although grammatical aspects of the oral register in Spanish may transfer to the English oral register, there is little evidence that grammatical components of the oral register will transfer to the more complex grammatical system underlying the academic language register (Clahsen & Felser, 2006).

Lucia and the Development of Academic Language Proficiency: A Case Study

Lucia (pseudonym) was born in rural Mexico and emigrated to an urban area in the southern United States with her parents at the age of 6.

Spanish is the home language; neither of Lucia's parents is fluent in English beyond functional use of the oral language register. When Lucia entered school, as a kindergartener, she was placed in an English-as-a-second-language program. The goal of the program was to transition students as quickly as possible to English-only classrooms.

As required by state mandates, Lucia was tested annually on a bilingual language survey. Based partly on the results of those tests, she repeated both kindergarten and first grade. Test results found that at age 9 Lucia had limited proficiency in speaking, reading, and writing English. Moreover, Lucia appeared to be experiencing some degree of attrition of her Spanish oral language register.

Now 11 years, 7 months old and in a grade 4 English-only class, Lucia is experiencing significant struggles with oral listening comprehension and vocabulary acquisition, as well as decoding and reading comprehension. With grade 4 state tests in reading, math, and science approaching, Lucia describes her science textbook as "very hard" to understand.

Lucia's classroom was observed by a graduate student pursuing a master's degree in communication sciences and disorders. The instrument of observation was the Early Language and Literacy Classroom Observation Toolkit (ELLCO; Smith & Dickinson, 2002). The tools employed were the Literacy Environment Checklist and the Classroom Observation (general classroom environment and language, literacy, and curriculum), and the follow-up teacher interview. The graduate student also assessed Lucia's perspective about reading activities and strategies through an informal, one-on-one reading interview (McKenna & Stahl, 2003).

According to the ELLCO criteria, some evidence was found of systematic reading and writing instruction that supported student development. As a quality indicator, the designation of "some evidence" translates into a "basic" level (Smith & Dickinson, 2002). In the follow-up interview, the teacher, who does not speak Spanish, reported that students were grouped according to their reading levels, a tactic she believes reduces their frustration.

The primary reading program being used was Reading Mastery. The teacher said it was especially appropriate for use with ELL students such as Lucia because of its emphasis on decoding. The U.S. Department of Education's What Works Clearinghouse (WWC; 2007) found only one study of Reading Mastery being used with ELLs and English-only students in grades K–4 that also met evidence standards. WWC found potentially positive effects on the reading achievement of ELLs when Reading Mastery was used as a supplement to standard reading instruction. However, because of the small ELL sample in the specific study evaluated, the WWC urged caution in interpreting this finding.

Lucia's teacher developed student portfolios that, along with the developmental reading assessment, were used to evaluate individual student progress. In general, instructional activities were planned to prepare students for the annual state assessments. The teacher also reported that computer use in the classroom was limited to educational games, writing of final drafts, and watching videos of previously read stories. Finally, the teacher conveyed that she communicated with parents at least twice a year during parent–teacher conferences.

When Lucia was asked what she did when she came to a word that she did not know, she responded that she used two strategies: "Stop and read it again" and "Try to sound it out." She identified her mother and big sister as good readers because "they can read recipes." She said her teacher helped someone with an unfamiliar word by "telling him the different sounds." She said she learned to read "when my mom helps [by] spelling some words and sometimes sounding out." Finally, when asked what she would like to do better as a reader and whether she thought that she was a good reader, Lucia replied that she wanted to "learn how to read the words" and that she was a good reader because she tried to "sound the words out." Based on Lucia's responses to the orally administered reading interview, it seems clear that her experiences with reading instruction have yet to convey that the real purpose of reading is to construct meaning.

Lucia was then engaged, outside of the classroom, in shared book-reading activities, which she enjoyed. In one such activity, she was asked to write about her favorite section of a book she was reading jointly with the graduate student. This task was essentially an expository activity because Lucia was being asked why she liked a particular section. The story's theme concerned a partially paralyzed dog named Willy who—after many trials and tribulations—was eventually adopted by a woman named Deborah who loved him. The "favorite" section that Lucia chose to write about involved Willy's attempts to find a toy to play with that was out of his reach. On the one hand, Lucia's composition reflected her struggles with coordinating the phonological, orthographic, and morphological components of English spelling. For example, one pattern of misspellings indicated that she had yet to master the use of the early acquired suffix -er as in closer and smaller.

Another pattern involved significant problems with English vowel variations in single-syllable words, such as *ham* for *him* and *side* for *said*, among other issues.

But the composition could be analyzed along a number of other dimensions similar to Mike's PowerPoint presentation. These aspects might include the quality of Lucia's text structure, selection of vocabulary, and correct grammatical constructions. (It should be noted that Lucia's recall of story events was accurate.) Because she was asked to provide an opinion, one might also expect Lucia to provide some "expository-like generalizations" (Berman & Nir-Sagiv, 2007, p. 94) such as the reason why she enjoyed this section, as well as pertinent background information, which she did not do. Instead, Lucia constructed her text as a narrative with the only tool she had available—the oral language register. This approach is distinguished by Lucia's exclusive use of Tier 1 (high frequency) words and the absence of any complex clauses or expanded noun phrases. She does, however, demonstrate the use of coordinate clauses in the sentence "Willy was going to play with the big black bear, but it was too heavy for him."

In sum, Lucia is expected to manage the academic discourse register of the classroom with only an oral language register available to her. The register distance between Lucia and Mike, who is three years younger, is a metaphor for the obstacles that many ELLs must overcome if they are ever to become full members of a learning community.

Best Practices

The question remains, Can academic language proficiency be taught? The extant research literature provides some basis for drawing implications for best practices, ideas, and programs related to the development of academic language. However, there is a dearth of scientific research evidence from which to draw such implications, in part because of the nature of the early research on literacy. The earliest studies described language functions, the communicative demands of classrooms, and individual differences; researchers posited that teaching and learning was both socially based and integrated. But even though such sociolinguistic studies revealed the complexity of classroom practices, they failed to provide a scientific research base from which to draw pedagogical implications. Descriptive studies function best to generate new hypotheses about causal mechanisms but do not yield broad generalizations. Future research may need to take an approach that combines the tools of both the cognitive and sociocultural sciences.

One area in which the research is potentially positive is related to the acquisition of Tier 2 words by students like Lucia. The Vocabulary Improvement Program for English Language Learners and Their Classmates (VIP; Lively, August, Carlo, & Snow, 2003) provides a curriculum for supporting the development of vocabulary breadth and depth of ELL and English-only students in grades 4–6. Adapted from a research program with ELLs, VIP's premise is that words found in grade-level narrative and expository texts are best learned in rich semantic contexts, with students engaging in deeper processing to make connections between concepts and multiple word meanings. The semester-long curriculum consists of 10 eight-day lessons at each grade level and 2 five-day review sessions. Targeted words are incorporated into the weekly reading assignments.

A two-year randomized, controlled trial of VIP that met the evidence standards for evaluation by WWC (2007) found potentially positive effects on reading achievement and (academic) English vocabulary development (Carlo et al., 2004). However, according to WWC's evaluation, some reservations are warranted, due to attrition in the research sample over the two-year period and the fact that the VIP intervention did not distinguish between students' language status (i.e., ELLs vs. English-only speakers).

Other initiatives that have been studied and reported on in the research literature include (a) Collaborative Strategic Reading, with an emphasis on vocabulary and comprehension development strategies (Klingner & Vaughn, 1999); (b) Vocabulary Power, an intervention program that addresses multiple meanings and figurative language (Seals, Pollard-Durodola, Foorman, & Bradley, 2007); and (c) Curtis and Longo's (2001) vocabulary intervention activities aimed at improving the reading comprehension of adolescents reading two to three years below grade level. Curtis and Longo's work is based on the work of Beck and colleagues (2002) on robust vocabulary instruction at the early elementary level. All of these studies provide evidence of promising programmatic interventions for more literate vocabulary learning across grade levels.

Summary of Main Ideas

To succeed in school, students must be proficient in academic language, the language of classroom instruction. Yet, for students learning English as a second language, developing full academic language proficiency can be daunting. That's because academic language—the "language of books" that students must master to meet the academic discourse expectations of content areas—is markedly different from everyday oral language.

Vocabulary is an element of the oral language register that is strongly linked to the development of academic language proficiency. That's because the depth of one's vocabulary is tied, in turn, to proficiency both in decoding and reading comprehension. The extant research literature, although limited, provides some basis for drawing implications for best practices, programs, and interventions with a special emphasis on integrated approaches that have the potential to support students' development of academic language proficiency.

Implications for Research, Practice, and Policy

One outcome of NCLB is to define a teacher of quality as an individual of high cognitive and verbal ability, with knowledge of subject matter taught and sufficient experience to successfully teach all students. Students of highly qualified and effective educators

- Achieve at the proficient level on high-stakes state assessments
- Are prepared to achieve at each grade level and ready to learn the curriculum at the next level
- Will graduate from high school having completed the required curricula and passed any mandated high-stakes assessments (Silliman et al., 2004)

Yet, despite the requirements of NCLB, we believe a major group of students—namely ELLs—remain at risk of academic failure. As argued previously (Silliman et al., 2004), a major source of the persistent achievement gap between ELLs and their counterparts is the disparity between what teachers know and what they need to know about ELLs and other at-risk students. The existing knowledge base of many practitioners appears disconnected from what is necessary for promoting and

maximizing successful educational outcomes for individual students—
and even more so for ELLs.

One concern is that ELLs often enter school without background
experiences and literacy tools that form the foundation of future literacy. These children require "teachers who are capable of accelerating
the learning of students who experience the greatest difficulty acquiring
literacy" (Dozier, Johnston, & Rogers, 2006, p. 11). The quality of classroom instruction is, by far, the most significant element in formal education. To improve ELL learning, we must provide innovative ways to
educate preservice teachers about not only the unique challenges facing
ELL students but also these students' strengths. Further, we must provide future teachers with paths to develop their own effective pedagogy
with ELLs.

Such a commitment requires us to move beyond the minimal requirements of traditional teacher preparation programs so that teachers
can meet the challenges of educating ELLs to the same standards as
other American children. Clearly, cultural and linguistic differences matter. "The classroom is a meeting ground of cultures where the worlds of
the students meet the worldview of schools and teachers" (Cymrot,
2002, p. 14). Only those future teachers who are prepared for cultural
and linguistic diversity and have developed a deep understanding of
how to help diverse students acquire academic literacy will be prepared
to make a difference in the lives of ELL students.

Because the majority of teacher candidates are unfamiliar with the
vast range of backgrounds and cultures of students attending urban
schools, teacher preparation institutions must assist teacher candidates
in learning about the backgrounds, experiences, and languages of their
students and also in how to most effectively teach them.

In conclusion, both sociocultural and linguistic components define
the conceptual knowledge base of highly qualified and effective teachers.
With such a storehouse of information, urban teachers will be better able
to build educational bridges for ELLs. These bridges, in turn, will enrich the interdependence of students' linguistic and discourse repertoires
in comprehension, speaking, reading, spelling, and writing.

*Authors' Note: We are indebted to Mabel Atez for her help in gathering infor-
mation about Lucia and for her dedication to advancing the oral language and
other literacy abilities of Spanish-speaking children learning academic English.*

REFERENCES

August, D., & Shanahan, T. (2006). *Developing literacy in second-language learners: Report of the National Literacy Panel on Language-Minority Children and Youth.* Mahwah, NJ: Erlbaum.

Bailey, A.L., & Butler, F.A. (2007). A conceptual framework of academic English language for broad application to education. In A.L. Bailey (Ed.), *The language demands of school: Putting academic English to the test* (pp. 68–102). New Haven, CT: Yale University Press.

Bailey, A.L., Butler, F.A., Stevens, R., & Lord, C. (2007). Further specifying the language demands of school. In A.L. Bailey (Ed.), *The language demands of school: Putting academic English to the test* (pp. 103–156). New Haven, CT: Yale University Press.

Beck, I.L., & McKeown, M.G. (2007). Different ways for different goals, but keep your eye on the higher verbal goals. In R.K. Wagner, A.E. Muse, & K.R. Tannenbaum (Eds.), *Vocabulary acquisition: Implications for reading comprehension* (pp. 182–204). New York: Guilford.

Beck, I.L., McKeown, M.G., & Kucan, L. (2002). Bringing words to life: Robust vocabulary instruction. New York: Guilford.

Berman, R.A. (2007). Developing linguistic knowledge and language use across adolescence. In E. Hoff & M. Shatz (Eds.), *Blackwell handbook of language development* (pp. 347–367). Oxford, England: Blackwell.

Berman, R.A., & Nir-Sagiv, B. (2007). Comparing narrative and expository text construction across adolescence: A developmental paradox. *Discourse Processes, 43,* 79–120.

Berninger, V.W. (in press). Defining and differentiating dysgraphia, dyslexia, and language learning disability. In M. Mody & E.R. Silliman (Eds.), *Brain, behavior, and learning in language and reading disorders.* New York: Guilford.

Cain, K., & Oakhill, J. (2007). Reading comprehension difficulties: Correlates, causes, and consequences. In K. Cain & J. Oakhill (Eds.), *Children's comprehension problems in oral and written language: A cognitive perspective* (pp. 41–75). New York: Guilford.

Carlo, M.S., August, D., McLaughlin, B., Snow, C.E., Dressler, C., Lippman, D.N., et al. (2004). Closing the gap: Addressing the vocabulary needs of English-language learners in bilingual and mainstream classrooms. *Reading Research Quarterly, 39,* 188–215.

Chouinard, M.M. (2007). *Children's questions: A mechanism for cognitive development.* Oxford, England: Blackwell.

Christian, B., & Bloome, D. (2004). Learning to read is who you are. *Reading & Writing Quarterly, 20,* 365–384.

Clahsen, H., & Felser, C. (2006). How native-like is non-native language processing? *Trends in Cognitive Sciences, 10*(12), 564–570.

Cummins, J. (2000). *Language, power and pedagogy: Bilingual children in the crossfire.* Clevedon, England: Multilingual Matters.

Curtis, M., & Longo, A. (2001). Teaching vocabulary to adolescents to improve comprehension. *Reading Online.* Retrieved February 10, 2008, from www.readingonline.org/articles/art_index.asp?HREF=curtis/index.html

Cymrot, T. (2002). What is diversity? In L. Darling-Hammond, J. French, & S. Garcia-Lopez (Eds.), *Learning to teach for social justice* (pp. 13–17). New York: Teachers College Press.

Danzak, R.L., & Silliman, E.R. (2005). Does my identity speak English? A pragmatic approach to the social world of an English language learner with language impairment. *Seminars in Speech and Language, 26*(3), 189–200.

Dozier, C., Johnston, P., & Rogers, R. (2006). *Critical literacy/critical teaching: Tools for preparing responsive teachers.* New York: Teachers College Press.

Duursma, E., Romero-Contreras, S., Szuber, A., Proctor, P., Snow, C., August, D., et al. (2007). The role of home literacy and language environment on bilinguals' English and Spanish vocabulary development. *Applied Psycholinguistics, 28*(1), 171–190.

Fisher, R. (2005). Teacher–child interaction in the teaching of reading: A review of research perspectives over twenty-five years. *Journal of Research in Reading, 28*, 15–27.

Foorman, B.R., Anthony, J., Seals, L., & Mouzaki, A. (2002). Language development and emergent literacy in preschool. *Seminars in Pediatric Neurology, 9*(3), 173–184.

Foorman, B.R., & Nixon, S.M. (2006). The influence of public policy on reading research and practice. *Topics in Language Disorders, 26*(2), 157–171.

Fuste-Herrmann, B., Silliman, E.R., Bahr, R.H., Fasnacht, K.S., & Federico, J.E. (2006). Mental state verb production in the oral narratives of English- and Spanish-speaking preadolescents: An exploratory study of lexical diversity and depth. *Learning Disabilities Research & Practice, 21*, 44–60.

Gee, J.G. (1999). *An introduction to discourse analysis.* New York: Routledge.

Klingner, J., & Vaughn, S. (1999). Promoting reading comprehension, content learning and English acquisition through collaborative strategic reading (CSR). *The Reading Teacher, 52*, 738–747.

Lively, T., August, D., Carlo, M., & Snow, C. (2003). *The vocabulary improvement program for English language learners and their classmates.* Baltimore: Paul Brookes.

Martínez-Roldán, C.M., & Malavé, G. (2004). Language ideologies mediating literacy and identity in bilingual contexts. *Journal of Early Childhood Literacy, 4*(2), 155–180.

McKenna, M.C., & Stahl, S.A. (2003). *Assessment for reading instruction.* New York: Guilford.

Nagy, W., Berninger, V.W., & Abbott, R.D. (2006). Contributions of morphology beyond phonology to literacy outcomes of upper elementary and middle-school students. *Journal of Educational Psychology, 98*, 134–147.

National Institute of Child Health and Human Development Early Child Care Research Network. (2005). Pathways to reading: The role of oral language in the transition to reading. *Developmental Psychology, 41*, 428–442.

Ordonez, C.L., Carlo, M.S., Snow, C.E., & McLaughlin, B. (2002). Depth and breadth of vocabulary in two languages: Which vocabulary skills transfer? *Journal of Educational Psychology, 94*, 719–728.

Ouelette, G.P. (2006). What's meaning got to do with it: The role of vocabulary in word reading and reading comprehension. *Journal of Educational Psychology, 98,* 554–566.

Pappas, C.C., Varelas, M., Barry, A., & Rife, A. (2002). Dialogic inquiry around information texts: The role of intertextuality in constructing scientific understandings in urban primary classrooms. *Linguistics and Education, 13*(4), 435–482.

Purcell-Gates, V., Duke, N.K., & Martineau, J.A. (2007). Learning to read and write genre-specific text: Roles of authentic experience and explicit teaching. *Reading Research Quarterly, 42,* 8–45.

Riley, P. (2006). Self-expression and the negotiation of identity in a foreign language. *International Journal of Applied Linguistics, 16*(3), 295–318.

Roberts, T., & Neal, H. (2004). Relationships among preschool English language learner's oral proficiency in English, instructional experience and literacy development. *Contemporary Educational Psychology, 29,* 283–311.

Seals, L.M., Pollard-Durodola, S.D., Foorman, B.R., & Bradley, A.M. (2007). *Vocabulary power: Lessons for students who use African American Vernacular English.* Baltimore: Paul H. Brookes.

Shanahan, T., & Beck, I.L. (2006). Effective literacy teaching for English-language learners. In D. August & T. Shanahan (Eds.), *Developing literacy in second-language learners: Report of the National Literacy Panel on Language-Minority Children and Youth* (pp. 415–488). Mahwah, NJ: Erlbaum.

Silliman, E.R., & Scott, C.M. (in press). Research-based language intervention routes to the academic language of literacy: Finding the right road. In S. Rosenfield & V.W. Berninger (Eds.), *Translating science-supported instruction into evidence-based practices: Understanding and applying the implementation process.* New York: Oxford University Press.

Silliman, E.R., Wilkinson, L.C., & Brea-Spahn, M.R. (2004). Policy and practice imperatives for language and literacy learning: Who will be left behind? In C.A. Stone, E.R. Silliman, B.J. Ehren, & K. Apel (Eds.), *Handbook on language and literacy: Development and disorders* (pp. 97–129). New York: Guilford.

Smith, M.W., & Dickinson, D.K. (2002). *Early Language & Literacy Classroom Observation (ELLCO) toolkit* (Research ed.). Baltimore: Paul H. Brookes.

Snow, C.E., & Kim, Y.-S. (2007). Large problem spaces: The challenge of vocabulary for English language learners. In R.K. Wagner, A.E. Muse, & K.R. Tannenbaum (Eds.), *Vocabulary acquisition: Implications for reading comprehension* (pp. 123–129). New York: Guilford.

Snow, C.E., Porche, M.V., Tabors, P.O., & Harris, S.R. (2007). *Is literacy enough? Pathways to academic success for adolescents.* Baltimore: Paul H. Brookes.

Swanson, H.L., Howard, C.B., & Sáez, L. (2007). Reading comprehension and working memory in children with learning disabilities in reading. In K. Cain & J. Oakhill (Eds.), *Children's comprehension problems in oral and written language: A cognitive perspective* (pp. 157–189). New York: Guilford.

U.S. Census Bureau. (2005, May). *School enrollment—social and economic characteristics of students: October 2003.* Washington, DC: Author. Retrieved May 17, 2007, from www.census.gov/prod/2005pubs/p20-554.pdf

U.S. Census Bureau. (2006, September 5). *Hispanic heritage month: Sept. 15–Oct. 15, 2006*. Retrieved May 17, 2007, from www.census.gov/Press-Release/www/releases/archives/facts_for_features_special_editions/007173.html

U.S. Census Bureau. (2007, May 17). *Minority population tops 100 million*. Retrieved May 17, 2007, from www.census.gov/Press-Release/www/releases/archives/population/010048.html

Varelas, M., & Pappas, C.C. (2006). Intertextuality in read-alouds of integrated science-literacy units in urban primary classrooms: Opportunities for the development of thought and language. *Cognition and Instruction, 24*, 211–259.

Wallis, C., & Steptoe, S. (2007, May 24). How to fix No Child Left Behind. *Time, 169*(23) 34–41.

Westby, C., Dezale, J., Fradd, S.H., & Lee, O. (1999). Learning to do science: Influences of culture and language. *Communication Disorders Quarterly, 21*(1), 50–94.

What Works Clearinghouse. (2007). *Intervention: Vocabulary improvement program for English language learners and their classmates*. Washington, DC: U.S. Department of Education, Institute of Education Sciences. Retrieved May 9, 2007, from ies.ed.gov/ncee/wwc/reports/english_lang/vip

Wilkinson, L.C., & Silliman, E.R. (2000). Classroom language and literacy learning. In M.L. Kamil, P. Mosenthal, P.D. Pearson, & R. Barr (Eds.), *Handbook of reading research* (Vol. 3, pp. 337–360). Mahwah, NJ: Erlbaum.

Wilkinson, L.C., & Silliman, E.R. (in press). Academic language proficiency. In C. Clauss-Ehlers (Ed.), *Encyclopedia of cross-cultural school psychology*. New York: Springer-Verlag.

Zimmerman, C. (2007). The development of scientific thinking skills in elementary and middle school. *Developmental Review, 27*(2), 172–223.

CHAPTER 7

The Importance of Professional Development for Teachers of Reading in Urban Settings

Lesley Mandel Morrow
Rutgers, The State University of New Jersey

Heather Casey
Rider University

Linda B. Gambrell
Clemson University

P rofessional development is crucial for creating exemplary teach- ers of reading in urban settings. In fact, without both school- wide and individualized professional development best practice cannot be achieved. Teachers must view themselves as lifelong learners within their school community. They must also look to professional or- ganizations and consider supplementing their education with advanced degrees and certifications to improve their skills.

We've found that once teachers get involved in quality research- based professional development programs, they are anxious to continue. Consider, for example, the following comments from a teacher who par- ticipated in such a program:

> I'm learning that there is a lot I didn't know about early literacy devel- opment. I'm also finding that through the staff development program I can always get better at teaching my kids. In the beginning, I didn't think the program would have much effect on me; I've been to work- shops before. Somehow, what was presented in this program made things come together for me. I needed a literacy coach to model new strategies in my classroom with my children. I needed to see my chil- dren achieving more from changes I was making, and I needed the support and time to reflect upon the changes being made with my

Improving Literacy Achievement in Urban Schools: Critical Elements in Teacher Preparation edited by Louise C. Wilkinson, Lesley Mandel Morrow, and Victoria Chou. © 2008 by the International Reading Association.

peers. This professional development program allowed for all of this to happen and for me to make progress and change.

This teacher describes what research suggests. Effective professional development programs are comprehensive and responsive to the individual needs of teachers (Morrow & Casey, 2004). The "one size fits all" approach does not work, particularly in urban contexts where so many variables influence teaching and learning (Morrow, Casey, & Haworth, 2003).

Purposes of This Chapter

In this chapter we review the research and theory related to the creation of excellent professional development programs in schools and discuss successful models. We also present the results of a study we conducted on what urban reading teachers say they need to support their work and sustain their development. Finally, we elaborate on the implications we see for practice, policy, and research surrounding the issue of professional development.

Review of Research and Theory

To best support the professional development of urban educators, it is important to understand the relationship between research on effective teaching and professional development initiatives. Implicit in this understanding is a belief that teacher practice and student learning is rooted within the specific socioeconomic, sociocultural, and sociopolitical environment of urban schools.

Putting Professional Development in Context

As was noted in the introduction to this volume, sociocultural theory suggests that student learning is dependent upon what a teacher knows, how students come to understand that knowledge, and the context in which such learning takes place (Vygotsky, 1978, 1934/1986). "School," therefore, is viewed as a collaborative community in which students form relationships with more capable adults and peers and learn as a result of such relationships. The learning that occurs is constructed by the individual agents (teachers and students) positioned in the classroom and influenced by the larger community in which the school is situated.

Recognizing teaching as situated in this way is important when considering the professional development of urban educators. Many urban teachers work in settings where No Child Left Behind (NCLB), for example, presents unique challenges, such as the need to use a wider variety of strategies to teach reading. They also face more testing requirements than teachers who work in more affluent settings. Professional development programs that motivate teachers to change their practice in ways that help them better meet these kinds of challenges and sustain that change over time address these and other contextual issues.

Effective Teaching and Professional Development

Studying effective teaching gives us additional valuable information we can use to design effective professional development programs. Once we have criteria against which to evaluate teachers, we can do so and then use that information to determine the type of professional development programs they need. As described in depth in the introduction to this volume, such studies (Clark & Peterson, 1986; Coker, 1985; Duffy & Hoffman, 1999; Genishi, Ryan, & Ochsner, 2001; Roehler & Duffy, 1986; Ruddell, 1995; Ruddell & Harris, 1989; Ruddell & Kern, 1986) have examined effective teachers' teaching strategies and the ways in which the physical environment in their classrooms supports those strategies. Researchers have also looked at how good teachers make decisions, establish routines and schedules, interact with their students, and set up classrooms that function as communities.

The results of such studies, as indicated earlier, find that effective teachers (a) use highly motivating and effective teaching strategies, (b) build strong affective relationships with their students, (c) create a feeling of excitement about what they are teaching, (d) adjust instruction to meet students' individual needs, (e) create rich physical environments to support their teaching, and (f) demonstrate strong organizational and management skills with schedules and routines (Block, 2001; Morrow & Casey, 2003; Pressley, Rankin & Yokoi, 1996; Taylor, Pearson, Clark, & Walpole, 1999; Taylor, Peterson, Pearson, & Rodriguez, 2002; Wharton-McDonald et al., 1997). Professional development that makes teachers aware of these and other similar research findings and that targets the development of the kinds of strategies routinely used by effective teachers can significantly influence teaching practice and, in turn, student achievement.

Exemplary teachers also, on their own, earn graduate degrees, belong to and participate in professional organizations, and independently seek out opportunities for professional development (Morrow & Casey, 2003). School-based professional development has the potential to instill these goals as well.

As we have seen, the research paints rich portraits of effective teachers that suggest students are motivated by individuals who have strong content knowledge, exhibit a keen awareness of pedagogy, are responsive to the individual and community in which the students are situated, and employ careful organization and management strategies (Center on English Learning and Achievement [CELA], 2002; Morrow & Casey, 2004; Strickland, 2002; Taylor, Pressley, & Pearson, 2002). While this list may read like a standard recipe for good teaching, its implementation is far from formulaic. How do we, in fact, motivate practicing teachers in urban settings to embrace these portraits as their own? The answer is largely through professional development.

The Qualities of Effective Professional Development

The next issue to consider is how best to make that professional development highly effective. Research in this area finds that the most popular form of professional development has long been the single-session workshop (Hoffman & Pearson, 2004). It is appealing in its affordability and efficiency. Research suggests, however, that these "single doses" of professional development fail to bring about significant change among teachers unless these initiating events are paired with ongoing support.

Professional development models that have been studied the most are those that are (a) externally driven or imposed on teachers; (b) teacher-generated with some teacher control; and (c) collaborative, with many individuals within the school and outside the school involved (Richardson, 1990). Recent research has focused on the individual teacher's role and responsibilities in relation to the support network of the school system and larger community (CELA, 2002; Morrow & Casey, 2004; Morrow et al., 2003). This research suggests that effective professional development begins with teacher input. Teachers identify areas of need and professional communities evolve in response to this shared interest. Throughout, teachers drive the areas of professional study and the format for learning. Effective professional development involves partnerships between teachers, administrators, and the communities in which they work. This shift to teacher-driven professional development is particularly critical in urban contexts where, in addition to traditional curricular demands, teachers often navigate multiple languages and dialects, a lack of resources in the homes and schools, and increasing state and national pressure because of poor achievement on standardized tests (Anderson & Olsen, 2006; Rhodes, Wolf, & Rhodes, 2005).

The findings of the National Reading Panel (National Institute of Child Health and Human Development, 2000) reveal that professional development related to reading can change teachers' practices and attitudes. The panel also reports that for professional development to be successful, it needs to occur over a long period of time and with a great deal of support. Anders, Hoffman, and Duffy (2000) contend that professional development that is most likely to bring about change involves voluntary participation, choice, collaboration, monitoring, coaching, reflection, deliberation, dialogue, negotiation, administrative support, and commitment on the part of both those providing and those participating in the professional development.

According to Guskey (1986), the first goal of any professional development initiative should be to improve classroom practice. Taylor, Peterson et al. (2002) report on an effort to significantly change reading instruction in 13 schools that relied on a research-based professional development model. The collaborative effort involved the sharing of information about literacy curriculum and pedagogy as well as modeling and coaching for classroom teachers. Student achievement, as measured by test scores, increased over a two-year period, with the greatest increases coming after two years of teacher training.

This initiative was also notable for the degree of collaboration evident among teachers, administrators, and providers; the opportunities given participants for reflection; participants' commitment to the program; and the degree of support available to teachers who had problems or questions.

Effective professional development experiences motivate teachers to revise entrenched practice (Bean & Morewood, 2007; Lyons & Pinnell, 2001; National Staff Development Council [NSDC] & National Association of Elementary School Principals [NAESP], 1995). NSDC in collaboration with NAESP (1995) emphasizes the importance of drawing on adult learning theory when developing professional development experiences. Such an approach calls for

- Research-based experiences
- Teachers who direct their own learning

- Opportunities for independent and interdependent learning
- Clear and measurable objectives and outcomes
- An awareness that change requires time, resources, and support structures
- Initiatives that are responsive to the structures and systems within the organization

The understanding that lasting change requires time, resources, and support structures while being responsive to the unique sociocultural contexts situating the experience is crucial (Anderson & Olsen, 2006; MacGillivray & Rueda, 2004; Morrow, 2003; Morrow & Casey, 2004).

Professional Development Models That Work

A review of the research on urban professional development initiatives that support teachers' work in literacy suggests these programs "work" because they (a) encourage teacher involvement from the outset; (b) are developed in collaboration with multiple partners, including teachers, administrators, university faculty, and the larger community; (c) offer multiple resources and ongoing support; and, perhaps most importantly, (d) are unique to the urban settings in which they are situated (Fisher, 2001; Indrisano, Birmingham, Garnick, & Maresco, 1999; Morrow, 2003; Morrow & Casey, 2003, 2004; Rhodes et al., 2005).

A study of teacher retention in urban settings suggests strong professional development is crucial to minimizing high teacher turnover rates (Anderson & Olson, 2006). Case studies of urban teachers suggest that effective professional development in these settings (a) is responsive to the "developmental" needs of the teacher (i.e., novice vs. veteran), (b) is aware of school contexts, (c) offers opportunity for extended teacher collaboration, and (d) capitalizes on teachers' interests in assuming new roles and responsibilities (Anderson & Olsen, 2006).

In Massachusetts, a collaborative effort between university and school faculty was forged to bridge the "divide" between classroom literacy instruction and Title I support (Indrisano et al., 1999). Literacy teachers and Title I teachers were literally "united" in a coteaching model based on a shared vision of the value of authentic literacy experiences for students. Working together, along with university faculty, the teachers identified areas of professional need. Those included a better understanding of explicit instruction, strategic teaching and learning, and the gradual release of responsibility model, a scaffolding of instruction where teachers guide students to independence (Indrisano et al.). A series of seminars, inservice experiences, and collaborative work sessions helped these teacher partners adopt a more unified, and arguably more effective, system of literacy instruction.

Similarly in an urban high school in California, teachers attributed a 12% increase in reading scores to focused staff development over two years (Fisher, 2001). A staff development committee identified a number of research-based strategies (writing to learn, incorporating K-W-L charts, understanding concept mapping, involving students in reciprocal teaching, and infusing read-alouds into the literacy curriculum) designed to support literacy development in their students. The strategies were shared initially with teachers at inservice training, followed by monthly meetings at which teachers discussed successes and challenges and supported each other's classroom application (Fisher, 2001).

In New York City, three professional development labs have been developed and physically "placed" directly in the schools and communities they are designed to support. Seminars and workshops are developed around student, faculty, and family interests and have focused on topics such as classroom management techniques and strategies for supporting English-language learners (Rhodes et al., 2005). Unique to this initiative are the literacy education services offered to the surrounding community; such services meet a need for more focused family literacy initiatives in urban settings, often identified as a necessary resource (Anderson & Olsen, 2006; MacGillivray & Rueda, 2004). A number of factors have contributed to the success of these labs. They include (a) strong administrative leadership in the building, (b) a sense of community among the faculty, (c) the presence of a full-time literacy liaison, (d) interest in school–university partnerships, and (e) ongoing support that is responsive to shifting needs (Fisher, 2001).

In an urban area in New Jersey, a three-year professional development project that included teachers, administrators, and university faculty motivated significant changes in established literacy teaching practices (Morrow & Casey, 2003, 2004). Teachers tenuously entered into the project, fearful of "top-down" initiatives, but soon found they were directing the initiative based on the needs of their students. Teachers self-selected their areas of focus. Some ambitious teachers began with topics such as guided reading and centers, while others chose to work on classroom design and management systems. Through a course of university seminars, monthly meetings, opportunities for peer coaching, and individual reflection, all of the teachers made positive changes in their instructional practice and, in turn, saw their students' literacy skills improve. Beginning at a point where teachers felt *comfortable* and providing ongoing support were critical to the project's success (Morrow & Casey, 2004). Comments from teachers who participated in the program underscore that point.

One teacher who participated in the program said the university consultant who led the seminars and monthly meetings, disseminated information, and provided support for change played a valuable role in the teachers' growth. This teacher also found the discussions among teachers who observed each other in their classrooms to be an effective way to exchange ideas and advice. Particularly helpful, she said, was the opportunity to work with teachers from the same grade level she was teaching.

Another teacher spoke favorably of the information sessions led by the university consultant in which she was able to learn about and view demonstrations of best practices via videotapes and classroom visitations. This teacher enjoyed sharing the work of her students and discussing the changes in her classroom environment and teaching techniques. She said that the comprehensive nature of the program helped bring about the changes and that she felt she could rely on the support of the university consultant.

These professional development projects work because they are responsive to the needs of teachers and students and offer multiple resources to support lasting change. While this description holds true for professional development in general, it is particularly crucial in urban settings because of the myriad challenges these teachers and students negotiate daily. Being responsive to the contexts in which these urban schools are situated means offering professional development initiatives that balance research on effective practices with an awareness of effective implementation. It is not enough to "tell" teachers how to teach reading and writing. It is not even enough to "show" teachers how to teach reading and writing. Instead, urban language arts teachers should be given opportunities to identify areas of inquiry and need based on their unique experiences; these descriptors, paired with research on effective practice, become the basis for effective professional development initiatives that can bring about enduring and lasting change in teacher practice and improved student achievement.

A Survey of Teachers of Reading in Urban Settings Concerning Their Needs

To organize our work with urban literacy teachers, it is important to both examine prior models of urban professional development that have prompted significant change and determine the needs of current urban educators. To that end, we conducted a survey of early childhood and elementary teachers situated in urban environments. Our goal was to gain a better understanding of how to support these teachers' work with developing students' literacy skills and strategies. We distributed 125 surveys in one urban district, and 65 teachers responded.

The teachers were asked to describe the knowledge they believe is essential for those working with urban youth in the primary and elementary grades. A number of common themes emerged, several of which related to the development of new content knowledge and pedagogical understanding. These include motivating children, understanding systems of classroom management, and becoming more responsive to the unique cultural and economic backgrounds of diverse classrooms.

While each of these themes is discussed separately below, in working with these teachers it became clear to us that it is the relationship between these needs that provides a cohesive framework for developing effective professional development initiatives. To build effective professional development programs for these teachers, each of these three areas needs to be considered in relation to the others.

What is unique to the teachers surveyed is their sense of urgency; they recognize that as their elementary-grade students move into middle school and beyond, the gap in achievement between struggling and achieving students grows ever wider. What's more, the contextual challenges that urban students and their teachers face often become exacerbated.

Motivating Children

Seventy-two percent of the teachers surveyed reported the need to learn more strategies to motivate their students. That is due in large part to the widespread use in urban settings of carefully controlled curricula and resources reflective of NCLB mandates. The teachers reported that their students become disinterested and disengaged during literacy events and said they were interested in learning about reading and writing resources that engaged their students' interest and integrating those resources into the existing curricula. There was a general belief among those surveyed that if the students saw their school literacy activities as purposeful and connected to their experiences within the community they would be more productive.

Implicit within this view is the need to better differentiate instruction within diverse classrooms. Thirty-two percent of the teachers surveyed described the need for tools and techniques to better accommodate the academically diverse learners in their classroom. They were specifically interested in making use of homogeneous and heterogeneous groups to support learning objectives, matching readers to texts, and scaffolding instruction appropriately to begin to bridge the achievement gap for those in their classroom struggling with reading and writing.

Understanding Systems of Classroom Management

Classroom management demands often elude the best of teachers. Creating an environment that responds to student needs and motivates literacy learning is not an easy task. Our findings are consistent with that of other researchers: Urban teachers often describe classroom management as one of the most demanding areas of their daily work (Anderson & Olsen, 2006; MacGillivray & Rueda, 2004). In fact, 61% of the teachers surveyed reported that one of their primary concerns was classroom management. This area is broad; for these teachers, classroom management is perceived as disciplining some students for behavioral disruptions while simultaneously monitoring other students' academic progress. It is noteworthy that classroom management becomes more of a concern in the upper grades as the unique demands of early adolescence begin to surface.

Becoming More Responsive to Unique Cultural and Economic Backgrounds

Urban settings include populations that are culturally and economically diverse (Rhodes et al., 2005). Often, the teachers working in such settings do not have sufficient knowledge of the cultural and economic backgrounds of the students in their classrooms (Willis, Garcia, Barrera, & Harris, 2003). Ninety-two percent of the teachers surveyed reported wanting to know more about how students' backgrounds situate their learning and how best to use that knowledge in the classroom. Specifically, these teachers were interested in using reading and writing resources that reflected the unique cultures of their students, finding ways to reach beyond language barriers to include parents, and understanding more about the communities in which they worked.

Summary of Main Ideas

The rich landscape of research on effective language arts teaching has offered multiple models and strategies for teachers to consider when developing their own pedagogical approaches. This research incorporates an understanding of the content, contexts, and pedagogy of literacy instruction (Morrow, Tracey, Woo, & Pressley, 1999; Pressley, Allington, Wharton-McDonald, Block, & Morrow, 2001). Situating these teaching models and strategies within their specific sociocultural context deepens our understanding of effective instruction (Taylor, Pressley et al., 2002). Recent work linking this growing research base with effective professional development frameworks has the potential to positively influence teacher change (Morrow & Casey, 2004; Morrow et al., 2003).

Professional development is often seen as the solution to deficiencies in student learning; frequently, a dose of a single-session workshop is expected to "cure" the problem. It is now understood, however, that to be effective professional development must sustain inquiry through larger, more involved, and more complicated systems of investigation (Lyons & Pinnell, 2001). Exemplary professional development engages teachers in the change process, is multifaceted and based on teachers' needs, pairs information sessions with ongoing support, and provides tangible student and teacher resources (CELA, 2002). When tailored to urban educators, this kind of systemic approach to professional development is also culturally responsive to the community in which the teachers and students are positioned (Anderson & Olsen, 2006). Model urban professional development programs and strategies, such as those in Massachusetts, California, New York, and New Jersey as described in this chapter, are effective because they begin with teachers identifying their needs; offer ongoing support; and are rooted within the community where the teachers and students work, offering opportunities for families to become involved.

The survey data we collected found teachers requesting more information on motivating children, understanding systems of classroom management, and becoming more responsive to the unique cultural and economic backgrounds of diverse classrooms. It is clear to us that the relationship between these three themes cannot be ignored. Other research, for example, suggests children are more likely to be motivated to engage in literacy events that are purposeful. Such events allow children to make links to experiences outside of the classroom (Pahl & Rowsell, 2006). To engage children in that kind of learning, teachers need to understand and be responsive to both the cultural backgrounds and academic needs of their students (Morrow, Reutzel, & Casey, 2006). Linking the collective pursuit of these three themes with effective professional development has the potential not only to better support the teachers we surveyed but also to inform the professional development of urban teachers in general.

Implications for Research, Practice, and Policy

Professional development offers a useful resource for enriching the literacy experiences of our historically most underrepresented and underserved youth. Focused partnerships that bring teachers, administrators, the community, and knowledgeable experts together offer a framework for positively supporting teacher change and student learning (Morrow et al., 2003). This approach is admittedly less efficient and more expensive than the single-session workshop. The possibility to create sustainable change for teachers and students, however, seems well worth the time and money.

There are multiple possibilities available when it comes to creating these types of partnerships. It is important to first contextualize the needs of the teachers and students. While there is consistency among urban education, for example, urban settings themselves are culturally, linguistically, and economically unique. The New Jersey initiative we described, for example, serves a student population distinctly different from that served by the California program we noted. It is important, then, to begin with what is known and to look to the educators within a specific urban setting to describe their own challenges and needs. The next step is to develop frameworks for supporting teacher development, in the form of both input from area experts and the teachers themselves. In fact, one reason for the tremendous success of the projects described in this chapter is that teachers were simultaneously supported by experts in the field while using their own individual expertise to support one another. Teacher collaboration, in the form of peer coaching, frequent focused meetings, and providing workshops for one another, is a valuable component of effective professional development systems.

One of the most important lessons taken from our work with teachers is that effective, enduring change takes time. All of the programs we described, for example, have been in place for several years and are now part of the professional fabric of the districts in which they were implemented. The professional development labs set up in the New York City schools, for example, are seen not as external entities but as part of each school's culture.

We have learned a lot from our reading in the field on professional development and our work with teachers across contexts. Urban educators face myriad daily challenges and frustrations. We need to look to professional development as an established link within the urban setting, offering teachers the resources they need to meet those challenges and reduce those frustrations.

To that end, large-scale intervention studies are needed to determine which professional development models are most likely to create exemplary teachers of literacy—teachers whose students learn to be fluent readers in urban settings.

REFERENCES

Anderson, L., & Olsen, B. (2006). Investigating early career urban teachers' perspectives on and experiences in professional development. *Journal of Teacher Education, 57*, 359–377.

Anders, P.L., Hoffman, J.V., & Duffy, G.G. (2000). Teaching teachers to teach reading: Paradigm shifts, persistent problems, and challenges. In M.L. Kamil, P.B. Mosenthal, P.D. Pearson, & R. Barr (Eds.). *Handbook of reading research* (Vol. 3, pp. 719–742). Mahwah, NJ: Erlbaum.

Bean, R., & Morewood, A. (2007). Best practices in professional development for improving literacy instruction. In L.B. Gambrell, L. Morrow, & M. Pressley (Eds.), *Best practices in literacy instruction* (3rd ed., pp. 373–394). New York: Guilford.

Block, C.C. (2001, December). *Distinctions between the expertise of literacy teachers preschool through grade 5.* Paper presented at the annual meeting of the National Reading Conference, San Antonio, TX.

Center on English Learning and Achievement. (2002, Winter). Effective professional development begins in the classroom. *English Update*, 1–2.

Clark, C.M., & Peterson, P.L. (1986). Teachers' thought processes. In M.C. Wittrock (Ed.), *Handbook of research on teaching* (3rd ed., pp. 255–296). New York: Macmillan.

Coker, H. (1985). Consortium for the improvement of teacher evaluation. *Journal of Teacher Education, 36*, 12–17.

Duffy, G.G., & Hoffman, J.V. (1999). In pursuit of an illusion: The flawed search for a perfect method. *The Reading Teacher, 53*, 10–16.

Fisher, D. (2001). "We're moving on up": Creating a schoolwide literacy effort in an urban high school. *Journal of Adolescent & Adult Literacy, 45*, 92–101.

Genishi, C., Ryan, S., & Ochsner, M. (with Yarnall, M.M.). (2001). Teaching in early childhood education: Understanding practices through research and theory. In V. Richardson (Ed.), *Handbook of research on teaching* (4th ed., pp. 1175–1210). Washington, DC: American Education Research Association.

Guskey, T. (1986). Staff development and the process of teacher change. *Educational Researcher, 15*(5), 5–12.

Hoffman, J., & Pearson, P.D. (2004). Reading teacher education in the next millennium: What your grandmother's teacher didn't know that your granddaughter's teacher should. In R. Robinson, M.C. McKenna, & J.M. Wedman (Eds.), *Issues and trends in literacy education* (pp. 5–29). Upper Saddle River, NJ: Pearson Education.

Indrisano, R., Birmingham, N., Garnick, S., & Maresco, D.K. (1999). A co-teaching model for literacy education. *Journal of Education, 181*, 75–102.

Lyons, C.A., & Pinnell, G.S. (2001). *Systems for change in literacy education: A guide for professional development.* Portsmouth, NH: Heinemann.

MacGillivray, L., & Rueda, R. (2004). Listening to inner city teachers of English language learners. In R. Robinson, M.C. McKenna, & J.M. Wedman (Eds.), *Issues and trends in literacy education* (pp. 96–119). Upper Saddle River, NJ: Pearson Education.

Morrow, L.M. (2003). *Organizing and managing the language arts block: A professional development guide.* New York: Guilford.

Morrow, L.M., & Casey, H.K. (2003). A comparison of exemplary characteristics in 1st and 4th grade teachers. *The California Reader, 36*, 5–17.

Morrow, L.M., & Casey, H. (2004). A professional development project with early literacy teachers: Partners in change. *The Reading Teacher, 57*, 662–669.

Morrow, L.M., Casey, H., & Haworth, C. (2003). Staff development for early literacy teachers: A plan to facilitate change. In D. Barone & L.M. Morrow (Eds.), *Literacy and young children: Research-based best practices* (pp. 3–22). New York: Guilford.

Morrow, L.M., Reutzel, D.R., & Casey, H. (2006). Organization and management of language arts teaching: Classroom environments, grouping practices, and exemplary instruction. In C. Evertson & C. Weinstein (Eds.), *Handbook of classroom management* (pp. 559–581). Mahwah, NJ: Erlbaum.

Morrow, L.M., Tracey, D., Woo, D., & Pressley, M. (1999). Characteristics of exemplary first-grade literacy instruction. *The Reading Teacher, 52*, 462–476.

National Institute of Child Health and Human Development. (2000). *Report of the National Reading Panel. Teaching children to read: An evidence-based assessment of the scientific research literature on reading and its implications for reading instruction* (NIH Publication No. 00-4769). Washington, DC: U.S. Government Printing Office.

National Staff Development Council & National Association of Elementary School Principals. (1995). *Standards for staff development: Elementary school edition.* Alexandria, VA: National Staff Development Council.

Pahl, K., & Rowsell, J. (2006). *Literacy and education: Understanding the New Literacy Studies in the classroom*. Thousand Oaks, CA: Sage.

Pressley, M., Allington, R.L., Wharton-McDonald, R., Block, C.C., & Morrow, L.M. (2001). *Learning to read: Lessons from exemplary first-grade classrooms*. New York: Guilford.

Pressley, M., Rankin, J., & Yokoi, L. (1996). A survey of instructional practices of primary grade teachers nominated as effective in promoting literacy. *The Elementary School Journal, 96*, 363–384.

Rhodes, C.S., Wolf, L.B., & Rhodes, G. (2005). Professional development laboratory: Center for literacy and community services. *Journal of Children & Poverty, 11*, 76–85.

Richardson, V. (1990). Significant and worthwhile change in teaching practice. *Educational Researcher, 19*, 10–18.

Roehler, L.R., & Duffy, G.G. (1986). What makes one teacher a better explainer than another. *Journal of Education for Teaching, 12*, 273–284.

Ruddell, R.B. (1995). Those influential literacy teachers: Meaning negotiators and motivation builders. *The Reading Teacher, 48*, 454–463.

Ruddell, R.B., & Harris, P. (1989). A study of the relationship between influential teachers' prior knowledge and beliefs about teaching effectiveness: Developing higher order thinking in content areas. In S. McCormick & J. Zutell (Eds.), *Cognitive and social perspectives for literacy research and instruction* (38th yearbook of the National Reading Conference, pp. 461–472). Chicago: National Reading Conference.

Ruddell, R.B., & Kern, R.B. (1986). The development of belief systems and teaching effectiveness of influential teachers. In M.P. Douglas (Ed.), *Reading: The quest for meaning* (pp. 133–150). Claremont, CA: Claremont Reading Conference.

Strickland, D.S. (2002). Improving reading achievement through professional development. In M. Kamil, J.B. Manning, & H. Walberg (Eds.), *Successful reading instruction* (pp. 103–117). Greenwich, CT: Information Age Publishing & Laboratory for Student Success.

Taylor, B.M., Pearson, P.D., Clark, K.F., & Walpole, S. (1999). *Beating the odds in teaching all children to read* (CIERA Tech. Rep. #2-006). Ann Arbor, MI: Center for the Improvement of Early Reading Achievement.

Taylor, B.M., Peterson, D.S., Pearson, P.D., & Rodriguez, M.C. (2002). Looking inside classrooms: Reflecting on the "how" as well as the "what" in effective reading instruction. *The Reading Teacher, 56*, 270–279.

Taylor, B.M., Pressley, M., & Pearson, P.D. (2002). Research supported characteristics of teachers and schools that promote reading achievement. In B.M. Taylor & P.D. Pearson (Eds.), *Teaching reading: Effective schools, accomplished teachers* (pp. 361–374). Mahwah, NJ: Erlbaum.

Vygotsky, L.S. (1978). *Mind in society: The development of higher psychological processes* (M. Cole, V. John-Steiner, S. Scribner, & E. Souberman, Eds. & Trans.). Cambridge, MA: Harvard University Press.

Vygotsky, L.S. (1986). *Thought and language* (A. Kozulin, Trans.). Cambridge, MA: The MIT Press. (Original work published 1934)

Wharton-McDonald, R., Pressley, M., Rankin, J., Mistretta, J., Yokoi, L., & Ettenberger, S. (1997). Effective primary-grades literacy instruction = Balanced literacy instruction. *The Reading Teacher, 50*, 518–521.
Willis, A.I., Garcia, G.E., Barrera, R., & Harris, V.J. (Eds.). (2003). *Multicultural issues in literacy research and practice*. Mahwah, NJ: Erlbaum.

CHAPTER 8

What We Have Learned About Teacher Education to Improve Literacy Achievement in Urban Schools

Kathryn H. Au
University of Hawaii

Taffy E. Raphael
Kathleen C. Mooney
University of Illinois at Chicago

U rban schools are beehives of activity, abuzz with programs, initiatives, and assessment systems, coping with one new mandate after another. Much of this activity is directed toward a single goal: raising scores on state tests. While we decry the overemphasis on test scores, we do not deny the reality that the literacy achievement of students in urban schools continues to lag behind that of their mainstream peers. In fact, by grade 12, many students in urban schools are reading at a level similar to that of typical mainstream students in grade 8 (Grigg, Daane, Jin, & Campbell, 2003). It is fitting, then, that teacher educators seek to join educators working in urban schools in the quest to improve students' literacy achievement.

What can we do to make such collaborations successful? As implied above, one of the ways to build successful school–university collaborations is to organize them around the goal of improving students' literacy achievement. When the school and university partners direct their efforts toward this shared goal, professional development assistance provided by the university partner becomes central to the mission of the urban school.

Improving Literacy Achievement in Urban Schools: Critical Elements in Teacher Preparation edited by Louise C. Wilkinson, Lesley Mandel Morrow, and Victoria Chou. © 2008 by the International Reading Association.

Purposes of This Chapter

In this chapter, we share the lessons we have learned about how teacher education can be organized to help urban schools improve their students' literacy achievement. Our insight comes from working with urban schools through an approach called the Standards Based Change (SBC) Process (Au, 2005; Au, Raphael, & Mooney, in press; Raphael, Goldman, Au, & Hirata, 2006), a systematic school improvement framework that leads to improved literacy achievement. Our view builds on and extends the concept of professional development schools, institutions based on partnerships between teacher education programs and P–12 schools that focus on increasing student achievement (National Council for the Accreditation of Teacher Education, 2001).

We begin by discussing the roots of the SBC Process in Hawaii and its scaling up to schools in Chicago, as well as the underlying principles of social constructivism that have framed our work. Our research suggests that schools that succeed in improving student achievement through their work with the SBC Process move through a seven-level developmental model. To facilitate schools' progress through the levels, we have designed four school-based teacher education courses taught through a combination of whole-school workshops and small-group coaching sessions at specific grade levels or for members of specific departments. The four courses, each of which is discussed in detail, focus on (1) the professional learning community and a system for improving student achievement, (2) student learning, (3) curriculum guides, and (4) portfolio assessment. Finally, we describe how we have reinforced our work with the SBC Process at the school level by making connections to a master's degree program in literacy.

Review of Research and Theory

The work in urban teacher education we describe grows from research on the SBC Process, which was developed in schools in Hawaii beginning in 1997 (Au, 2005). In 2002, the SBC Process was scaled to Chicago as the basis for the work of Partnership READ, a project directed by Taffy Raphael at the University of Illinois at Chicago (UIC), with funding from the Searle Funds of the Chicago Community Trust. While the SBC Process had been used in a wide range of schools in Hawaii, it had not been tested in an urban environment comparable to that of the Chicago Public Schools (CPS). The school systems are markedly different. The average poverty level in public schools in Hawaii, for example, is approximately 50%. That compares to a poverty rate of approximately 85% among public schools in Chicago. Results of a hierarchical linear modeling analysis showed that students in Hawaii Title I schools following the SBC Process had significantly higher test scores on the state reading test than did students in Title I schools not following this approach (Au, 2005). Similar growth was seen in Chicago schools that stayed with the process for five years (Destefano, 2007; Mooney & Raphael, 2006).

When observations made in the Chicago schools were combined with those made in the Hawaii schools, the results led to a developmental model of school change with the following seven levels (Raphael, Goldman, et al., 2006):

1. Recognizing a need—An individual or small group recognizes the need to pull the school together to improve students' literacy achievement.

2. Organizing for change—A core group of leaders focuses professional development efforts on literacy and adjusts the school's schedule to give teachers time to work together.

3. Working on the building blocks—The school's university (or other external) partner introduces the SBC Process as a means of pulling the school together as a professional learning community and guides teachers to identify the school's philosophy and vision of the excellent reader or writer.

4. Moving as a whole school—The external partner supports the schoolwide professional learning community by helping teachers develop grade-level benchmarks (end-of-year outcomes) in literacy and a rubric-based assessment system to monitor student progress.

5. Establishing the system—The external partner sets up opportunities for teachers to participate in schoolwide conversations at the beginning, middle, and end of the year in which they share assessment results and talk together about how they are using standards to improve students' literacy achievement.

6. Implementing the staircase curriculum—Teachers create literacy curriculum guides that define *progress* at each grade level in terms of "steps" on a coherent "staircase" curriculum; completed guides are shared with everyone in the school.

7. Fully engaging students and families—Teachers, through portfolio assessment, engage students in self-assessment, goal setting, and three-way conferences (Davies, Cameron, Politano, & Gregory, 1992) as a way of expanding the learning community to include students and their families.

Schools in Hawaii generally saw gains in literacy achievement when they reached Level 6. In Chicago, some schools saw gains as early as Level 5, although teachers did not necessarily experience ownership over the change effort at that level.

When we work with schools at Levels 1 and 2, we focus on helping them create the infrastructure needed to support a schoolwide professional learning community. Once a solid infrastructure is in place, we provide the school with four teacher education courses based on the levels in the developmental model. The first course guides teachers at a school through Levels 3 and 4, the second takes them through Level 5, the third through Level 6, and the fourth through Level 7. Descriptions of each of the four courses appear later in this chapter. In each course, we seek to build teachers' knowledge of literacy, literacy instruction, and literacy assessment as well as their ability to be effective change agents who support efforts to refine the staircase curriculum and promote literacy achievement.

Social constructivist theory, particularly the work of Vygotsky (see Gavelek & Bresnahan, in press), has led to many insights about learning, particularly with respect to students' literacy learning in classrooms (e.g., Au & Mason, 1981; Goatley, Brock, & Raphael, 1995; Palincsar & Brown, 1984). We have conceptualized the SBC Process as a social constructivist approach to school literacy improvement, building on parallels between the learning of students and teachers.

The first parallel stems from Vygotsky's (1978) assertion that learning begins on the social plane, in interactions with a more knowledgeable other. Just as students learn reading through participation in a community of readers with the assistance of teacher and peers, we suggest that teachers learn to teach effectively through participation in a professional learning community, where the facilitator may be a university professor or other external partner. The facilitator brings an outsider's perspective, along with knowledge of research on literacy and school change, and can facilitate the exchange of professional knowledge and practical experiences among teachers in a school.

A second parallel is found in the embodied nature of experience, recognizing the limitations of "book learning." Just as students develop proficiency in literacy by engaging in activity settings with authentic purposes for reading and writing, teachers develop proficiency in improving their students' literacy achievement by working within authentic activity settings in their own schools—or within close approximations to such settings. We have found that teachers' introduction to and participation in the SBC Process is most effective when conducted within the school setting and with the entire faculty. Alternatively, when teachers from different schools enroll in graduate course work to improve their literacy instruction, we establish activity settings that allow them to participate as members of a virtual school. Regardless of the setting, our sessions include time for teachers to work together to improve their practice. Typically, while teachers in urban settings may learn the content needed for effective instruction, this content is seldom embodied in the practices needed to actually implement and sustain high-quality practice. We fill this gap by preparing teachers to become change agents in their schools through the teaching they model in their own classrooms and through their work as part of their school's professional learning community.

A third parallel is found in the importance of ownership: students' ownership of literacy and teachers' ownership of literacy improvement efforts. Au (1997) defines *ownership* in terms of students valuing literacy so much that they will use reading and writing for purposes they set for themselves, in home and community settings as well as at school. Au argues that ownership of literacy, rather than just proficiency, should be the overarching goal of literacy instruction in urban and other schools with high proportions of students of diverse cultural and linguistic backgrounds. This argument will resonate with many educators in urban settings, who often report that students appear to lack the motivation to become excellent readers and writers.

Likewise, curriculum leaders cite teachers' lack of ownership over literacy improvement efforts as a chief barrier to change efforts in their schools. The standards movement began in the 1980s, and many veteran teachers have grown weary of mandate after mandate demanding that they address standards and raise test scores. This weariness is understandable given that most teachers have never received adequate support, which we believe must come in the form of systematic professional development and extensive time to work with colleagues. Urban teachers rarely have the opportunity to gain a deep understanding of higher standards for student achievement, to work out the implications for changes in their practice, or to receive feedback related to continued improvements in practice. When teachers, such as those working in SBC Process schools, do get this opportunity, they feel ownership over literacy improvement efforts. A high degree of teacher ownership lays the foundation for sustainability of the improvement effort over a period of years.

The final parallel is related to the importance of a well-planned curriculum in which learning experiences occur within what Vygotsky (1978) called the zone of proximal development, the region of sensitivity to instruction. In the classroom, students are guided through increasingly challenging experiences that they are able to address successfully because they can draw on what has come before. Similarly, in SBC Process schools, we created a series of four courses, each building on the previous one, to help teachers take on increasingly challenging tasks related to schoolwide literacy improvement. Teachers are guided through these courses, which are designed to help them create and implement a coherent, or staircase, literacy curriculum for students across the grades.

Best Practices

Schools in Chicago, like many of their urban counterparts, often adopt comprehensive reform models such as Success for All (Slavin & Madden, 2001) or other packaged programs in an effort to improve students' literacy achievement. On some occasions, these adoptions occur at the district level, as evidenced by the CPS's 2007 Core Program Initiative, in which schools were asked to select one of three basal reading programs to guide their literacy instruction and assessment. While such programs may provide an appropriate starting point for school literacy improvement, we find that preset programs foster a tendency for schools to downplay reflective practice and to promote teaching that overemphasizes lower-level skills. This situation raises issues of equity, as preset programs overemphasizing basic skills are most often adopted by schools serving high proportions of students of diverse backgrounds, thus moving teachers away from reflective practice and students away from higher-level thinking (Au, 2006). Lack of reflective practice by teachers is an equity issue because teachers who are not encouraged to think for themselves are less likely to be prepared to teach students to think for themselves.

In the SBC Process, we distinguish between a program and a curriculum. We define *curriculum* as all the materials and experiences—both instructional and assessment-related—that teachers use to help their students achieve high standards. Teachers use the SBC Process to develop their own effective literacy curricula. Rather than relying on materials or lesson plans dictated by preset programs, they choose the best materials available from a variety of sources and determine exactly which instructional activities they will use in the classroom. Teachers who develop a curriculum through the SBC Process understand it deeply, are committed to its implementation, and realize that the curriculum is never finished. Rather, it is in a state of continual refinement (Au, 2005).

Our goal when we work with urban schools in the SBC Process is to support teachers in creating what we call their school's own staircase curriculum (the same concept as curriculum coherence, espoused by Newmann, Smith, Allensworth, & Bryk, 2001). The staircase curriculum, which is based on benchmarks carefully coordinated across grade levels, is broader than any preset reading or writing program. We work with the reading or writing programs already in place in a school, inviting teachers to build on the strengths of these programs while correcting the weaknesses. Obviously, if we want teachers in urban schools to be creators and not just receivers of curriculum, we must be committed to involving them in a multiyear process of systematic professional development, a process that not only allows them to become familiar with current research on literacy but also values their knowledge of their students and the community.

The results of the research have guided our work with urban schools and provided the outline of a teacher education curriculum for those teaching in such settings. This research-based curriculum, designed to promote school change, is made up of a series of four year-long, on-site courses in literacy. In fact, four years is a good estimate of the time it is likely to take a typical urban school to achieve sustainable success, though evidence of student gains in achievement typically emerges within approximately two years. We depart from the way typical on-site courses operate in our insistence that professional development in the SBC Process involve all teachers, not just volunteers (for details, see Au, 2005). Each course centers on teachers working together on specific tasks related to improving students' literacy achievement, and a new course is introduced only when teachers have successfully completed the previous one. Our experience suggests that a school needs to provide teachers with *the equivalent of* eight full days (a combination of half-day inservice days, professional development days, grade-level meeting time, etc.) to participate in each of these year-long courses; curriculum leaders tell us that most teachers devote many additional hours on their own.

Supporting Best Practices

Course #1: Professional Learning Community and System for Improving Student Achievement

In the first course we often begin by helping the teachers in an urban school to come together as a professional learning community (DuFour, 2004). This course centers on a To-Do List that is integral to the SBC Process. Although the first two items on the list are relatively straight-forward issues, they address areas teachers typically have not explicitly considered for many years. The items call for discussing beliefs about teaching, learning, and literacy and creating a vision statement describing the excellent reader or writer who will graduate from the school. Professional development focuses on knowledge building about literacy and in particular on current research related to reading and writing (Farstrup & Samuels, 2002) and national expectations for students' literacy performance as inferred from the current framework of the National Assessment of Educational Progress (Donahue, Daane, & Jin, 2003). Teachers work in grade-level or content area teams or create vertical teams as they explore these issues.

A CPS literacy coordinator who works at Reid Elementary (pseudonym) described her school's experience with the beginning phase of Partnership READ, the UIC project based on the SBC Process, as follows:

> In our first year, we met as a faculty in August before the students began classes. After being introduced to the SBC Process and Partnership READ's To-Do List, we worked on our philosophy. The faculty broke into teams to discuss and record their philosophy of what a good literacy program would look like. We then came together and reported out on our philosophy of literacy and found commonalities. From this we worked on a vision statement. A committee took the rough draft created as a whole group and worked to make it clear and concise. A few versions were then shared with the staff and one was chosen. (interview with literacy coordinator, May 20, 2005)

At Drake Elementary School, teachers began the school year by forming four teacher teams that included teachers across K–8 grade levels and curricular areas. Each team generated a list of concepts that characterized their beliefs about teaching (e.g., the importance of "being clear on objectives" and "differentiated learning"), learning (e.g., "connecting to prior knowledge and extending it" and "every child can learn"), and literacy (e.g., components of the Chicago Reading Initiative—comprehension, word study, writing, fluency and "reading for meaning").

After the philosophy and vision statements have been drafted, grade-level teams tackle the next two items on the list: creating grade-level benchmarks that support the vision of the excellent reader or writer and "I Can" statements (rewordings of each of the benchmarks in student-friendly language). Teachers check their benchmarks and "I Cans" against state standards and bring their work into alignment.

Grade-level discussions are often intense and thoughtful. We find it critical for teachers to draft their own grade-level benchmarks rather than simply selecting state or district benchmarks from a list. Benchmarks form the foundation for both instruction and assessment in the SBC Process. Our experience suggests that teachers will neither feel ownership over nor have deep understanding of benchmarks prepared by others. We have encountered teachers who refused to develop their own benchmarks. These teachers made slower progress when it came to understanding both the SBC Process and standards-based education and had more difficulty mastering instruction and assessment strategies that promoted students' higher-level thinking abilities and literacy achievement than those who did prepare their own benchmarks.

Once the benchmarks are in place, we focus on the remaining key elements in the SBC Process To-Do List, which was developed in Hawaii and used by Partnership READ in scaling up the SBC Process for use in Chicago schools. The elements in the To-Do List are as follows:

- Identifying the evidence needed to determine how well students are meeting the established year-end benchmarks
- Constructing a system for collecting this evidence at the beginning, middle, and end of the year
- Creating and refining rubrics for evaluating the evidence and for assessing inter-rater reliability
- Analyzing student work
- Designing instructional improvements

In short, this first course provides teachers with grounding in standards-based instruction and assessment in literacy and stresses the importance of coherence across grades and school subjects in a staircase curriculum.

Course #2: Focus on Student Learning

By the time teachers at a school have completed the To-Do List, they have come together as a professional learning community and put in place a rudimentary system for improving student achievement through standards. However, teachers have typically focused their work within grade levels and have spent little time coordinating their benchmarks and assessments across grade levels. In other words, grade levels have created their own steps but have not explored how well the steps come together to form a "staircase." This is why we focus closely on student learning in the second course and use teachers' observations about student progress to promote development of the staircase curriculum.

The task we present to the teachers is that of establishing a system for three-times-per-year reporting of results: pretest, midyear check, and posttest. We ask teachers to administer assessments measuring students' progress toward meeting grade-level benchmarks during three evidence windows set by the school, typically periods of a week or two weeks. We facilitate sessions during which teachers meet in grade levels to score the assessment evidence collected, refining their rubrics if necessary and checking for reliability. We guide teachers to discuss the results obtained; create bar graphs showing the percentage of students meeting, exceeding, or working on the benchmarks; identify strengths and weaknesses in students' performance; and design instructional improvements.

Information presented in this course centers on two areas. The first is assessment. Basics of assessment—such as the difference between formative and summative assessment, the advantages of performance assessment, the role of large-scale state and standardized tests—are all addressed. Exploring such topics in the context of examples from one's own school, district, and state makes lessons real to teachers. We teach about rubrics, including distinctions between task-specific and generalizable, holistic, and analytic. Because teachers are working on refining rubrics of their own, they can immediately apply what they learn to real-life situations.

After the second year of work with the SBC Process in Chicago, both the teachers and literacy coordinators working at Partnership

READ schools became aware of their need for a deeper understanding of assessment. In response, UIC faculty members developed a summer assessment course for the literacy coordinators, with the expectation that they would subsequently share the course content and processes with faculty members at their schools. The four-week course, specifically crafted for literacy coordinators at schools that were participating in the SBC Process, focused on several aspects of assessment:

- Various forms of assessment
- Relative quality of assessment instruments
- Alignment of instructional goals with assessment methods
- Design of standards-based literacy assessments

Feedback subsequent to the course suggested that this focused study of assessment empowered the literacy coordinators to better teach and support their teachers in classroom-based assessment work. The course also enabled the literacy coordinators to become critical consumers of assessment and led to extended, on-site professional development courses in assessment at several of the Partnership READ schools the following year.

The second topic covered in this course is instruction aimed at higher-level thinking in literacy. For example, at Shields School in Chicago, teachers had adopted Question–Answer Relationships (QAR; Raphael, Highfield, & Au, 2006) as a schoolwide framework for comprehension instruction, but they continued to have difficulty making connections between the instructional strategies they used to teach comprehension skills and comprehension assessment results. In response, Partnership READ staff members worked collaboratively with the two literacy coordinators at Shields during the second semester of one school year, designing a series of professional development workshops aimed at supporting evidence-based comprehension instruction. The workshops featured activities on the purposes of different forms of comprehension assessment, analysis by grade-level teams of the content and results of the comprehension assessments teachers had administered in their classrooms, and modeling of instructional strategies related to these assessment results. These whole-school workshops were followed by Partnership READ staff members' participation in grade-level team meetings, arranged to support the teachers' application of the professional development information and processes.

When it comes to sharing their assessment results, we guide teachers in reaching agreement on the approach they will follow. We draw on the concept from the arts known as a "gallery walk," in which artists' products are displayed for the public. A gallery walk in the SBC Process takes place three times a year and consists of

- The schoolwide reporting, by grade levels, of students' achievement levels on classroom-based assessments along with information on how the teachers plan to respond instructionally to what they have learned from these assessments
- Schoolwide reflection activities on both the grade-level benchmarks and "I Can" statements and on the related assessment system as it reflects progress in constructing a staircase curriculum
- Individual teachers' reflections on what they and their grade-level peers need to do in response to the schoolwide sharing session and the information that has emerged from the discussions
- An opportunity to acknowledge and celebrate the hard work that has gone into the gallery walk

We provide teachers with templates for their presentations while encouraging them to experiment with formats that will allow them to communicate their findings effectively. We guide teachers in how to provide constructive feedback to teachers at other grade levels following presentations. We promote the building of a staircase curriculum by asking teachers to make observations about what the presentations as a whole indicate about continuities and discontinuities in benchmarks, assessment, and instruction across the grade levels, a move that contributes to their vision of the excellent reader or writer. Because experienced teachers will participate in many gallery walks over time, we find it important to vary the format of the gallery walk—for example, in the ways teachers share their results or give feedback to others—so that the event does not lose its power to foster change.

Whole-school discussion of student learning has proven to be a particularly powerful tool for promoting teacher and school change, whether schools are just beginning their work with the SBC Process or are veterans of several years. In the second year of the SBC Process at Reid School, teachers' reflections following their grade-level presentations revealed a trend related to word study that appeared to exist throughout the grade levels. Teachers used the gallery walk conversations as the impetus for identifying word study as an important schoolwide focus. They also agreed on the need to align instruction in this area across grade levels. A middle school language arts teacher kicked off this part of the discussion, stating,

> I notice a trend of word knowledge and vocabulary needs throughout the grades. In third grade, they talked about vocabulary in context; in second grade, they talked about word calling; in the upper grades, the needs are the same. This seems to be a trend in every grade that affects our [students' reading] comprehension. Because of a lack of advanced vocabulary, our kids are behind.... This is especially true in the content areas; reading is very difficult if you don't have this.

A second-grade teacher added that it was important to connect students' home and school languages—that it was solely a matter of teaching vocabulary. A middle school math teacher noted that vocabulary knowledge was fundamental to both fluency and comprehension and raised this question about the alignment in the "I Can" statements:

> We seem weak, as a whole, in fluency and vocabulary in context— and vocabulary connects directly to comprehension. We need to emphasize prefixes and suffixes in content vocabulary.... The gaps might be in the "I Can" statements. Maybe there are some disconnects there.

And the assistant principal reinforced the importance of alignment: "We've done a lot of grade-level planning, but we need to look at vertical alignment so that teachers across grades are talking to each other" (field notes, January 28, 2005). As a result of this particular gallery walk and discussion, Reid School faculty members identified vocabulary as their school's greatest need; it became a primary focus area for that year's SBC Process work. The importance of these three-times-per-year schoolwide reports is reflected in the literacy coordinator's comments about their impact on development of the staircase curriculum at Reid School. She characterized her school's experience as follows:

> Our focus on vocabulary did come directly from our discussion following the fall gallery walk [schoolwide reports by each grade level]. Word knowledge "I Cans" and assessments were so different across the school. Some grades looked at word knowledge as reading a list of words while others looked at word analysis or the use of context clues.... After the gallery walk, grade levels were expected to revisit their "I Cans," to either add additional "I Cans" to address vocabulary or redo their existing ones. Of course, this meant changing assessments and instruction. So this gallery walk discussion generated

a lot of work for all the grades. But it came directly from teacher observations of grade-level presentations. (personal communication, May 27, 2007)

Course #3: Curriculum Guides

Once teachers at a school have made three-times-per-year reporting of results a routine, we can be quite certain that they are engaging in schoolwide conversations about what everyone is doing to improve students' literacy achievement through standards. As a result of these conversations across—as well as within—grade levels, a staircase curriculum gradually begins to come together. At this point we introduce alignment activities in which teachers make observations about continuities or discontinuities between the benchmarks developed by their peers at different grade levels.

Once the teachers have had the opportunity to align and fine-tune their benchmarks, they are ready to begin creating their grade-level curriculum guides. When this chapter was written, most Chicago schools had not worked with the SBC Process long enough for teachers to have begun working on their curriculum guides. However, teachers in more than a dozen SBC Process schools in Hawaii had been involved in curriculum development efforts on a smaller scale, having worked on author study or genre units for their grade level. Most had not attempted to create a year-long curriculum in reading or writing, but they were well prepared to tackle this challenge because of the work they had completed in the first two courses.

In the third course, we build on this foundation by using Tyler's (1949) classic work on curriculum as a structure for the guides. Tyler suggests that a curriculum has four necessary components:

1. Goals for student learning
2. Instructional strategies
3. Instructional materials
4. Assessment

We tell teachers that we will guide them through the process of creating curriculum guides based on Tyler's model. Teachers are pleasantly surprised to learn that through their work with the SBC Process To-Do List they have already created many products that can go directly into their curriculum guides. Their grade-level benchmarks and "I Can" statements, aligned to state standards, address the section on goals. Furthermore, they have completed the section on assessment by writing procedures for collecting evidence, developing rubrics, and selecting anchor papers (exemplars of student work at a given level of performance).

Components 2 and 3 of Tyler's (1949) list, dealing with instructional strategies and instructional materials, often require considerable effort for teachers to assemble. Examples of instructional strategies include (a) QARs, a way to help students answer questions based on a specific text; (b) thematic units such as those for author studies; or (c) minilessons designed to teach particular concepts such as the sequence of events. Instructional materials are items that may be intended for student use, such as short texts to be read to or by students, forms for concept maps, and peer editing checklists. They may also be references for teachers, such as an article providing guidelines for conducting literature discussions or a list of phonics skills and spelling patterns typically taught at a particular grade level.

Experienced teachers usually have access to a wide array of resources related to instructional strategies and materials, scattered among professional books, file folders, binders, teachers' guides, and the like. We encourage teachers to gather these resources together in one place and to match resources to their grade-level benchmarks. Teachers can then engage in discussions to determine the specific resources they want to use to help their students meet or exceed grade-level benchmarks. These resources are placed into master curriculum guide binders for each grade level. All teachers receive copies of the relevant pages in the master curriculum guide, which they then use as the basis for their customized, individual curriculum guides. For example, all teachers at grade 3 may have agreed on a list of read-aloud books to use in teaching students how authors engage in character development. However, individual teachers may choose to supplement this list with their personal favorites.

At the time this chapter was written, teachers at 13 schools in Hawaii had completed curriculum guides in reading and writing. In most Hawaii schools, the process of developing good drafts of the curriculum guides has taken teachers about a year. When teachers have their drafts ready, a carousel is held in the school library. Each grade level is assigned a table, on which the teachers place their curriculum guides. In the span of about an hour, groups of grade-level teachers rotate among the tables, looking at the guides their peers in other grade levels have created. When all teachers have reviewed all the guides, teachers discuss their observations with their grade levels: what they have learned about what other grade levels are doing, implications for improvements to their own curriculum guides, and where their school seems to be in terms of building a staircase curriculum. At this point, teachers understand that the process of curriculum writing is never really finished, although changes in the future are likely to be refinements rather than complete overhauls.

A teacher at Holomua Elementary School in Hawaii explained the benefits of working with the SBC Process and creating a curriculum guide in the following way:

> I have no fear when it comes to curriculum. I've been through the process. I created a curriculum from scratch. It's not just that we went through the process, but [rather that] what we ended up with was such a good product that we could really use and that we could really see growth in our students. (Hokutan, 2005, p. 24)

Teachers in Hawaii report that they use their guides on a daily basis because they built the guides with the resources they know they need to teach reading or writing effectively. Guides can often be found open on teachers' desks, and teachers can be seen pulling pages out of the guides. Schools provide time periodically for teachers to revise and update their guides, particularly when new teachers arrive at a grade level. The use of curriculum guides in Chicago is discussed later in this chapter in the context of UIC's master's degree in literacy program.

Course #4: Portfolio Assessment

By the time teachers have completed the third course and have their curriculum guides in hand, they have gained a deep understanding of their grade level's curriculum in reading or writing and they are familiar with the staircase curriculum that extends across the grades. Because the curriculum has become transparent to the teachers, they are now in a position to make the curriculum transparent to their students. This is the reason that we make portfolio assessment—which includes student self-assessment, goal setting, and three-way conferences (Davies et al., 1992)—the subject of the fourth course.

We have introduced portfolio assessment in the context of the SBC Process to five schools in Hawaii. (As of this writing, Chicago schools had not worked with the SBC Process long enough to implement portfolios.) At each of these schools, some teachers were using the process in their classrooms, and almost all had attempted to use it at some point. Many, however, were doing so with limited success. Our experience indicates that unless they have taken a graduate course on literacy assessment, teachers have not had the opportunity to gain a conceptual understanding of portfolio assessment. Therefore we begin by providing teachers with an intellectual framework for identifying the purpose of portfolio assessment and the specific portfolio model that will help them accomplish that purpose. The basis for this framework is Valencia's (1998) outline of six portfolio models: (1) the showcase model, which highlights students' best efforts; (2) the progress model, which shows an individual student's growth over time; (3) the process model, which presents a student's work in different phases of a process, such as the writing or inquiry process; (4) the ownership model, which features evidence of the student's identity as a reader and writer; (5) the evaluation model, which shows evidence of a student's performance evaluated against an external standard; and (6) the composite model, which is a combination of two or more of the other models. In deciding among models, Valencia emphasizes, teachers must think of both the purpose of and audience for the portfolios.

In SBC Process schools, we explain to teachers that they have a ready-made basis for evaluation portfolios, provided by the evidence of student performance they have been collecting three times per year to determine progress toward meeting grade-level benchmarks. We suggest that teachers work together in grade levels to determine whether an evaluation portfolio will suffice or whether they want to create a composite portfolio that addresses an additional aspect of assessment. To date, teachers at all grade levels at all schools have opted to design composite portfolios. The vast majority has decided on composite portfolios with an evaluation component plus a progress component. Teachers indicate that the progress component is valuable in providing evidence of growth even when students are not meeting grade-level standards. Some kindergarten teachers have chosen to include a showcase component, reasoning that children and parents enjoy having a record of the best work produced that year, including drawings and CDs of children reading aloud. Because they wanted to improve students' attitudes toward literacy, some upper-grade teachers have chosen to include an ownership component.

It is an extremely challenging task for teachers to work out all the details of a portfolio assessment system and successfully implement that system in an ongoing manner. Most teachers have had the experience of starting the process in the fall only to see it languish as the school year proceeds. The fourth course in the SBC Process helps teachers come to understand the reasons behind portfolios and gain clarity about what they need to do to make portfolios a part of the everyday process of teaching and learning. Many products that teachers have previously developed become part of the process. For example, teachers come to understand that copies of the "I Can" statements should not only be posted on classroom walls but also placed in students' portfolios. This is also the case with rubrics, which teachers can rewrite in student-friendly language for students to use in self-assessment and teacher-designed student reflection sheets.

Once students are involved in self-assessment, they can also engage in goal setting, with their goals based on the parts of rubrics they are unable to meet. For example, first-grade teachers at one school established a benchmark indicating that students would produce a piece of writing with an identifiable beginning, middle, and end. Many students were able to write a good beginning before they learned how to produce an effective middle or ending to their narratives. Based on the results of self-assessments of their writing, the students came to understand that their next goal was to better develop the middle and end of their drafts.

Teachers taught students how to prepare for three-way or student-led conferences with their parents by following procedures outlined by Wong-Kam, Kimura, Sumida, Ahuna-Ka'ai'ai, and Maeshiro (2001). Such conferences were well received by parents. At all schools, teachers discovered that parents became quite well versed in expectations for their children, due to the jargon-free wording of the "I Can" statements and the clarity of the rubrics. These understandings enabled parents to support their children's progress more effectively than in the past. Thus, the end result of the fourth course is to expand the learning community beyond teachers to encompass students and their parents.

Connections to a Master's Degree in Literacy Program

Clearly, our approach to whole-school reform requires knowledgeable staff members who can work collaboratively to construct the systems foundational to the SBC Process. Also critical is the ability to differentiate literacy instruction in strategic ways so that all students can achieve appropriate end-of-year targets. In Chicago, we learned through the first two years of implementing the SBC Process in eight K–8 and two K–5 schools that success requires more than leadership from key administrative leaders and a school-based curriculum or literacy coordinator. It also demands a core group of teachers willing to both buy into the process and take the steps necessary to acquire literacy content knowledge and grade-level leadership skills. Moreover, CPS recognized that this kind of leadership—by teachers and curriculum/literacy coordinators—was necessary for district improvement on a wide scale. Consistent with national trends, CPS leaders began to encourage and provide funds for district teachers to work toward highly qualified status. In Illinois, that meant certification as a reading specialist or becoming endorsed as a reading teacher. The Partnership READ Fellows Program was born in response to these needs and trends.

Since 2004, there have been three, 30-member cohorts (2004–2005, 2005–2006, 2006–2007) of Partnership READ fellows. Most have been CPS classroom teachers, although a few literacy coordinators have participated in the program as well. Because the basis of the SBC Process is a collaborative construction of curriculum, assessment, and research-based instructional practices, we created a virtual school—the Partnership READ Fellows Academy—within each cohort. Each Academy includes representatives from grades K–8, and a UIC faculty member serves as "principal." Over the course of the year, fellows work together in "whole-school" meetings and in leadership and grade-level teams, paralleling the activities that occur in their own schools and learning the leadership skills needed to promote active teacher participation and ownership in each of these settings. At the end of the program, the fellows leave with competencies in literacy teaching, learning, and assessment, as well as the ability to participate in and guide the construction of their own school's literacy staircase curriculum.

The Partnership READ Fellows Program consists of 12 credits (three courses) of advanced graduate study in literacy education. Approximately one-third of the fellows go on to apply for admission to the UIC master's degree program in literacy, language, and culture (LLC), applying their 12 credits to the 39 required for specialization or endorsement. Two of the three courses parallel those in the MEd program but are tailored to teachers involved in the SBC Process in their schools; the third is one of the regularly scheduled MEd courses in the LLC program.

The first course, Advanced Methods of Literacy Instruction, is a one-semester course that is framed in terms of the Chicago Reading Initiative, which emphasizes four topics in literacy instruction: comprehension, writing, word study, and fluency. Thus, the course is structured with 3–4 week "units" on each of these topics, followed by synthesis work (e.g., lesson sets) that brings the individual topics together. Each unit draws on a professional text that would be appropriate for use in school-based teacher study groups or as a curriculum planning resource, such as one of the following:

- *Strategies That Work* (Harvey & Goudvis, 2000)
- *QAR Now* (Raphael, Highfield, & Au, 2006)
- *Assessment and Instruction of Reading and Writing Difficulties* (Lipson & Wixson, 2008)
- *Words Their Way* (Bear, Invernizzi, Templeton, & Johnston, 2007)
- *The Fluent Reader* (Rasinski, 2003)
- *Teaching Writing: Balancing Process and Product* (Tompkins, 2007)
- *Writing Workshop: The Essential Guide* (Fletcher & Portalupi, 2001)

The Partnership READ Fellows Program website, oce.uic.edu/oce/ocepublic/programs/DisplayProgram.asp?ProgramID=48, provides additional course information.

The second course, Seminar on Literacy Teacher Leadership, meets one day a month during the school year (i.e., two semesters). While the district covers tuition, each school pays for a substitute teacher for its fellow. In the course, fellows master the leadership skills and strategies they need to effectively share what they learn in their advanced methods course work with their colleagues through grade-level team meetings and inschool professional development coplanned with their school's literacy coordinator. They also work within grade-level teams to construct curriculum guides that they can take back to their schools to serve as examples and models of exemplary staircase curriculum guides.

The third course each fellow takes is selected from among those offered in the LLC master's degree program. Selection is based on factors such as whether a fellow is planning to apply to the program, areas of greatest need, and course availability.

Over the course of the year of their targeted work in the program, fellows experience a range of contexts that develop professional leadership in literacy:

- Participating in the course work
- Creating and delivering an informal presentation on effective instruction of a comprehension strategy within a writing genre to

other fellows in their cohort, using a PowerPoint presentation and related materials

- Presenting formally at a fellows-organized and fellows-run winter strategy conference within a poster fair model
- Collaborating with grade-level colleagues to create a lesson set designed to integrate literacy content areas in the teaching of a small text set
- Participating as a faculty member in the SBC Process to create a vision statement describing the excellent reader or writer who graduates from the school; identify grade-level, end-of-year targets; develop relevant assessment systems; and align instructional activities with anticipated needs of students
- Creating a grade-level specific literacy curriculum guide

Occasionally, the literacy coordinators from the fellows' schools were asked to attend the monthly seminars—occasions the fellows said enhanced communication within their schools and their ability to support the literacy coordinators in their work. With each new cohort, principals of the Partnership READ participating schools became increasingly strategic in nominating fellows, using criteria that included a teacher's commitment to staying in the school at least three years, his or her relationship to other teachers in the school, his or her leadership potential, and the grade level taught (i.e., using fellows to help jump-start grade-level teams in need of additional support). In short, the Partnership READ Fellows Program created a support system wherein the university's master's program became a vehicle for providing high-quality professional development in literacy education to Partnership READ schools. In return, university faculty received feedback from the fellows that could be used to ensure that graduate course work remained highly relevant to those teaching in the urban setting.

While space does not permit a detailed discussion of the implications for preservice teacher education programs, the principles and procedures are much the same as at the graduate level. SBC Process ideas can just as easily be embedded in undergraduate language arts methods courses. Preservice teachers take on the roles of faculty members of a virtual school, working their way through the SBC Process To-Do List. At the University of Hawaii, Au (2002) found this approach to be particularly effective if preservice teachers' field placements were in schools where teachers were working with the SBC Process.

Summary of Main Ideas

We suggest that collaborations between universities and urban schools be grounded in the shared goal of improving students' literacy achievement. The SBC Process we have used to structure our teacher education efforts in urban schools was developed with schools in Hawaii in 1997 and then scaled up in 2002 to use with schools in Chicago through a partnership with UIC. Schools in the project seek to improve students' literacy achievement by moving through the SBC Process's seven-level developmental model of change.

Teacher education in the form of courses conducted at participating schools is the primary vehicle we use to help schools progress through the levels in the developmental model. The courses, which are taught in order and build on the content of earlier courses, present teachers with increasingly challenging tasks related to improving students' literacy achievement through standards-based education.

The first course centers on the SBC Process To-Do List, which consists of nine items teachers must put in place to implement a rudimentary system for boosting achievement. Simultaneously, the teachers come together to form a schoolwide professional learning community. The second course requires teachers to take a close look at student learning for the purpose of creating what we call a staircase curriculum. During this course, teachers learn to establish a system of three-times-per-year reporting of assessment results, tracking students' progress toward meeting important end-of-year outcomes in literacy. The third course focuses on curriculum guides, and the fourth on portfolio assessment. In the process of preparing their portfolios, students engage in self-assessment, work with "I Can" statements and student-friendly rubrics, and participate in three-way conferences with their parents and teachers. Thus, at this highest level of the SBC Process developmental model, the learning community expands to encompass students and their parents as well as teachers.

Finally, UIC's Partnership READ Fellows Program supplements the four school-based courses in the SBC Process and is linked to the UIC master's degree program in literacy. The fellows receive instruction in the change process, literacy curriculum, instruction, assessment, and facilitation and leadership skills in the context of graduate-level courses tailored to address urban education. In return, the fellows program supports schools moving through the SBC Process developmental model by providing them with highly knowledgeable teacher leaders.

Implications for Research, Practice, and Policy

In discussing implications of our work on urban teacher education within the framework of the SBC Process, we recall the social constructivist themes introduced earlier:

- The social nature of learning and the importance of the school-wide professional learning community
- The embodied nature of experience and the importance of teachers' work on curriculum, instruction, and assessment being embedded within the context of their own schools, grade levels, and classrooms
- Ownership and motivational factors and the importance of teachers seeing themselves—and being seen by others—as creators rather than receivers of curriculum
- The zone of proximal development and the importance of a teacher education curriculum based on a developmental model of school change

We have shown in this chapter how these principles were applied to the design of teacher education courses within long-term school change efforts supported by systematic professional development as the means to help urban schools raise students' literacy achievement.

Our stance is that research, practice, and policy must be undertaken as a coordinated enterprise in urban school districts, where teachers face tremendous challenges in improving literacy achievement. In the case of our work with the SBC Process, research led us to identify seven levels of development through which schools passed as they became successful in raising literacy achievement. We are now able to apply this developmental model as a road map to guide other schools toward success. The four on-site teacher education courses we described provide teachers working in urban schools with the kind of professional learning experiences appropriate to the level their school has reached on the developmental model.

Research thus shapes practice—both our practice as teacher educators and the practice of the teachers with whom we collaborate in SBC Process schools. As a school reaches each new level in the developmental model, we proceed with teachers to the next course and prepare them to take on new challenges related to strengthening their practice. As teachers become more knowledgeable about literacy curriculum, assessment, and instruction, they become more effective in fostering literacy learning in the classroom. Soon the effects of schoolwide implementation of the staircase curriculum become evident, and students' literacy achievement rises. School progress is further supported when professional development based in urban schools is supplemented with graduate courses for teacher leaders, as demonstrated in the Partnership READ Fellows Program. Teacher leaders emerge from the program ready to promote change schoolwide and within grade-level teams.

The policy implications of our work on teacher education in urban settings are clear. If we are to raise the literacy achievement of students in urban schools, we must have a policy environment that treats teachers as creators—not just receivers—of curriculum. If the goal is to improve students' literacy achievement, especially in areas involving higher-level thinking, policymakers should emphasize systematic professional development related to the improvement of literacy curricula, instruction, and assessment. They should avoid imposing packaged programs on schools and reducing professional development to the kind of "training" needed to implement such programs. We urge policymakers to focus less on specifying which program a school uses and more on professional development that helps teachers to analyze the strengths and weaknesses of programs already in place and to build the strongest literacy curriculum they can.

Often, federal, state, and district mandates narrowly focused on specific literacy or assessment programs make it difficult for schools to stay the course with multiyear school change efforts such as the SBC Process. Mandates that threaten to derail long-term school change efforts should be avoided, and care should be taken not to impose incompatible external initiatives on urban schools that are beginning to show success in improving student achievement.

Few efforts are more critical to the future of the United States than making sure all students—including those in urban school districts—reach the high levels of literacy vital to participation as citizens in a democratic society faced with meeting the demands of globalization. Our repeated observation in urban schools is that success is fragile, while failure is robust. We must renew our efforts to reverse this unfortunate situation. Empowering urban teachers to be creators of literacy curricula, through on-site and graduate courses such as those described in this chapter, will enable them to teach their students to use literacy in thoughtful, constructive, and insightful ways. Long-term professional development efforts—in which teacher educators partner with urban schools—offer a promising avenue toward the accomplishment of this ambitious goal.

REFERENCES

Au, K.H. (1997). Ownership, literacy achievement, and students of diverse cultural backgrounds. In J.T. Guthrie & A. Wigfield (Eds.), *Reading engagement: Motivating readers through integrated instruction* (pp. 168–182). Newark, DE: International Reading Association.

Au, K.H. (2002). Communities of practice: Engagement, imagination, and alignment in research on teacher education. *Journal of Teacher Education, 53,* 222–227.

Au, K.H. (2005). Negotiating the slippery slope: School change and literacy achievement. *Journal of Literacy Research, 37,* 267–288.

Au, K.H. (2006). *Multicultural issues and literacy achievement.* Mahwah, NJ: Erlbaum.

Au, K.H., & Mason, J.M. (1981). Social organizational factors in learning to read: The balance of rights hypothesis. *Reading Research Quarterly, 17,* 115–152.

Au, K.H., Raphael, T.E., & Mooney, K. (in press). Improving reading achievement in elementary schools: Guiding change in a time of standards. In S.B. Wepner & D.S. Strickland (Eds.), *Supervision of reading programs* (4th ed.). New York: Teachers College Press.

Bear, D.R., Invernizzi, M., Templeton, S.R., & Johnston, F. (2007). *Words their way: Word study for phonics, vocabulary, and spelling instruction* (4th ed.). Upper Saddle River, NJ: Prentice Hall.

Davies, A.C., Cameron, C., Politano, C., & Gregory, K. (1992). *Together is better: Collaborative assessment, evaluation & reporting.* Winnipeg, MB: Peguis.

Destefano, L. (2007, April). *Evidence of ARDDP's impact on students, teachers, and schools.* Paper presented at the annual conference of the American Educational Research Association, Chicago, IL.

Donahue, P.L., Daane, M.C., & Jin, Y. (2003). *The nation's report card: Reading, 2003.* Washington, DC: National Center for Educational Statistics.

DuFour, R. (2004). What is a "professional learning community"? *Educational Leadership, 61*(8), 6–11.

Farstrup, A.E., & Samuels, S.J. (Eds.). (2002). *What research has to say about reading instruction.* Newark, DE: International Reading Association.

Fletcher, R., & Portalupi, J. (2001). *Writing workshop: The essential guide.* Portsmouth, NH: Heinemann.

Gavelek, J.R., & Bresnahan, P. (in press). Ways of meaning making: Sociocultural perspectives on reading comprehension. In S. Israel & G.G. Duffy (Eds.), *Handbook of reading comprehension.* New York: Routledge.

Goatley, V.J., Brock, C.H., & Raphael, T.E. (1995). Diverse learners participating in regular education "book clubs." *Reading Research Quarterly, 30,* 352–380.

Grigg, W.S., Daane, M.C., Jin, Y., & Campbell, J.R. (2003). *The nation's report card: Reading 2002* (No. NCES 2003-521). Washington, DC: U.S. Department of Education, Institute of Education Sciences.

Harvey, S., & Goudvis, A. (2000). *Strategies that work: Teaching comprehension to enhance understanding.* York, ME: Stenhouse.

Hokutan, C. (2005). *The effects of the Standards Based Change Process on teachers.* Unpublished master's paper, University of Hawaii, Honolulu, HI.

Lipson, M.Y., & Wixson, K.K. (2008). *Assessment and instruction of reading and writing difficulties: An interactive approach.* Boston: Allyn & Bacon.

Mooney, K., & Raphael, T. (2006, December). *Turning points in school reform: One school's journey through the standards-based change process.* Paper presented at the annual meeting of the National Reading Conference, Los Angeles, CA.

National Council for the Accreditation of Teacher Education. (2001). *Standards for professional development schools.* Washington, DC: National Council for the Accreditation of Teacher Education. Retrieved February 1, 2008, from www.ncate.org/documents/pdsStandards.pdf

Newmann, F.M., Smith, B., Allensworth, E., & Bryk, A.S. (2001). Instructional program coherence: What it is and why it should guide school improvement policy. *Educational Evaluation and Policy Analysis, 23,* 297–321.

Palincsar, A.S., & Brown, A.L. (1984). Reciprocal teaching of comprehension-fostering and comprehension-monitoring activities. *Cognition and Instruction, 2,* 117–175.

Raphael, T.E., Goldman, S., Au, K.H., & Hirata, S. (with Mooney, K., Weber, C., Glasswell, K., Dong, H., Madda, K., Kim, J.Y., et al.). (2006, April). *A developmental model of the Standards-Based Change Process: A case study of school literacy reform.* Paper presented at the American Educational Research Association, San Francisco, CA.

Raphael, T.E., Highfield, K., & Au, K.H. (2006). *QAR now: A powerful and practical framework that develops comprehension and higher-level thinking in all students.* New York: Scholastic.

Rasinski, T.V. (2003). *The fluent reader: Oral reading strategies for building word recognition, fluency, and comprehension.* New York: Scholastic.

Slavin, R.E., & Madden, N.A. (2001). *One million children: Success for all.* Thousand Oaks, CA: Corwin Press.

Tompkins, G.E. (2007). *Teaching writing: Balancing process and product* (5th ed.). Englewood Cliffs, NJ: Prentice Hall.

Tyler, R. (1949). *Basic principles of curriculum and instruction.* Chicago: University of Chicago Press.

Valencia, S.W. (1998). *Literacy portfolios in action.* Fort Worth, TX: Harcourt Brace.

Vygotsky, L.S. (1978). *Mind in society: The development of higher psychological processes* (M. Cole, V. John-Steiner, S. Scribner, & E. Souberman, Eds. & Trans.). Cambridge, MA: Harvard University Press.

Wong-Kam, J., Kimura, A.K., Sumida, A.Y., Ahuna-Ka'ai'ai, J., & Maeshiro, M.H. (2001). *Elevating expectations: A new take on accountability, achievement, and evaluation.* Portsmouth, NH: Heinemann.

SECTION 3

Key Resources
for the Preparation
of Teachers of Reading
for Urban Settings

©2008 Jupiterimages

CHAPTER 9

Literacy Development in the Urban Elementary and Middle School: A Syllabus

Erica C. Boling
Jeanine Beatty
Rutgers, The State University of New Jersey

Course Overview

This course serves as an introduction to the teaching of literacy in urban schools. The major focus of the course will be literacy instruction in grades 4 through 8 with some discussion of literacy learning at other levels. Throughout the semester, we will examine the ways in which the term *literacy* is constantly evolving in today's society. In addition, we will explore the relationship between various areas of literacy, as well as the role of literacy across the curriculum. The course is designed to assist future teachers in developing the fundamental knowledge, skills, strategies, and dispositions needed to carry out a literacy program where students' expertise in reading, writing, and oral language is nurtured.

Because of its focus on urban education, this course is strongly grounded in the belief that students and teachers in urban schools often have the advantage of working with—and learning from—people of varied cultural and linguistic backgrounds. The course is designed to prepare teachers for the responsibility of providing high-quality instruction to students who come to school with a wide range of literacy knowledge and experiences. Although teachers setting out to work in urban areas often wonder if they can make a difference in the lives of students facing economic, social, and academic challenges, research has shown that we have reason to be optimistic about the impact that good teachers can have. Good teaching, regardless of where that teaching occurs, matters for students who struggle (Haycock, 2005).

Improving Literacy Achievement in Urban Schools: Critical Elements in Teacher Preparation edited by Louise C. Wilkinson, Lesley Mandel Morrow, and Victoria Chou. © 2008 by the International Reading Association.

Major Themes

Three themes related to the specific needs, challenges, and advantages of working in urban areas will be part of the ongoing focus of the course. These themes are

- Questioning how we can effectively address cultural, linguistic, and socioeconomic diversity
- Rethinking how we approach students through re/mediation. In the context of urban education, we define *re/mediation* as "changing the ecology of classroom teaching and learning" (Alvermann, 2005, p. 10)
- Redefining "text" to include visual and digital modalities and using technology/multiliteracies to reach reluctant students (Alvermann, 2005)

Student Objectives

Students will

- Articulate a philosophy of literacy instruction that emphasizes the interactive and integrative nature of language and builds upon these connections when creating learning opportunities in urban classrooms
- Demonstrate the knowledge and skills needed for creating and implementing a literacy curriculum using small- and large-group work, collaborative learning, conferences, and individual work based on professional standards
- Identify, plan, and design literacy instruction based on students' needs, developmental progress, learning styles, and prior knowledge
- Identify and understand the characteristics, uses, advantages, and limitations of different types of assessments for evaluating how students learn, what they know and are able to do, and what kinds of experiences will support students' growth and development
- Critically reflect on their teaching and learning
- Identify and use available resources and materials for instructional planning

- Articulate how educational research can be used as a means for continual learning and development

Required Texts

Gunning, T.G. (2008). *Creating literacy instruction for all students in grades 4 to 8* (2nd ed.). Boston: Allyn & Bacon.

Various articles (see Course Topics and Related Readings)

A children's or young adult novel of the student's choice

Supplemental Text

Strickland, D.S., & Alvermann, D.E. (Eds.). (2004). *Bridging the literacy achievement gap, grades 4–12*. New York: Teachers College Press.

Web Resources

www.ReadWriteThink.org—an IRA- and NCTE-sponsored website featuring high-quality lesson ideas

www.4Teachers.org—a website offering a wealth of teacher resources such as RubiStar and Classroom Architect

www.ReadingRockets.org—U.S. Department of Education, Office of Special Education Programs website featuring articles, video clips, and other information related to supporting the literacy needs of diverse learners

Course Topics and Related Readings

Literacy in Our Lives

What does it mean to be literate? How is the term *literacy* constantly evolving? How do our environment and experiences affect how we define *literacy*? How might literacy take on different forms in different contexts?

- No related readings

Nature of Literacy

What is the reading process? How can culture and prior experiences influence a person's perspective on learning to read? How might culture and prior experiences influence what we value about literacy?

- Anderson, J., & Gunderson, L. (1997). Literacy learning from a multicultural perspective. *The Reading Teacher, 50,* 514–516.
- Gunning, chapter 1

Re/mediation and Redefining "Text"

What is the literacy achievement gap? What can teachers do to help close the literacy achievement gap? How might access to resources such as technology have an impact on the gap between economically unequal groups?

- Alvermann, D.E. (2005). Literacy on the edge: How close are we to closing the literacy achievement gap? *Voices From the Middle, 13,* 8–14.
- Neuman, S.B., & Celano, D. (2006). The knowledge gap: Implications of leveling the playing field for low-income and middle-income children. *Reading Research Quarterly, 41,* 176–201.

Evaluation

How can teachers assess reading, writing, listening, and speaking? How can teachers use assessments to inform classroom instruction?

- Gunning, chapter 2

Word Recognition and Fluency

What is fluency and why is it important? What aspects of the English language might create difficulties for those students who are nonnative English speakers? How can teachers build upon students' prior knowledge while avoiding ineffective, repetitive instruction?

- Gunning, chapter 3
- Gunning Table 11.1, p. 470

Vocabulary

What are the stages of word knowledge? What are some techniques for teaching vocabulary? How do teachers design vocabulary instruction that builds upon students' varied background knowledge and experiences?

- Gunning, chapter 4

Comprehension: Theory and Strategies

What theories drive reading comprehension instruction? What strategies support reading comprehension across various types of texts?

- Gunning, chapter 5

Comprehension: Text Structures and Teaching

How do good readers and writers comprehend texts? Why is knowledge of text structure important? Which teaching procedures support students' comprehension of both online and offline texts?

- Gunning, chapter 6

Writing and Reading

What are the stages of the writing process? How can reading improve writing? How can writing improve reading? How can writing and technology be used for social purposes, identity formation, and the development of learning communities?

- Gunning, chapter 10

Creating and Managing a Literacy Program

What are the basic principles for planning and managing a literacy program? How can teachers create an environment that fosters thoughtful literacy in the classroom?

- Gunning, chapter 12

Technology and Literacy Instruction

What online resources are available for teachers? How do teachers and students evaluate and use online resources? What is the role of visual and media literacies in elementary and middle schools?

- Smolin, L.I., & Lawless, K.A. (2003). Becoming literate in the technological age: New responsibilities and tools for teachers. *The Reading Teacher, 56*, 570–577.

Literacy in the Content Areas

What instructional techniques support reading and writing in the content areas? How do students use reading and writing as tools for learning across content areas?

- Gunning, chapter 7

Reading Literature

What are some basic principles for teaching literature? How can teachers use literature to develop communities of readers and writers? What are book clubs and how can teachers use them to enhance students' critical literacy skills?

- Gunning, chapter 8
- Book chosen for the class book club project

Approaches to Teaching Reading

What are some approaches to teaching reading and writing? How have these approaches changed over time?

- Gunning, chapter 9

Revisiting Diversity in the Literacy Classroom

What have you learned throughout the course about the special needs and characteristics of diverse populations of students? In your future classrooms, how will you implement literacy programs that account for both the strengths and the needs of these students?

- Gunning, chapter 11

Course Format and Major Assignments

During each class session, participants will explore research-based practices for building literacy in diverse learners. Classes will involve a variety of collaborative activities such as discussing readings, examining curriculum and assessment materials, analyzing and developing lesson plans, and engaging in other cooperative learning activities related to content and pedagogy. Lessons will also be modeled by the instructor.

Reading Responses

Each student is responsible for completing the required readings. Activities related to readings will take the form of written reflections, small-group discussions, and group-generated lesson plans. Students will also complete narrative writing assignments related to the themes of the course. Some of these writings will be posted in the online discussion forum. Topics will be determined throughout the semester based on student interest.

One such assignment is Narrative Writing #1, in which students are required to write a two- to three-page narrative describing their literacy learning experiences and how those experiences influenced their knowledge, beliefs, and feelings. Such experiences may include early memories of learning to read and write and events related to your K–12 or university education.

Consider the following when writing:

- Describe your memories of becoming literate.
- Describe the ways in which your reading and writing habits changed during adolescence.
- Provide examples of your literacy learning that occurred both in and out of school.
- Reflect upon and discuss the variety of ways that you have defined the concepts "literacy" and "being literate."

(Note: These prompts are meant to serve as a guide. You do not need to address every point in your narrative.)

Lesson Development and Reflection

Throughout the course students will have opportunities to plan, develop, and implement lessons. Students are required to develop at least two literacy-related lessons that will be taught in field placement settings. These lessons can be taught one-on-one, in small groups, or to the entire class. Students are encouraged to use peers, classroom teachers, and course-related lesson plans as resources. After teaching each lesson, students will write a two- to three-page reflection evaluating their experience. At the end of the semester, students will meet in a small group of peers to discuss teaching experiences.

Keep in mind the following when planning lessons:

- Include all of the information listed in the class-generated lesson plan template.
- Review the grading checklist before submitting your assignment.
- You may adapt lessons from the Gunning text or from other resources. If you choose to do so, be sure to cite your source(s) on the lesson plan.
- You are encouraged to plan together but must teach the lesson separately.

Your reflection should address at least four of the following questions:

- How did the lesson go?
- What evidence do you have that students met or did not meet your objective(s)?
- What was surprising or unexpected about the lesson?
- If you had to teach the lesson again, what would you do differently? Why?
- What did you learn about yourself and your students by teaching the lesson?
- How would you (or your supervising teacher) scaffold student learning in future lessons to help students gain independence using the strategy that you taught?

(Note: Do not be afraid to talk about the things that did not go well. It is important for you to be able to acknowledge weaknesses and identify what you would do differently in future lessons. You are expected to be well prepared, but you are not expected to be perfect!)

Literacy Investigation Paper

At the beginning of the course, each student will choose a literacy topic to investigate. In order to choose a topic, students should think of a number of "burning questions" that they have about literacy instruction or student learning in urban schools. Students are encouraged to use field experiences to guide this process. Once each student chooses an area to investigate, he or she will decide on the types of resources needed to sufficiently answer the question(s). Parent, teacher, student, and librarian interviews are encouraged. Each student will share what he/she has learned in a paper and in a small-group discussion. The final paper will be six to eight pages in length. Students are encouraged to investigate issues related to urban education and the themes of the course.

Your inquiry paper should include

- Introduction (1/2 to 1 page): Describe your inquiry question(s) and the rationale for your choice.
- Methodology (1/2 page): Describe how you searched for answers to your question(s). You might list some of the keywords used for article and Internet searches, explain why you chose to use specific articles and online resources, describe who you interviewed and why, and so on. In this section, you can also describe if or how your inquiry changed, became more focused, and so on.
- Findings or Results (3 to 5 pages): This is the most important part of your paper. In this section you describe what you learned. Many times authors also discuss the strengths and weaknesses of their findings in this section. (For example, they might explain the limitations of their findings, additional areas to investigate, etc.). If applicable, include interview information in this section.
- Discussion/Implications (2 or 3 pages): This section highlights your key findings and describes implications for teachers, students, and future research.

Book Club Project

Students will create lessons and activities as part of a unit to be shared with all course participants. Students will be given class time during the second half of the course to collaborate and develop the components of the project. Students will produce a document including the information outlined below, create a brief PowerPoint slideshow, and deliver a five-minute presentation.

Your book club project document should include

- Introduction (2 to 4 paragraphs): Describe your group's philosophy of literacy instruction. You might want to refer to Gunning chapters 1 and 12 to assist you in writing this. Also include an explanation of how your book club book will fit into your literacy program, specifically in terms of how it will be used to meet the needs of diverse learners in urban classrooms.

- "About the Novel" (1 to 2 paragraph synopsis of the book): In your synopsis, provide a bulleted list of any unique characteristics of the book or "red flags" that parents, teachers, and students should know about (i.e., difficult vocabulary).

- Instruction: Describe the overarching purpose of the instruction, how much time you will devote to this book, and ways in which you intend to assess students prior to and after reading the book. Next, outline five minilessons. (You must include an objective/assessment for each, but you do not need to include fully developed lesson plans.) If you choose to use this book to teach a strategy, the lesson must follow Pearson and Gallagher's (1983) Gradual Release of Responsibility model of instruction.

- Additional Resources: Provide information and websites related to the author and websites and resources related to the book— for example, websites that will help the teacher build background related to historical events. (These topics can and should be a part of one or more of your lessons.)

Discussion Leader/Contributor

Each student is responsible for organizing 8 to 10 minutes of one class session. Students may choose to organize a discussion, share a professional resource or children's book, teach a short demonstration lesson, or plan some other type of presentation. Students must make connections between the readings and topics for that week and the themes of the course. Students may work individually or with up to two other students. When working in pairs, the presentation should be 15 to 20 minutes long. If students choose to work in a group of three, they should take 25 to 30 minutes.

A formal paper is not required for this assignment, but you must submit, for approval, a bulleted list that should include

- A description of the purpose of the activity shared

- An explanation of the activity and how you will engage the class
- An explanation of how the activity connects to urban issues and course themes (i.e., how instruction and assessment relate to the education of English-language learners, at-risk students, and diverse families)
- A list of sources

(Note: Be sure to explicitly state the purpose of your activity and cite your sources in class.)

REFERENCES

Alvermann, D.E. (2005). Literacy on the edge: How close are we to closing the literacy achievement gap? *Voices From the Middle, 13,* 8–14.

Haycock, K. (2005). Choosing to matter more. *Journal of Teacher Education, 56,* 256–265.

Pearson, P.D., & Gallagher, M.C. (1983). The instruction of reading comprehension. *Contemporary Educational Psychology, 8,* 317–344.

CHAPTER 10

Content Area Literacy in the Multicultural Secondary School: A Syllabus

Patricia L. Anders
University of Arizona

Kathleen A. Hinchman
Syracuse University

Course Overview

The public secondary school is a rich and diverse community where literacy serves as a common bond. This course brings together future middle and high school teachers representing multiple subject areas to explore the concepts of literacy and culture and their relationship to teaching and learning. In this course we will also examine how language, specifically reading and writing, can be used to better understand not only curricular content but also ourselves, our colleagues, and our students.

Content area teachers who integrate literacy instruction within the context of their teaching see a payoff in content learning because their students become familiar with the kind of precise written language needed to describe important concepts within a discipline. This, in turn, helps them to remember key constructs and to recognize them on assessments and in situations that call for application of knowledge. It also helps them see which of their literacy strategies can be applied across content areas, fostering their development as independent learners. Teachers who integrate literacy into their instruction in a way that values both academic literacy and the ideas and experiences of youth from a variety of backgrounds give their students access to literacy in a way that will have a profound impact on their lives.

Improving Literacy Achievement in Urban Schools: Critical Elements in Teacher Preparation edited by Louise C. Wilkinson, Lesley Mandel Morrow, and Victoria Chou. © 2008 by the International Reading Association.

The goal of this course, then, is twofold: to familiarize teachers with the nature of diverse school populations and to explore principles of literacy that support the teaching of reading comprehension, composition, and study skills and their practical application in various subject areas. Class meetings will be structured in a variety of formats: workshop, small- and large-group discussion, lecture, and presentation.

Major Themes

A number of themes related to the teaching of literacy across the curriculum in urban school settings provide the framework for this course. Those themes are

- Literacy is the use of language tools (speaking, reading, writing) in various contexts to construct meaning, communicate, and evaluate experience.

- Students develop and engage in multiple literacies; one may be literate in one context or culture and illiterate in others.

- The content area educator provides a context within which students become literate in the culture and discourse of a specific discipline.

- A teacher's literacy-related experiences and values affect his or her stance on promoting literacy.

- Enactments of literacy vary across cultures; an understanding of this concept increases teachers' sensitivity to diverse students.

- The process of becoming a reader and writer is a sociopsycholinguistic process. As such, the acquisition of literacy tools required to understand the world and to adequately communicate is ongoing; one achieves literacy as one participates in constructing meaning in various contexts and cultures.

- Efficient and effective reading, writing, and study skills can be taught and must be taught across the curriculum; students need discipline-specific language and cultural practice to access content areas.

- Linguistic and experiential diversity in our classrooms is a strength, providing a resource for enriching and enhancing the quality and quantity of teaching and learning.

- Teachers balance several considerations when orchestrating effective instruction: their own knowledge, the curriculum and related materials, the background knowledge and needs of their students, and the sociocultural context of the classroom.
- Student evaluation is a necessary part of good teaching and learning. It is embedded in teachers' practice and related to social and political issues.

Student Objectives

Students will

- Reflect upon and evaluate their own literacy experiences
- Relate their own literacy experiences to the plans they make for incorporating literacy instruction in the classes they plan to teach
- Describe the role of literacy in society and the secondary school's responsibility to prepare literate citizens
- Demonstrate familiarity with at least two cultures
- Describe the culture of a particular group of students and suggest implications for practice
- Relate their personal observations of discipline-specific and peer-associated literacy activity to the sociopsycholinguistic nature of the process
- Relate generally accepted principles of adolescent development to literacy processes
- Select, use, and modify comprehension, composition, and study skills strategies to scaffold their students' engagement with and learning of content knowledge and related literacies
- Evaluate and use a variety of materials to accommodate students' varying background knowledge, experience, and interests
- Select print and digital resources that support secondary students' content learning and literacy development
- Use research-based practices to create instructional units that integrate reading, writing, and study skills instruction with discipline-specific inquiry
- Establish a classroom environment that promotes critical thinking, diversity, and risk taking

- Assess their students' background knowledge and existing literacies and use the assessment results for planning purposes
- Develop and use methods of evaluation that reflect student experiences
- Recognize potential linguistic and cultural biases of existing assessment instruments, texts, and other instructional materials and curriculum
- Create or adopt assessment practices appropriate for assessing reading and writing in the content areas

Required Texts

Anders, P.L., & Guzzetti, B.J. (2005). *Literacy instruction in the content areas*. Mahwah, NJ: Erlbaum.

Buehl, D. (2001). *Interactive classroom reading strategies*. Newark, DE: International Reading Association.

Various examples of adolescent literature representative of various cultures

Supplemental Texts

Allen, J. (2004). *Tools for teaching content area literacy*. Portland, ME: Stenhouse.

Alvermann, D., Phelps, F., & Ridgeway, V.G. (2006). *Content area reading and literacy*. Boston: Allyn & Bacon.

Bear, D.R., Invernizzi, M., Templeton, S.R., & Johnston, F. (2004). *Words their way* (3rd ed.). Upper Saddle River, NJ: Prentice Hall.

Fisher, D., Brozo, W.G., Frey, N., & Ivey, G. (2007). *50 content area strategies for adolescent literacy*. Upper Saddle River, NJ: Prentice Hall.

Fisher, D., & Frey, N. (2004). *Improving adolescent literacy: Strategies at work*. Upper Saddle River, NJ: Prentice Hall.

Gere, A.R., Christenbury, L., & Sassi, K. (2005). *Writing on demand: Best practices and strategies for success*. Portsmouth, NH: Heinemann.

Ivey, G., & Fisher, D. (2006). *Creating literacy-rich schools for adolescents*. Alexandria, VA: Association for Supervision and Curriculum Development.

Keene, E.O., & Zimmermann, S. (1997). *Mosaic of thought: Teaching comprehension in a reader's workshop*. Portsmouth, NH: Heinemann.

Moore, D.W., & Hinchman, K.A. (2006). *Teaching adolescents who struggle with reading: Practical strategies*. Boston: Allyn & Bacon.

Readence, J.E., Bean, T.W., & Baldwin, R.S. (2004). *Content area literacy: An integrated approach* (8th ed.). Dubuque, IA: Kendall/Hunt.

Ruddell, M.R. (2006). *Teaching content reading and writing* (4th ed.). New York: Wiley.

Tatum, A. (2005). *Teaching reading to black adolescent males: Closing the achievement gap*. Portland, ME: Stenhouse.

Tovani, C. (2004). *Do I really have to teach reading? Content comprehension, grades 6–12*. Portland, ME: Stenhouse.

Vacca, R.T., & Vacca, J.L. (2001). *Content area reading: Literacy and learning across the curriculum*. Boston: Allyn & Bacon.

Web Resources

www.curry.edschool.virginia.edu/go/clic—a Content Literacy Information Consortium website that features opportunities for adolescent literacy experts and students to exchange ideas

www.literacymatters.org—a website hosted by Education Development Center, Inc., a nonprofit educational and health organization supported by the Annenberg Foundation, that features teaching ideas

www.wested.org—a website describing WestEd's Strategic Literacy Initiative

www.reading.org—the website of the International Reading Association

www.ncte.org—the website of the National Council of Teachers of English

Course Topics and Related Readings

Introduction

What are the goals and objectives of the course? What texts and other materials will be used in the course? What are the course requirements? Why should content area teachers take a course in literacy?

- Anders & Guzzetti, Preface and chapter 1

Generalizations About Schooling and Culture

What are some generalizations we can make about schooling, particularly in multicultural settings? What are some generalizations we can make about the relationship between culture, schooling, and student achievement?

- Anders & Guzzetti, chapter 2
- Press/media article about literacy

Literacy Processes: Theory and Practice

What is literacy and what is its role in society? What are the various forms of literacy? How does one achieve literacy? What is meant by "multiliteracies" and why is that concept particularly important in a multicultural setting? How does the enactment of literacy vary across cultures? What is the relationship between adolescent development and the literacy process?

- Anders & Guzzetti, chapter 3

Principles/Concepts of Learning

How is content area literacy related to content area curriculum? What is meant by "literacy across the curriculum"? Why and how do the literacy demands of various content areas differ from each other? What are the literacy implications, demands, and expectations of various content areas? How are relevant literacy skills taught and reinforced by content area teachers?

- Adolescent novel

Curriculum Planning and the Role of Concepts

How do teachers develop content area curricular goals, objectives, and strategies that incorporate opportunities for literacy development? How do teachers develop a curriculum that meets the content area and literacy needs of diverse students?

- Anders & Guzzetti, chapter 4

Collecting and Analyzing Resources

How does one analyze a content area text in terms of its literacy demands? Why is this important?

- No related readings

Literacy and Life

How do personal life experiences, and in particular those related to literacy, affect a teacher's stance on promoting literacy? How do such experiences affect teaching practice as it pertains to integrating literacy into the content area curriculum?

- No related readings

Reading Strategies

What are the criteria used to select reading strategies best suited to various content areas? How are such strategies taught and reinforced?

- Review Anders and Guzzetti, chapter 6

Study Skills, Note-Taking, and Writing to Learn

What is the role of the content area teacher when it comes to teaching study skills, note-taking techniques, and writing strategies? How should such skills be taught?

- Anders & Guzzetti, chapters 5 and 6
- Buehl, chapter or chapters that pertain to each student's specific content area

Assessment

How can teachers develop and use methods of evaluation that reflect student experiences? How can teachers use students' literacy skills to effectively assess achievement in various content areas? How can teachers recognize potential linguistic and cultural biases of existing assessment instruments, texts, and other instructional materials and curriculum? How can teachers find or create tools and practices appropriate for assessing reading and writing in the content areas?

- Anders & Guzzetti, chapters 7 and 8

Course Format and Major Assignments

This course is planned so that students are actively engaged in examining their own literacy development and the literacy demands of their content area. The assignments are designed to provide opportunities for reflection and self-evaluation; as more sophisticated ideas about literacy develop, students are required to apply their increased understandings to their instructional plans.

This class requires active participation. Students must complete all readings. Pop quizzes on the reading assignments may be given.

Literacy and Life Essay

Students will be actively involved in experiencing—both realistically and vicariously—alternative culture groups. These experiences will involve interviewing each other and an adolescent, reflecting upon and comparing their experiences, and writing a "Literacy and Life" essay summarizing the interviews and reflections and drawing appropriate conclusions.

Reading Response

Students will read adolescent literature and literature related to various content areas. Students will participate in literature groups about adolescent novels. Each group will make a presentation to the class on the novel its members studied and provide classmates with a one-page abstract of the book.

Planning Portfolio

Each student will create a planning portfolio, the preparation a teacher does before designing a unit of study. Each portfolio will include

- A list of content area curricular goals and objectives—conceptual, performance, and state standards—in the form of a conceptual map
- A list of possible digital, media, and print resources that relate to the conceptual objectives
- An analysis of one possible core text (using the text analysis procedures described in Anders & Guzzetti, chapter 4)

- An example of a prereading activity, a midreading activity, and a postreading activity to be used with the core text
- A description of the formative and summative assessments that could be used with this yet-to-be-planned, potential unit

This planning portfolio may be completed individually or collaboratively, either by content area teams of students or teams made up of students representing several different content areas. Those students choosing to collaborate will develop a common concept map, resource list, and description of possible assessment instruments. Each member of the team will analyze a different but potentially usable core text and develop literacy instructional strategies to be used with that text.

Journals

Students will keep a journal made up of 14 entries—one based on the activities of each class meeting—and will e-mail their entries to the instructor. The last journal entry should be a reflection on the journal-writing experience and how well it helped clarify the course concepts.

Text Set

Each student will create and present to the class a "text set," a celebratory account of a personally meaningful literacy learning experience. For example, if a student finds the poetry of a particular poet to be personally meaningful, he or she might present examples of that poetry and explain what it is about the poet's work that made it especially relevant to the development of the student's own life or literacy experiences. Another student might explain the role a particular teacher or other significant adult played in his or her literacy development. These unique accounts provide examples of how personal literacy development influences one's identity as a future teacher. Depending on the number of students in the class, one or two presentations will be made at each class meeting throughout the semester on dates self-selected by the students.

CHAPTER 11

Children's Literature for Urban Classrooms: A Syllabus

Diane Barone
University of Nevada, Reno

Course Overview

Children's Literature for Urban Classrooms presents a traditional over-view of children's literature through an exploration of the general history of children's literature and children's book genres that is geared toward preschool through elementary students. Students will discover numer-ous children's books and authors in this course. What is unique to this course is the additional focus on children's literature that is appropriate and supportive of children in urban schools. Students will consider each piece of literature with a view to cultural understanding, values, and per-spectives of a worldview. In addition, students will explore numerous websites that support an understanding of children's literature, espe-cially literature that is multicultural or shares important themes for children in urban circumstances.

Major Themes

The major themes addressed within this course are

- A historical overview of children's literature and its relationship to changing sociopolitical and cultural issues
- A deeper understanding of the genres of children's books
- A reframing of views about children's books and how they meet the needs of urban students

Improving Literacy Achievement in Urban Schools: Critical Elements in Teacher Preparation edited by Louise C. Wilkinson, Lesley Mandel Morrow, and Victoria Chou. © 2008 by the International Reading Association.

Student Objectives

Students will

- Increase their knowledge of children's literature by reading and reviewing children's books in a variety of literary genres
- Develop an understanding of the history of children's literature
- Recognize and evaluate multicultural literature
- Understand the multiple ways children's books can be interpreted
- Recognize children's book authors and illustrators
- Become aware of awards granted to quality children's books
- Develop the ability to select books and collections of books appropriate to children in urban schools
- Become aware of professional resources surrounding children's literature

Required Text

Mitchell, D. (2003). *Children's literature: An invitation to the world.* Boston: Allyn & Bacon.

(Note: While there are a number of high-quality children's literature textbooks, this one was chosen because it has an explicit focus on diversity. It challenges the reader to examine his or her own worldviews—from cultural heritage to life experiences—and to reflect on how these views may manifest as biases when interpreting and teaching children's literature.)

Supplemental Texts

Children's books available at the university library, local libraries, school libraries, and bookstores

Web Resources

General

www.ReadWriteThink.org—a website with lesson plans centered on children's literature www.reading.org—the International Reading Association's website, which includes book lists and articles about children's literature

Periodicals

www.ala.org/BookLinks—website of *Book Links*

www.cbcbooks.org/cbcmagazine—website of the Children's Book Council

www.education.wisc.edu/ccbc—website of the Cooperative Children's Book Center

www.hbook.com/magazine—website of *The Horn Book Magazine*

www.childrensliteratureassembly.org/journal3.htm—website of the *Journal of Children's Literature*

www.publishersweekly.com—website of *Publishers Weekly*

www.schoollibraryjournal.com—website of the *School Library Journal*

scholar.lib.vt.edu/ejournals/ALAN/—website of *The ALAN Review*

www.bookwire.com/bbr/bbr-home.html—website of *The Boston Book Review*

www.lis.uiuc.edu/puboff/bccb—website of *The Bulletin of the Center for Children's Books*

muse.jhu.edu/journals/lion_and_the_unicorn—website of *The Lion and the Unicorn*

www.lib.latrobe.edu.au/ojs/index.php/tlg—website of *The Looking Glass*

Video Clips

www.reading.org/publications/bbv/videos/v655/index.html—*Read to Me* video, which can be borrowed from the International Reading Association, stressing the importance of parents' reading aloud to their children

pbskids.kids.us/program-lions.html—tips on reading and clips from the PBS television series *Between the Lions*

www.readingrockets.org—Reading Rockets website that includes interviews with authors such as Gail Gibbons and techniques for reading aloud

Professional Organizations

www.ala.org—website of the American Library Association

www.cbcbooks.org—website of the Children's Book Council

www.reading.org—website of the International Reading Association

www.ncte.org—website of the National Council of Teachers of English

Course Topics and Related Readings

Introduction to Children's Literature

What is children's literature? How is children's literature related to child development? What are the general trends in children's literature?

- Mitchell, chapter 1
- Selection of grade-level books for service learning assignment
- Visit one of the following websites to find children's literature resources: www.reading.org, www.carolhurst.com, www.ala.org, or www.ucalgary.ca/~dkbrown.

History of Children's Literature

How has children's literature developed since the 1800s? What has been the effect of changing sociopolitical and cultural issues on children's literature?

- Mitchell, chapter 2

Books for Young Children

What are the characteristics of quality books for young children? Who are some of the noted authors and illustrators of young children's books?

- Mitchell, chapter 3
- Visit the children's art gallery at www.arts.uwaterloo.ca/ENGL/courses/engl208c/gallery.htm to explore the artwork in picture books.

Picture Books

What is a picture book? What are the characteristics of quality picture books? What is the best way to read picture books to children?

- Mitchell, chapter 4
- Visit one of the author or illustrator websites listed on pp. 96, 97, and 98 of the Mitchell text.

- Visit www.acpl.lib.in.us/children/readalouds.html to find read-aloud books or www.reading.org to explore children's or teachers' favorite annual picture book choices.

Responding to Literature

How does one respond to literature through speech, art, writing, movement, drama, and music? What are the differences between literal and inferential responses to literature?

- Mitchell, chapter 5
- Visit www.readingrockets.org/books/interviews/bunting to listen to an interview with Eve Bunting. You will learn why she often writes about immigrants and her immigrant experience.

Poetry

What are the characteristics of poetry? What are the best ways to share poetry with students?

- Mitchell, chapter 6

Context of Children's Literature

Where can one find bigotry and bias in children's books? What effect do worldviews have on bigotry and bias in children's books? How does one evaluate children's books in terms of bigotry and bias?

- Mitchell, chapter 7
- Visit www.tolerance.org/teach to find activities to reduce hatred and bigotry.

Multicultural and International Books

What are the reasons for using multicultural literature in urban classrooms? What variants of children's literature are found in other cultures? Who are the major authors and illustrators of children's books from other countries?

- Mitchell, chapter 8
- Visit www.newhorizons.org/strategies/multicultural/higgins.htm to find additional ways to evaluate multicultural literature.

Traditional and Folk Literature

What are rhymes, fables, myths, and folk tales, and what are the characteristics of each?

- Mitchell, chapter 9
- Visit www.acs.ucalgary.ca/~dkbrown/storfolk.html or www.ipl.org/cgi-bin/youth/youth.out to further explore traditional literature.

Realistic and Historical Fiction

What are the different forms of realistic and historical fiction? How can realistic and historical fiction be used to support students?

- Mitchell, chapter 10
- Visit www.nytimes.com/learning/teachers/lessons/archive.html to find teaching plans about current events or www.scholastic.com/dearamerica/index.htm to find books, timelines, and discussion guides.

Modern Fantasy and Science Fiction

What are the different forms of modern fantasy and science fiction? How can modern fantasy and science fiction be used to support students?

- Mitchell, chapter 11
- Visit www.scholastic.com/harrypotter or www.redwall.org/dave/jacques.html for information about these books and authors and to find possible activities that would be engaging for students.

Nonfiction Books

What are some examples of award-winning nonfiction and narrative nonfiction texts in children's literature? How can students be supported with nonfiction and narrative nonfiction?

- Visit www.nsta.org/ostbc to find out about outstanding science trade books or visit www.nationalgeographic.com or www.nasa.gov; visit www.geocities.com/heartland/estates/4967/math.html or www.carolhurst.com/subjects/math/math.html for math.
- Explore websites for examples of nonfiction literature in content areas such as science, math, social studies, music, art, and so on.

Biography and Autobiography

How can biographical and autobiographical works be used to support students? How does one deal with issues of accuracy in biographical and autobiographical works?

- Mitchell, chapter 12
- Visit www.s9.com/biography or www.brain-juice.com/main.html to explore biographical information.

Reading Behaviors of Teachers and Students

How should one read aloud to students? How should teachers' and students' opinions about works of children's literature be explored?

- Visit the website of one of the journals listed in the Periodicals section of this syllabus and read one article that focuses on urban children or urban children's books.

Award Winners

What are the major awards in the field of children's literature?

- Visit two award websites, such as the Newbery or Caldecott sites, and explore the winner and runner-up books. Choose one book that you think would be beneficial to children in an urban school. Be prepared to share your book and why you believe it is appropriate for urban students.

Course Format and Major Assignments

Students are expected to attend each class and be prepared for class discussions, which will focus on sharing and discussing various works of children's literature.

Literature Response Notebook

Each student will read 50 children's books and in a notebook (electronic is the preferred format) provide for each book the following: a citation, a brief overview of the book that describes its theme, and the student's reaction to the book. Books to be read include

- *Books for young children.* Select five picture books for young children that deal with emotions, the world, people and relationships, or feelings.
- *Picture books.* Select five picture books by the same author or illustrator. Make comparisons across the books. There is a resource list on pages 96 and 97 of the Mitchell text. Visit the author's or illustrator's website.
- *Poetry.* Read three poetry anthologies or books. One must be written by a person of color.
- *Multicultural books.* Read five books representative of different cultures or ethnicities. Three of these books must be written by authors from those cultures, races, or ethnicities.
- *Traditional or folk literature.* Select one traditional tale or folk tale and read five different versions of the work. Observe the differences in each version.
- *Realistic fiction or historical fiction.* Select two novels that focus on the same individual. Compare how the individual is represented in each text.
- *Modern fantasy or science fiction.* Select two novels. Compare the plots of the books. What did the elements of fantasy or science fiction add to the stories?
- *Nonfiction.* Select five picture books and one longer text. Check to see how the content is delivered to students. Is the format appealing? Does it include features such as a table of contents, glossary, text boxes, charts, or figures? How do these features improve comprehension of the book's topic?
- *Biography or autobiography.* Select three picture books and one longer text that focus on the same individual.
- *Award winners.* Choose five books, each of which has won a different award. Visit an award website and learn about previous winners.

Service Learning

Students will spend a total of 15 hours reading to children at a local elementary school. This activity will occur outside class hours and must be arranged with the classroom teacher. Students may choose a grade level, from preschool through sixth grade, in which to read.

Students will keep a log of their reading visits that must be signed by the classroom teacher. In their logs, students will want to discuss with the classroom teacher the themes, genres, authors, or illustrators being studied in order to select books that will enrich children's learning. In addition to the log, students will keep a notebook that includes the titles of books read, the children's responses to those books, and a personal reflection on the reading activity.

During the time that you are reading in a classroom, schedule an interview with the teacher. You might use the following questions or develop others that you think are important:

- How often do you read to children each week?
- How do you select books?
- What are your favorite experiences with books?
- How do you involve children with books?

Then ask the teacher for permission to interview three children. You might use the following questions or others that you develop:

- What are your favorite books?
- Do you have favorite authors or illustrators?
- How often do you read?

Students will summarize what they learn from these interviews in a short paper (approximately three pages long).

CHAPTER 12

Literacy Development in the Early Years With a Focus on Children in Urban Settings: A Syllabus

Lesley Mandel Morrow
Rutgers, The State University of New Jersey

Heather Casey
Rider University

Course Overview

The purpose of this course is to introduce students to the principles of early literacy instruction. Students will study the history of literacy instruction as well as the theory, research, and public policy that have had an influence on instructional practice today. Students also will be introduced to key literacy concepts, including language acquisition, phonological and phonetic awareness, reading comprehension and fluency, written and oral language, characteristics of books and other print media, motivation, and family literacy. They will also study how to teach young children the skills and strategies they must master to become literate. Lastly, the course will address how best to organize and manage early literacy instruction. Although the course will address the teaching of children in all settings, it has been designed to focus in particular on literacy instruction in urban settings.

Major Themes

This course will focus on an exploration of the following themes:

- Early literacy instruction encompasses an array of topics, ranging from language acquisition to an appreciation of children's literature.

Improving Literacy Achievement in Urban Schools: Critical Elements in Teacher Preparation edited by Louise C. Wilkinson, Lesley Mandel Morrow, and Victoria Chou. © 2008 by the International Reading Association.

- Literacy instruction needs to be integrated into all content areas throughout the school day.

- Organizing and managing literacy instruction calls for a variety of teaching strategies and instructional models, including small-group, differentiated instruction in reading and writing; shared reading and writing; and independent reading and writing.

- Quality literacy instruction takes into account a child's cultural background, language, socioeconomic status, and exceptionalities.

Student Objectives

Students will

- Review research, theory, and policy related to early literacy development

- Identify ways to integrate literacy development into all content areas

- Organize and manage literacy instruction with an emphasis on small-group differentiated reading and writing instruction, shared reading and writing, and independent reading and writing

- Become familiar with standards for literacy achievement and how they are assessed in a developmentally appropriate manner

- Develop an awareness of the unique needs of culturally diverse students and English-language learners (ELLs) attending urban schools, as well as an understanding of how poverty and other issues of social justice affect their learning

- Plan early literacy instruction for children from diverse backgrounds, including those who are ELLs

- Become familiar with instructional strategies related to the instruction of children with physical impairments in the regular classroom

- Identify what is meant by *multiple intelligences* and how that term relates to literacy instruction

- Identify what is meant by *early intervention programs*

- Identify what is meant by *inclusion*

Required Texts

Bear, D.R., Invernizzi, M., Templeton, S.R., & Johnston, F. (2004). *Words their way* (3rd ed.). Upper Saddle River, NJ: Prentice Hall. (WW)

Morrow, L.M. (2002). *The literacy center: Contexts for reading and writing* (2nd ed.). Portland, ME: Stenhouse. (LC)

Morrow, L.M. (2003). *Organizing and managing the language arts block: A professional development guide.* New York: Guilford. (OMLAB)

Morrow, L.M. (2009). *Literacy development in the early years: Helping children read and write* (6th ed.). Boston: Allyn & Bacon. (LDEY)

Course Topics and Related Readings

History and Philosophy of Early Literacy

What are the major events in the history of literacy from the 1700s to the present? What are the major ways in which the teaching of literacy skills has changed over the years?

- Morrow (LDEY), chapter 1

Foundations of Early Literacy

What are the characteristics of the major approaches (direct instruction, balanced instruction, whole language instruction) to teaching early literacy? What are the components of the major theories (constructivist, explicit, behavioral) of teaching early literacy? What is meant by integrated-interdisciplinary language arts? What are the national and state standards that address literacy instruction? What are some of the ways teachers effectively organize and manage instruction in a language arts block?

- Morrow (LDEY), chapter 2
- Morrow (LDEY) and Appendix D; Integrated Language Arts Unit
- Brochures and class handouts on the Montessori method of instruction
- Class handout on the philosophy of the National Association for the Education of Young Children (NAEYC)
- U.S. Department of Education handout on Reading First booklet

Literacy and Diversity: Teaching Children With Special Needs

What are the issues that need to be addressed when teaching urban children with diverse cultural backgrounds how to read? What are the issues that need to be addressed when teaching urban children who are gifted, learning disabled, or physically disabled? What is meant by terms such as *early intervention programs* and *meeting special needs*? What is the Reading Recovery reading intervention program?

- Morrow (LDEY), chapter 3

Language, Literacy, and Vocabulary Development

What are the major theories and research findings related to early language, literacy, and vocabulary development? What kinds of objectives, strategies, materials, and types of assessment ideally guide instruction in these areas? How can teachers best address the language, literacy, and vocabulary development of students in urban areas, including those who are ELLs or who have special needs?

- Morrow (LDEY), chapter 4

Word Study: Phonemic Awareness and Phonics

What are the major theories and research findings related to early word study? What kinds of objectives, strategies, materials and types of assessment ideally guide instruction in this area? How can teachers best address the topic of word study with students in urban areas, including those from diverse backgrounds and those who are ELLs or who have special needs?

- Morrow (LDEY), chapter 5
- Morrow (LC), chapter 4 and resource section 3
- Bear et al. (WW), chapters 4, 5, 6, and 7

Developing Reading Comprehension and Fluency

What are the major theories and research findings related to the development of reading comprehension and fluency? What kinds of objectives, strategies, materials, and types of assessment ideally guide instruction in these areas? How can teachers best address the topics of reading comprehension and fluency with students in urban areas, including those from diverse backgrounds and those who are ELLs or who have special needs?

- Morrow (LDEY), chapter 6
- Morrow (LC), chapter 3 and resource section 2

Developing Writing Skills

What are the major theories and research findings related to the acquisition of writing skills? What are the developmental stages of writing acquisition? What kinds of objectives, strategies, materials, and types of assessment ideally guide instruction in this area? How can teachers best address the topic of writing with students in urban areas, including those from diverse backgrounds and those who are ELLs or who have special needs?

- Morrow (LDEY), chapter 7
- Morrow (LC), resource section 5

Motivating Literacy Development: Children's Literature, Technology, Play

How can children's literature be used to motivate literacy development, particularly children from diverse backgrounds? What kinds of objectives, strategies, and materials can be used to create motivated readers and writers, especially in urban settings? How can teachers use technology to create motivated readers and writers in urban settings? How can teachers use play to create motivated readers and writers in urban settings?

- Morrow (LDEY), chapter 8
- Morrow (LC), chapters 1 and 2 and resource section 4

Assessment Issues

How are instruments such as running records, portfolio assessments, and standardized high-stakes tests used to assess literacy, particularly with children from diverse backgrounds? How do teachers ensure that children, including those from diverse backgrounds, are able to meet state standards related to literacy as measured by high-stakes tests and other assessments? How do teachers carry out assessment-guiding instruction? What are the special issues related to assessment of children from diverse backgrounds?

- Morrow (LDEY), chapter 2

Commercial Materials and the Teaching of Reading

How do teachers evaluate and select materials for teaching reading and writing to children, including those from diverse backgrounds? How do teachers merge a school's curriculum and philosophy of instruction, their own philosophy of instruction, commercial instructional materials, and an array of classic children's literature into a cohesive instructional plan for teaching reading and writing?

- Morrow (LDEY)

Organizing and Managing Literacy Learning

How do teachers create literacy-rich classroom environments? How do teachers integrate literacy across the curriculum into all content areas? How can teachers use art, music, and play to integrate literacy across the curriculum? How do teachers organize small-group and differentiated instruction to meet the needs of all children? How do teachers use the strategy of guided reading to meet the needs of all children? How do teachers create learning centers that foster independent and collaborative learning?

- Morrow (LDEY), chapter 9
- Morrow (OMLAB), chapters 3 and 4
- Morrow (LC), chapter 5 and resource section 1

The Family and Literacy Development

What is family literacy and how is it best developed, particularly in families from diverse backgrounds?

- Morrow (LDEY), chapter 10

Professional Development

What are the characteristics of exemplary schoolwide professional development programs? What are the characteristics of exemplary personal professional development plans? How can professional development help literacy teachers address the special issues and challenges related to urban settings?

- Morrow (LDEY), afterword

Course Format and Major Assignments

Students should bring the text *Literacy Development in the Early Years* to class every day and bring other materials when requested for demonstrations and displays. Class attendance and participation are a major part of the course work. Students are expected to participate in class discussions.

Students are strongly encouraged to join a professional organization, such as the National Association for the Education of Young Children (NAEYC), the International Reading Association (IRA), or the New Jersey Education Association (NJEA); subscribe to a professional journal and a teacher magazine; and attend a professional literacy conference.

As part of their preservice education, students are required to participate in two field experiences. One must be in an urban setting and one in a suburban setting. One should be in a primary grade and one in an upper elementary grade. Students should schedule the primary-grade urban field experience to coincide with this course.

Case Study Analysis

Students will read and analyze several case studies that focus on ways to differentiate instruction for children from multicultural backgrounds, children who are ELLs, and children with special needs.

Case Study Research

Each student will complete an original case study of a child between the ages of 3 and 8. The subject of the case study may be a child the student encounters during the field placement experience, a relative, or the child of a friend. The student will work with the child using literacy strategies learned in class. Specifically, students will

- Complete a written case study that documents the child's performance on several learning tasks and, based on those outcomes, analyze the child's future learning needs

- Prepare a portfolio containing materials such as language and writing samples and running reading records, which will be shared with the class and the child's teacher

Readings

Students are expected to read all assigned readings and participate in class discussions. Each week designated students will be discussants for the readings.

Original Lesson Plan

Each student will select a specific literacy skill and create a lesson in which the skill is taught through a piece of children's literature. The one- to two-page lesson plan should include the title of the book being used, the name of the author, and the publisher. In addition, students will use storytelling materials to create a learning center activity designed to give children a chance to practice the skill being taught in the lesson plan. Students will also plan and make a five-minute presentation to the class that includes describing the lesson and displaying the materials used to teach it. If possible, students should provide each member of the class with a copy of the lesson plan.

Final Exam

There will be a final exam, in the form of an essay test, toward the end of the semester. The exam will deal with material covered in the readings and class discussions. Students will be required to reference information from three journal articles of their choice in their test. Some appropriate journals to reference include *The Reading Teacher*, *Reading Research Quarterly*, *Journal of Literacy Research*, *Reading Research and Instruction*, *The National Reading Conference Yearbook*, *Language Arts*, *Young Children*, and *Early Childhood Research Quarterly*.

CHAPTER 13

Classroom Language and Literacy Learning Focusing on the Teaching of Culturally, Linguistically, and Ethnically Diverse Students: A Syllabus

M. Kristiina Montero
Syracuse University

Course Overview

Teacher education programs are often criticized for not adequately preparing preservice and inservice teachers to meet the academic, linguistic, social, and psychological needs of students who are not members of the mainstream, dominant culture (Banks et al., 2001; Gay, 2000; Ladson-Billings, 2001). Furthermore, many public school teachers—90% of whom are members of the dominant cultural, ethnic, and linguistic group (National Education Association, 2003)—say they are unprepared to effectively teach students who come from backgrounds that differ from their own (Darling-Hammond, Chung, & Frelow, 2002; Karabenick & Noda, 2004). Yet when 88% of full-time faculty in the field of education are members of the same mainstream, dominant group (Ladson-Billings, 2001), the knowledge base supporting a transformative approach to teaching a culturally, ethnically, and linguistically diverse student population is diminished (Banks, 1995).

Typically, preservice teachers' only preparation in this area is a course or workshop on diversity or a field experience in an urban setting (Ladson-Billings, 2001). Such an approach is not sufficient, particularly when it comes to literacy education, which is not just for those who speak the discourse of mainstream schooling or who manage to figure it out on their own.

Improving Literacy Achievement in Urban Schools: Critical Elements in Teacher Preparation edited by Louise C. Wilkinson, Lesley Mandel Morrow, and Victoria Chou. © 2008 by the International Reading Association.

This course is designed to address the lack of attention given to culturally responsive teaching practices at the preservice and inservice teacher education level. Its purpose is to create learning opportunities for preservice and inservice teachers who teach or plan to teach in urban settings. To that end, the focus of the readings and assignments is not so much on how to teach reading and writing per se but instead on how to teach literacy, broadly defined. The course aims to give students the opportunity to investigate the theories, research, practices, pedagogies, issues, perspectives, and complexities of literacy acquisition from the point of view of mainstream teachers teaching in an ethnically, culturally, and linguistically diverse classroom. The course work will call upon students' personal experiences, expectations, research, and theories about the subject matter as well as upon the experiences, expectations, research, and theories of those working in the field. These efforts will culminate in projects that will be shared with all class members in order to expand the mutual and growing knowledge base of the subject matter.

Although an effort will be made to present an overview of classroom literacy and language development, this course will encourage depth of focus and personal investment. In essence, the more students put into this course, the more they will get out. In addition, all participants will be encouraged to ponder their current beliefs about both teaching and learning language and literacy. Students should also be able to document the ways that this course has changed, expanded, or deepened their knowledge base.

Major Themes

The course is designed to focus on the following major themes:

- The traditional text-based definition of *literacy* is inadequate and needs to be expanded.
- Students' home literacy practices need to be valued and incorporated into the teaching of school literacy practices.
- To teach in a culturally responsive way, teachers need to experience firsthand nondominant students' funds of knowledge (Moll, Amanti, Neff, & Gonzalez, 1992)—the knowledge and sociocultural practices children glean from their home culture and families.

- English-language learners (ELLs) have specific linguistic and language-learning needs.
- Cultural differences can play an integral role in determining the kind of teaching strategies and classroom materials used in urban classrooms.
- One's own knowledge and sociocultural practices, or funds of knowledge, influence one's literacy practices and influence one's teaching practices in significant ways.

Student Objectives

Students will

- Review the varying needs of students a teacher may encounter in a classroom located in a U.S. or Canadian urban school and, in particular, the sociocultural and sociolinguistics needs of culturally, ethnically, and linguistically nondominant students
- Reflect on their own culture of literacy and their own privilege in a literate society and understand how a teacher's culture of literacy influences her or his pedagogy
- Review research on how a mainstream teacher can learn to respond to all children's literacy development needs in a validating, comprehensive, and multidimensional manner (Gay, 2000)
- Understand how children's culture of literacy can either engage or disenfranchise them from literacy practices that are needed to become a full participant in today's society
- Identify ways in which instructional strategies should be modified in order to be culturally responsive, thus serving the literacy development needs of all students

Required Text

Gallego, M.A., & Hollingsworth, S. (Eds.). (2000). *What counts as literacy: Challenging the school standard*. New York: Teachers College Press.

Required Readings

Alexander, P.A., & Fox, E. (2004). A historical perspective on reading research and practice. In R.B. Ruddell & N.J. Unrau (Eds.), *Theoretical models and processes of reading* (5th ed., pp. 33–68). Newark, DE: International Reading Association.

Alvermann, D.E., & Montero, M.K. (2003). Literacy and reading. In J.W. Guthrie (Ed.), *Encyclopedia of education* (2nd ed., pp. 1513–1518). New York: Macmillan.

Banks, J.A. (1995). Multicultural education: Historical development, dimensions, and practice. In J.A. Banks & C.A.M. Banks (Eds.), *Handbook of research on multicultural education* (pp. 617–627). New York: Macmillan.

Bell, D., & Jarvis, D. (2002). Letting go of "letter of the week." *Primary Voices, 11*(2), 10–24.

Cunningham, J., Many, J., Carver, R.P., Gunderson, L., & Mosenthal, P. (2000). How will literacy be defined in the new millennium? *Reading Research Quarterly, 35,* 64–71.

Delpit, L. (1995). The silenced dialogue: Power and pedagogy in educating other people's children. In L. Delpit (Ed.), *Other people's children: Cultural conflict in the classroom* (pp. 21–47). New York: The New Press.

Duke, N.K., & Purcell-Gates, V. (2003). Genres at home and at school: Bridging the known to the new. *The Reading Teacher, 57,* 30–37.

Fitzgerald, J., García, G.E., Jiménez, R.T., & Barrera, R. (2000). How will bilingual/ESL programs in literacy change in the next millennium? *Reading Research Quarterly, 35,* 520–523.

Gay, G. (2000). Power pedagogy through cultural responsiveness. In G. Gay (Ed.), *Culturally responsive teaching: Theory, research, and practice* (pp. 21–44). New York: Teachers College Press.

González, N., Moll, L.C., Tenery, M.F., Rivera, A., Rendon, P., Gonzales, R., et al. (1995). Funds of knowledge for teaching in Latino households. *Urban Education, 29,* 443–470.

Hamilton, M. (2000). Using photographs to explore literacy as social practice. In D. Barton, M. Hamilton, & R. Ivani (Eds.), *Situated literacies: Reading and writing in context* (pp. 16–34). New York: Routledge.

Howard, G.R. (2006). White teachers and school reform: Toward a tranformationist pedagogy. In G.R. Howard (Ed.), *We can't teach what we don't know* (2nd ed., pp. 117–136). New York: Teachers College Press.

McCarthey, S.J., Dressman, M., Smolkin, L., McGill-Franzen, A., & Harris, V.J. (2000). How will diversity affect literacy in the next millennium? *Reading Research Quarterly*, *35*, 548–552.

Moje, E.B., Labbo, L.D., Baumann, J.F., & Gaskins, I.W. (2000). What will classrooms and schools look like in the new millennium? *Reading Research Quarterly*, *35*, 128–134.

Moll, L.C., Amanti, C., Neff, D., & González, N. (1992). Funds of knowledge for teaching: Using a qualitative approach to connect homes and classrooms. *Theory Into Practice*, *31*(2), 132–141.

National Institute of Child Health and Human Development. (2000). *Report of the National Reading Panel. Teaching children to read: An evidence-based assessment of the scientific research literature on reading and its implications for reading instruction.* (No. 00-4769). Washington, DC: U.S. Government Printing Office.

Neuman, S.B., Smagorinsky, P., Enciso, P.E., Baldwin, R.S., & Hartman, D.K. (2000). What will be the influences of media on literacy in the next millennium? *Reading Research Quarterly*, *35*, 276–282.

Rogers, T., Purcell-Gates, V., Mahiri, J., & Bloome, D. (2000). What will be the social implications and interactions of schooling in the next millennium? *Reading Research Quarterly*, *35*, 420–424.

Silin, J.G. (2003). Reading, writing, and the wrath of my father. *Reading Research Quarterly*, *38*, 260–267.

Smith, M.C., Mikulecky, L., Kibby, M.W., Dreher, M.J., & Dole, J.A. (2000). What will be the demands of literacy in the workplace in the next millennium? *Reading Research Quarterly*, *35*, 378–383.

Street, B. (2000). Literacy events and literacy practices: Theory and practice in new literacy studies. In M. Martin-Jones & K. Jones (Eds.), *Multilingual literacies: Reading and writing different worlds* (pp. 17–30). Philadelphia: John Benjamins.

Thompson, G.L. (2004). Standard English or Ebonics: Should we force them to speak "correctly?" In G.L. Thompson (Ed.), *Through ebony eyes: What teachers need to know but are afraid to ask about African American students* (pp. 132–148). San Francisco: Jossey-Bass.

Tierney, R.J., Moore, D.W., Valencia, S.W., & Johnston, P. (2000). How will literacy be assessed in the next millennium? *Reading Research Quarterly*, *35*, 244–250.

Yoon, J.C. (2001). Literacy practices in dark times: A reflective memoir. *Journal of Adolescent & Adult Literacy*, *45*, 290–294.

Supplemental Texts

Compton-Lilly, C. (2007). *Re-reading families: The literate lives of urban children, four years later.* New York: Teachers College Press.

Igoa, C. (1995). *The inner world of the immigrant child.* Mahwah, NJ: Erlbaum.

Thompson, G.L. (2004). *Through ebony eyes: What teachers need to know but are afraid to ask about African American students.* San Francisco: Jossey-Bass.

Valdés, G. (2001). *Learning and not learning English: Latino students in American schools.* New York: Teachers College Press.

Zentella, A.C. (2005). *Building on strength: Language and literacy in Latino families and communities.* New York: Teachers College Press.

Course Topics and Related Readings

Broadening the Definition of Literacy *and* Multiple Literacies *(two class sessions)*

How does one define *literacy*? What are some commonly held assumptions about literacy acquisition, learning, and development? When does language and literacy begin to develop? What was your classroom like in elementary school or high school? Was it urban, suburban, or rural? How would you describe the students and teachers and their learning and instructional styles? What was assessment like? How has today's classroom changed? How does literacy instruction need to change to meet the evolving literacy needs of all students?

- Gallego & Hollingsworth, Introduction and chapters 6 and 17
- Alvermann & Montero

Differences Between Home and School Literacy Practices (one class session)

How might the literacy practices of some of your students differ from your own? How can teachers validate home literacy practices?

- Gallego & Hollingsworth, chapters 1 and 2
- Bell & Jarvis
- González et al.

Linguistic and Cultural Capital (two class sessions)

What are the social, cultural, linguistic, and academic strengths of students who are members of the nondominant group? How has the traditional schooling system failed to address these students' strengths? What do teachers need to do in order to teach the "codes needed to participate fully in the mainstream of American life?" (Delpit, 1995, p. 45)

- Gallego & Hollingsworth, chapters 7, 10, 12, and 13
- Delpit

Examining Literacy Practices (two class sessions)

What are the social, cultural, historical, and political forces that influence your "culture of literacy?" How can we come to understand our own literacy practices? How can we come to understand the literacy practices of our students? How can we make use of this information to guide our instruction?

- Hamilton
- Silin
- Street
- Yoon

Culturally Responsive Teaching and Multicultural Education (one class session)

What is culturally responsive teaching? How are curriculum, instruction, and assessment typically set up in mainstream classrooms? How does such a curriculum engage some students while at the same time disenfranchise others?

- Gallego & Hollingsworth, chapters 8 and 14
- Banks
- Gay
- Howard

Evidence-Based Instructional Strategies and Historical Perspectives of the Field of Reading (two to three class sessions)

What is the origin of often used instructional strategies such as graphic organizers, read-alouds, and prediction activities? How can phonics and other mainstream literacy-fostering instructional strategies be taught in a culturally responsive way?

- Gallego & Hollingsworth, chapter 11
- Alexander & Fox
- National Institute of Child Health and Human Development

Course Format and Major Assignments

The course topics, readings, and assignments presented in this syllabus have been designed for a three-credit–hour course where class meetings are held on a weekly basis for three hours. Many of the topics explored in this course will be taught and communicated via class demonstrations, activities, and discussions. Therefore, regular attendance and participation are crucial for a full understanding of the course material. Students are expected to attend all classes, arrive on time, and contribute to our community of learners. Regular class attendance is mandatory.

Double-Entry Reading Journal

Students will keep a double-entry reading journal as a way of constructing meaning from the content of the class readings. On the left-hand side of the page, students will write a compelling quote, a paraphrased thought, or some key ideas from each reading; on the right-hand side of the page, the students will write a reflection describing the material's significance.

Student-Facilitated Class Discussions of Readings

Each student will facilitate one to two class discussions on assigned readings in order to help the group synthesize and summarize the information contained therein. Facilitating the discussion implies that the student is somewhat of an "expert" on the material assigned for the session. The assignment is also designed to improve students' oral literacy (speaking and listening) and group facilitation skills and to refine their ability to identify and share selected ideas.

Students are expected to synthesize and articulate information across multiple readings, facilitate a whole-class discussion that uses open-ended questions to explore and arrive at conclusions about the main ideas and themes in the readings, and demonstrate oral presentation skills that are organized and easy to follow. Students also should prepare and provide a handout that synthesizes the discussion's salient points.

Cultural Literacy Photography Project

This assignment is based on JoBeth Allen and Linda Labbo's (Allen et al., 2002; Allen & Labbo, 2001) PhOLKS project, which uses photography to understand more about the out-of-school lives and funds of knowledge (Moll et al., 1992) of urban students. This assignment requires each student to work with a child from a cultural, linguistic, or ethnic background that differs from that of the student and preferably from a cultural, linguistic, or ethnic minority group (e.g., African American, Hispanic American, Native American, Asian American, Native Hawaiian, Native Alaskan).

Students will need a disposable camera and are responsible for developing costs. They are encouraged to get the photographs burned to a CD to allow for the creation of a digital photograph journal.

The student should give the disposable camera to the child he or she is working with to take home and should explain how to use it. The student may also want to talk about how to frame objects and subjects in the frame of the camera's lens and show the child some sample photos demonstrating framing. The student should instruct the child to take photographs of people, places, or things that are important to him or her at home and in the neighborhood. Photography prompts could include "Take photographs of activities you enjoy doing around the house and in your neighborhood," "Take photographs of things you know a lot about," and "Take photographs about things you don't like or things you don't know a lot about but would like to."

The students should develop the photographs, give the child copies, and engage the child in a conversation about the photographs; ask why he or she took each photograph; and have the child write or dictate the "story" of each photograph. Next, the student should send the photographs home and ask a family member to narrate in writing one or more pictures in order to gain another perspective on the child's out-of-school life.

Students should then compile the photographs and narrations in a "photograph journal." Tech-savvy students can create electronic journals, scanning in copies of child- and family-produced text and using electronic copies of the photographs. Students should prepare a copy of the journal for the child and his or her family. For bilingual children, students may prepare a dual-language text. (For further ideas, see Chow, 2001 and Cummins et al., 2005.)

Once this portion of the project is complete, students will share their projects in small-group discussions in which they discuss with each other the different insights they gained from the project about the home, school, and community aspects of the children's lives. Students should draw upon their own diverse background experiences to help guide the discussion in a way that avoids stereotyping.

In preparation for the class discussions, students will track in a journal (e.g., traditional written journal, Web log) the insights they gained from working with the children, noting specifically what they discovered about the children's cultural and literate attributes as demonstrated outside the classroom. In their entries students should discuss what they learned about themselves as learners and as teachers—and specifically about creating classroom communities that validate, support, and take advantage of students' out-of-school lives—from this experience.

An Examination of My Culture of Literacy Journal

This assignment asks students to reflect upon and analyze their beliefs about their own literacy practices and the culture of literacy—the ways in which one's cultural background can influence these practices.

In written journal entries or Web logs, students will describe

- Their literacy skills
- How those skills were acquired and learned
- How those skills are practiced
- How their values; traditions; social, cultural, and political relationships; and worldview shape their understanding of their own culture of literacy
- How ethnicity, socioeconomic class, language, and religion inform their understanding of their own culture of literacy
- The thoughts, perceptions, and feelings that result from completing this assignment
- Three major issues related to classroom language and literacy
- How this assignment informs their understanding of major issues related to classroom language and literacy
- How one's culture of literacy influences one's access to literacy

Theory to Practice Presentation

Throughout the course we will read numerous articles about in-school, out-of-school, and personal literacies. We will come to a deeper understanding of the various needs (cultural, ethnic, racial, linguistic) diverse students may have in classrooms that follow a mainstream cultural discourse. This assignment is designed to help students think more deeply about how classroom instruction can better serve the linguistic, social, academic, and psychological needs of the students we teach. Through this assignment, students will experience a variety of teaching strategies used to develop literacy skills (e.g., fluency, comprehension, vocabulary acquisition, phonemic awareness, phonics, technology, writing) in a culturally responsive manner.

The assignment asks students to

- Choose five instructional strategies used to develop literacy
- For each strategy, describe the following:
  a. The strategy's intended instructional purpose
  b. How the strategy is implemented
  c. An example of the strategy
  d. Considerations one needs to make when using the strategy with nondominant groups of children (e.g., ELLs, members of cultural or ethnic minority groups)
- Prepare and deliver an instructional presentation to a small group of peers during class time on one of the five strategies

REFERENCES

Allen, J., Fabregas, V., Hankins, K.H., Hull, G., Labbo, L., Lawson, H.S., et al. (2002). PhOLKS Lore: Learning from photographs, families, and children. *Language Arts, 79,* 312–322.

Allen, J., & Labbo, L. (2001). Giving it a second thought: Making culturally engaged teaching culturally engaging. *Language Arts, 79,* 40–52.

Banks, J.A., Cookson, P., Gay, G., Hawley, W.D., Irvine, J.J., Nieto, S., et al. (2001). Diversity within unity: Essential principles for teaching and learning in a multicultural society. *Phi Delta Kappan, 83,* 196–203.

Chow, P. (2001). *The dual language showcase.* Toronto, ON: A Thornwood Public School (Peel District School Board), York University, and OISE/University of Toronto Project. Retrieved June 5, 2007, from thornwood.peelschools.org/Dual/index.htm

Cummins, J., Bismilla, V., Chow, P., Cohen, S., Giampapa, F., Leoni, L., et al. (2005). Affirming identity in multilingual classrooms. *Educational Leadership*, 63(1), 38–43.

Darling-Hammond, L., Chung, R., & Frelow, F. (2002). Variation in teacher preparation: How well do different pathways prepare teachers to teach? *Journal of Teacher Education, 53*, 286–302.

Delpit, L. (1995). Other people's children: Cultural conflict in the classroom. New York: The New Press.

Gay, G. (2000). *Culturally responsive teaching: Theory, research, and practice.* New York: Teachers College Press.

Karabenick, S.A., & Noda, P.A.C. (2004). Professional development implications of teachers' beliefs and attitudes toward English language learners. *Bilingual Research Journal, 28*(1), 55–75.

Ladson-Billings, G. (2001). *Crossing over to Canaan: The journey of new teachers in diverse classrooms.* San Francisco: Jossey-Bass.

Moll, L.C., Amanti, C., Neff, D., & Gonzalez, N. (1992). Funds of knowledge for teaching: Using a qualitative approach to connect homes and classrooms. *Theory Into Practice, 31*(2), 132–141.

National Education Association. (2003). *Status of the American public school teacher 2000–2001.* Retrieved December 2, 2004, from www.nea.org/edstats/images/status.pdf

AUTHOR INDEX

Note. Page numbers followed by *f* or *t* indicate figures or tables, respectively.

SUBJECT INDEX

Note. Page numbers followed by *f* or *t* indicate figures or tables, respectively.

A

AACTE News, 85

AAL. *See* African American Language

ABCTE. *See* American Board for Certification of Teacher Excellence

ACADEMIC FAILURE, 45

ACADEMIC LANGUAGE, 122–130; content area demands, 125–130, 126*f*; features typical of academic works, 127, 128*t*–129*t*; general vocabulary knowledge, 130–135; school registers, 124, 124*t*; science information texts, 126*f*, 126–127

ACADEMIC LANGUAGE PROFICIENCY, 123; best practices for teaching, 135–136; case study, 132–135; definition of, 122–125; development of, 124, 132–135; significance of, 122–125; social effects of, 123; in urban settings, 121–142

ACADEMIC LANGUAGE REGISTERS, 127

ACADEMY FOR URBAN SCHOOL LEADERSHIP (CHICAGO, ILLINOIS), 29

ACCOUNTABILITY, xiii

ACCREDITATION, 26–27; alternative certification programs, 28; National Council for Accreditation of Teacher Education (NCATE), 27, 94

ACHIEVEMENT, 116

ACHIEVEMENT GAP, 2

ACT ASSESSMENT, 31

ADULT LEARNING THEORY, 147

ADVANCED METHODS OF LITERACY INSTRUCTION (COURSE), 177–178

ADVOCACY: processes of, 33; for students, 74

AFRICAN AMERICAN LANGUAGE (AAL), 65

AFRICAN AMERICAN LEARNERS, 25

AFRICAN AMERICAN TEACHERS ACADEMY, 107

AFRICAN AMERICANS, 41, 43, 47, 65, 106

THE ALAN REVIEW, 209

ALTERNATIVE CERTIFICATION PROGRAMS, 28, 98

ALTERNATIVE URBAN TEACHER EDUCATION PROGRAMS, 97–99

AMERICAN BOARD FOR CERTIFICATION OF TEACHER EXCELLENCE (ABCTE), 28

AMERICAN INDIAN RESERVATION PROJECT, 108

AMERICAN LIBRARY ASSOCIATION, 209

AMOUNT OF INSTRUCTION, 112

ANNENBERG FOUNDATION, 202

ASIAN PACIFIC AMERICANS, 41

ASIAN/PACIFIC ISLANDERS, 47, 106

ASSESSMENT, 113–114, 204, 220–221; alignment of standards, curriculum, and, 32–33; final exam, 223; Portfolio Assessment (course), 174–176; self-assessment, 175

ASSIGNMENTS: Book Club project paper, 196; bulleted list assignment for discussion leaders/contributors, 196–197; Children's Literature for Urban Classrooms (syllabus), 213–215; Classroom Language and Literacy Learning Focusing on the Teaching of Culturally, Linguistically, and Ethnically Diverse Students (syllabus), 231–234; Content Area Literacy in the Multicultural Secondary School (syllabus), 205–206; Literacy and Life essay, 205; Literacy Development in the Early Years With a Focus on Children in Urban Settings (syllabus), 222–223; Literacy Development in the Urban Elementary and Middle School (syllabus), 192–197; Literacy Investigation paper, 194–195 Narrative Writing #1, 193; Theory to Practice presentation, 234

AUTOBIOGRAPHY, 213, 214

AWARD WINNERS, 213, 214

B

BASIC SKILLS ACT, 22

BEHAVIOR: classroom management systems, 152; reading behaviors, 213

BENITO JUAREZ COMMUNITY ACADEMY HIGH SCHOOL, 106–107

BEST PRACTICES: courses for supporting, 166–176; differentiating instruction using multiliteracies, 51–56; in field instruction, 110–117; for literacy achievement improvement, 164–166; promising practices, 69–74; for teacher education, 164–166; for teaching academic language proficiency, 135–136; for urban teacher preparation, 89

BETWEEN THE LIONS, 209

BILINGUAL STUDENTS, 65, 66; circumstantial bilinguals, 66; instruction for, 112–113; mastering two languages, 66–67

BILINGUAL VOCABULARY LEARNING, 131–132

BIOGRAPHY, 213, 214

BOOK CLUB PROJECT, 195–196

"BOOK LEARNING", 163

BOOK LINKS, 209

BOOKS: academic language registers of fifth-grade science textbooks, 127; for classroom study of DNA, 56, 56*t*; international books, 211; multicultural books, 211, 214; nonfiction, 212; picture books, 210–211, 214; read-aloud books, 211; for young children, 210, 214. *See also* Literature

THE BOSTON BOOK REVIEW, 209

BUILDINGS, 19